MUTINY AND ITS BOUNTY

PATRICK J. MURPHY AND RAY W. COYE

MUTINY
AND ITS
BOUNTY

*Leadership Lessons from
the Age of Discovery*

Yale UNIVERSITY PRESS/NEW HAVEN & LONDON

Frontispiece: Fifteenth-century caravel. © Bettmann/Corbis.

Yale University Press books may be purchased in quantity for educational, business, or
promotional use. For information, please e-mail sales.press@yale.edu (U.S. office) or
sales@yaleup.co.uk (U.K. office).

Designed by Mary Valencia.
Set in Minion and Fournier types by Integrated Publishing Solutions.
Printed in the United States of America.

Library of Congress Cataloging-in-Publication Data

Murphy, Patrick J.
Mutiny and its bounty : leadership lessons from the age of discovery /
Patrick J. Murphy, Ray W. Coye.
p. cm.
Includes bibliographical references and index.
ISBN 978-0-300-17028-3 (hardback)
1. Mutiny—History.   2. Insubordination—History.   3. Explorers—
History.   4. Organization—History.   5. Leadership—History.
I. Coye, Ray W.   II. Title.
VB860.M87 2013
658.3'14—dc23
2012040078

A catalogue record for this book is available from the British Library.

This paper meets the requirements of ANSI/NISO Z39.48–1992 (Permanence of Paper).

10 9 8 7 6 5 4 3 2 1

To Those Who Speak Truth to Power

CONTENTS

PREFACE

Almost nothing brings out both the best and the worst in human nature like a full-fledged mutiny. Consider everything that is involved in attempting to remove a leader or to invert authority in an organization. Mutiny hinges on timing, coordination, implicit and compound loyalties, risks, secrets, political dynamics, strategies, and even luck.

Terrifying and sometimes violent mutinies occurred on seafaring ships hundreds of years ago. Today, members of a department or team may take an organized stand to remove a leader. Surprisingly, there are significant parallels. Modern mutinies are less physical than their historic forerunners, but this book will show that they retain most of the same basic elements. Perhaps the leader's actions violated the shared values of members, or the ringleaders played important strategic roles in the organization, or the environment was highly uncertain.

Mutinies have always been intense. Although history's swords have become today's words, mutiny still entails the same distinct tendencies. Our purpose in this book is to draw from the richness of the past, particularly the Age of Discovery—when continents were being explored and lands were being claimed—to delineate those tendencies in ways that are relevant to leaders and members of enterprises and organizations in general.

Have you or one of your colleagues ever in fun cried out "Mutiny!" during a meeting or discussion at work? Doing so is taboo in a way, like shouting "Fire!" in a sold-out theater, and it also connotes a certain subtle passion. *Mutiny* is one of those peculiar words with its own built-in exclamation point. A mutiny occurs at a sharp juncture, a point of potential transformation in an organizational situation. Even though the juncture is definite, the road to it can be lengthy; the elements necessary for mutiny can simmer for a very long time. Immutable and irreversible aspects emerge at that juncture, and the opportunity to depose authority becomes real. Mutiny can shake the foundations of an organization. Mutiny is surprising to a leader, but it reveals what already exists under the surface. A mutiny's success or failure depends on the strategic counteractions of leaders and members. We will not focus on those elements until Part II. At first, in Part I, we shall explore historical cases of mutiny.

Mutiny can capture the imagination. Historically speaking, it was not so long ago that sailing ships traversed the world's oceans, regularly undertaking voyages lasting for months or years. Throughout the fifteenth to the eighteenth centuries, seafarers undertook tens of thousands of voyages during any given year, traveling the globe, undertaking conquest, and engaging in commerce. The earlier part of this era, until the early 1600s, involved mainly Portuguese and Spanish enterprises and is known as the Age of Discovery. The period gave way to the Age of Sail, which involved more English and American commercial enterprises and less discovery owing to greater knowledge of world geography. We will focus squarely on the highly entrepreneurial Age of Discovery.

Mutiny was an integral part of human achievement and enterprise during that age. Since seafaring enterprises could last for years, the duration of a single one can be compared to the average tenure of a professional member of a business organization. The number of enterprises that Age of Discovery seafarers undertook in one lifetime was about the same as the number of positions held by many of today's business professionals. And yes, mutinies in the wooden confines of a ship were as common as restructurings, layoffs, mergers, and acquisitions in most business settings. Mutiny was, and is, a natural part of enterprise.

Today's dominant form of commercial activity, the industrial organization, is only about two hundred years old. Humankind's current relationship with the industrial organization is much less mature than its past relationship with the seafaring enterprises that we will examine. Just as people learn from meaningful relationships and past experiences, so too do they benefit from historical lessons. Contemporary and historical cases of mutiny both entail skilled people working together in social and organized contexts defined by resources, structures, objectives, and strategies. In both contexts, mutinies result from similar constellations of elements and from such social aspects of human nature as leadership, purpose, belief, and value.

Defiance of authority is part of basic human development in both anthropological and personal terms. A mutinous feeling is deeply familiar; refined by life experience, it is something most of us have learned to act on carefully or to sublimate. The rebellious impulse is a ghost in the bureaucratic mechanisms of many governments. When defined by coordination and intent, this ghost is no stranger to people in organized settings. To the contrary, the spirit of an organized, upward, and defiant force is germane to some of humanity's most influential texts and stories.

We could, for a foundational example celebrating the virtues of this basic spirit, go back to Socrates. As the story is related in Plato's *Phaedo,* Socrates defied Athenian society by teaching his students lessons critical of the state. For refusing to cease his practices he was sentenced to death. Socrates' rebellious spirit made his work far more influential than it would otherwise be. It spurred the founding of Plato's academy (385 BCE) and Aristotle's lyceum (335 BCE). Scholars in the European Renaissance (early 1400s–1700s)—a period that encompasses the Age of Discovery—often cited Socrates' legacy as such a spur. Even the Bible's book of Genesis illustrates the primacy of this spirit sharpened by organization. Its original human action against authority occurred only after discreet planning and coordination, at a basic level, in defiance of God.

As business school professors with a love for historical research and as veterans of maritime services (Navy and Coast Guard), we have special advantages when it comes to extracting lessons about

mutiny from history and delineating them for organizational settings. Our work in this area emerged from Coye's experiences in the
1970s, Murphy's in the 1990s, and a shared passion for history. We
have perused rare archives and historic primary sources and studied contemporary cases. Our ideas have evolved into a distinctive
research stream.

Successful leaders in any sphere often have an interest in history's
lessons, which help them develop their own style. History can also
be instructive to members of organizations who would like to make
strategic improvements to their situation. Yet drawing leadership
lessons from the Age of Discovery, so far in the past, makes for an
unusual undertaking indeed. We provide far more background information and more complex illustrations than are found in most
business books. We tell detailed stories about such seafarers as Christopher Columbus, Ferdinand Magellan, Sebastian Cabot, and Henry
Hudson. Their cases are presented in chronological order and become increasingly complex, building on each other and spanning the
Age of Discovery. Within the complexity, certain conceptual themes
begin to resonate based on the connection between mutiny and
leadership.

This book goes against the grain on a few levels. First of all, we
researched and wrote it as historians first and as business scholars
second—an unusual approach to explaining business principles. Second, our view of mutiny as a positive force is provocative and uncommon. It is, in fact, more similar to how mutiny and leadership
were regarded during the Age of Discovery. Third, to undertake the
historical analysis, we describe these cases in great detail. Rigor is
vital in conveying context and culture. Finally, the material includes
some dramatic and violent scenes. There are instances of execution,
torture, and slavery. We deplore violence, colonialism, and slavery,
but noting them is important for an analysis of mutiny in this earlier
context.

By illustrating that leadership and mutiny draw their power from
much of the same foundation, we shift today's leadership paradigm.

The basic idea is that when an enterprise faces uncertainty and a leader's decisions clash with the shared values of members, mutiny may benefit the whole organization. In the Age of Discovery, leaders often harnessed that potential for improving the enterprise. The response to mutiny is different today. Most leaders are terrified, even though mutinies are not physical; they have become almost entirely social and intellectual. But business leaders have more in common with leaders in the Age of Discovery than one might think.

A historical researcher must navigate between interpretation and description, using the critical distance provided by time to reflect on past events. However, if the historian is not careful, the interpretation can admit biases that hinder accurate understanding. In our case, we sought to minimize bias by drawing from multiple sources, especially primary sources. These sources are cited in both text and notes; reference information is in the bibliography. Attention to the historical record enhanced the scholarly aspects of this work, but it also helped us keep track of the distinctive character of each case as well as linkages across cases. Events and people that seemed tertiary to one case ended up influencing events and people in another case. Tracing these links strengthens our procedural delineation of mutiny.

Given the importance of historical research for the derived lessons, we augment the discussion in the text with extensive historical notes. These notes clarify many of the obscure fifteenth-, sixteenth-, and seventeenth-century references, especially ones germane to a seafaring culture that is now mostly extinct, and they often cite rich evidence from primary sources that helps illustrate events and contexts. They are intended to enliven and enhance the reading of the chapters.

This book offers personal and practical lessons. Connecting the distant past to the present generates personal insights into mutiny and leadership, especially for members of enterprises taking big risks amid uncertainty. Many of the trials and tribulations of human achievement in the Age of Discovery are identical to those faced by today's professional managers and entrepreneurs. However, the historical cases (and the leaders they chronicle) are, in a very practical sense, as different from one another as business professionals are.

A business professional might wonder what he or she can really learn from the Age of Discovery in a practical sense. The answer to that question is simple: the differences between then and now are largely contextual. Almost everything that happens in the cases has some specific contemporary parallel. Our focus on a period of history that is gone forever sheds light on how mutiny is vital to all human enterprises. That realization opens up lessons that are as valuable to leaders who wish to quell a mutiny as they are to mutineers who wish to depose a leader. Indeed, there is a logic to coordinated upward force by members that can save an enterprise in spite of a leader's actions to the contrary.

This book is intended for both leaders and mutineers, after all. Leadership and mutiny are opposed in theory but are, in practice, part of the same force of human nature. Assuming that a leader is always right and a mutiny is always wrong is a fallacy of organizational life. Exploring mutiny thus clarifies some complexities of today's business enterprises in unorthodox ways. As historians know, viewing current topics through the lens of the past enables us to better understand them. And that may help shift today's dominant industrial organizational perception of mutiny.

ACKNOWLEDGMENTS

We are grateful to many individuals and various institutions for supporting our work. Mike O'Malley, former executive editor at Yale University Press, approached us with the initial suggestion to turn our mutiny research paper into a book. William Frucht, the Press's current executive editor, along with Jaya Chatterjee and Mary Pasti, gave consistently amazing support. Our research assistants, Lopilma Boldbataar, Mike Goode, Yitong Liu, and Wenqin Zhang, also provided many immensely valuable contributions.

The *Journal of Management History*, Emerald Publishers, and the Academy of Management have all helped promote our research widely. David Lamond, Jane Gibson, Regina Greenwood, John Humphreys, Milorad Novicevic, Pete Petersen, Chester Spell, and others have long offered helpful comments on various legal, historical, international, and cultural aspects of mutiny. We also acknowledge Greg Anderson, Robert Cooke, Debby Defranco, Robin Fang, Franz Lohrke, Monika Moehring, Bill Paczkowski, Marian Worth, and Lida Zhang.

At DePaul University, we have received support from across the entire institution. In the Driehaus College of Business, the research committee, chaired by Albert Muniz, gave us multiple research grants for this project. Our dean, Ray Whittington, our former dean, Leo Ryan, and our department chair, Scott Young, all endorsed our history research warmly. Colleagues Anne Clark Bartlett, Asun Borrás, Javier Monllor, Pablo Rincón Romero, Rob Ryan, Gina Sian, and Harold Welsch provided friendly readings and translations of primary sources. Robert Boeshaar, Cornell Lambert, Ben Miranda, and Rick Salisbury provided technological help. Jennifer Leopoldt provided early copy editing and formatting assistance.

Patricia Spencer helped write our original mutiny article that won the *Journal of Management History*'s 2011 Outstanding Paper Award. Finally, Nezih Altay, Kathy Dhanda, Lisa Gundry, Laura Pincus Hartman, Daniel Heiser, Marsha Katz, Daniel Koys, Helen Lavan, Ilya Meiertal, Charles Naquin, and many students offered helpful suggestions. These individuals and institutions helped us create a better book. Any deficiencies in the final product, of course, are ours alone.

Timeline of Key Events in the Age of Discovery

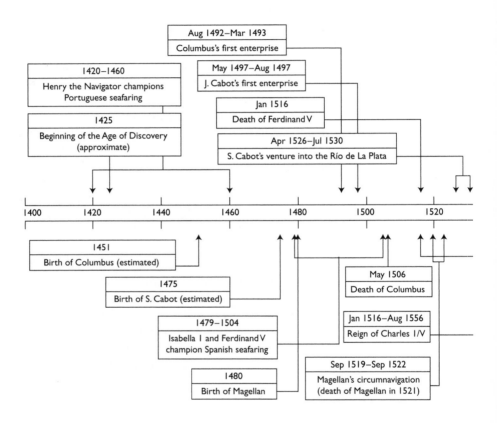

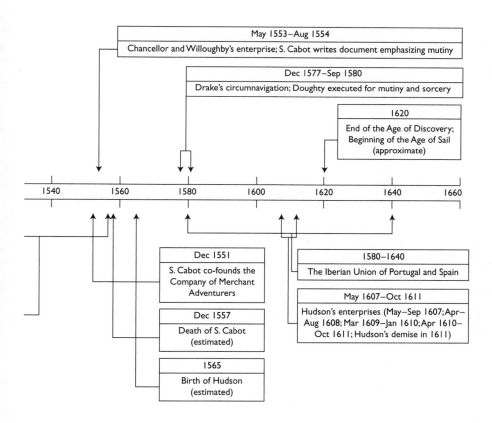

| May 1553–Aug 1554 |
| Chancellor and Willoughby's enterprise; S. Cabot writes document emphasizing mutiny |

| Dec 1577–Sep 1580 |
| Drake's circumnavigation; Doughty executed for mutiny and sorcery |

| 1620 |
| End of the Age of Discovery; Beginning of the Age of Sail (approximate) |

1540   1560   1580   1600   1620   1640   1660

| Dec 1551 |
| S. Cabot co-founds the Company of Merchant Adventurers |

| Dec 1557 |
| Death of S. Cabot (estimated) |

| 1565 |
| Birth of Hudson (estimated) |

| 1580–1640 |
| The Iberian Union of Portugal and Spain |

| May 1607–Oct 1611 |
| Hudson's enterprises (May–Sep 1607; Apr–Aug 1608; Mar 1609–Jan 1610; Apr 1610–Oct 1611; Hudson's demise in 1611) |

Introduction
Inversive Operations

First the Captaine general, with the pilot major, the masters,
merchants and other officers, to be so knit in unitie, love,
conformitie, and obedience in every degree on all sides, that
no dissention, variance, or contention may rise or spring be-
twixt them and the mariners of this companie, to the damage or hindrance of the voyage: for that dissention (by many
experiences) hath overthrown many notable intended and
likely enterprises and exploits.

—Sebastian Cabot, instructions to a venture seeking
a northeast passage, May 9, 1553

What is mutiny? It is when members of an organization
defy and depose an incumbent leader. Mutineers intend to influence the operations of an organization via
conflict, coordinated action, promotion of interests or values, or the
seizure of power and influence. Although a mutiny can remove a
leader, its aim is rarely to damage or destroy the organization. On the
contrary, improving the organization is a more common objective.

Mutiny and leadership are organizational corollaries; during the
period of their overlap the authority in an organization can invert
precipitously. The event is usually intense and may involve reckless
actions. Even if a mutiny fails horribly in its execution, its core intent is often constructive and utilitarian. A specific ideology or set

of basic values often drives and informs a mutiny. Like leadership, sometimes ignorance or miscommunication can drive a mutiny. A mutiny can also serve a cathartic or ritualistic function, helping to relieve tension. As such, the concept of mutiny is related to various kinds of revolts, including protests, strikes, coups d'état, rebellions, and whistle-blowing. Such dissonance movements have been constant acts throughout history. What has changed about them has more to do with their rationale, practical application, and perception than the underlying mechanisms.

In 1921, Ilya Tolstoy, who penned the quotation at the beginning of Part II, wrote that all such dissonance movements "are children of the same mother." That mother is liberty, or the simple freedom to do something about undesirable circumstances. Such acts to gain freedom oppose an existing order on principled and often passionate grounds. All are nurtured by the same basic belief in the importance of a larger purpose. However, the similarities among these particular "children of freedom" are merely skin-deep. Mutiny is distinct from those other forms of dissent in several important ways. These differences represent a potentially ameliorative force, and that particular perception of mutiny is lost to history. Let us examine its different elements briefly.

First, the most peculiar elements of an effective mutiny are a clear set of objectives and a strategic or tactical plan. Unlike in other organizational settings, however, if the mutiny's plan is uncertain, then its objectives are probably uncertain too. The direct relation between planning and objectives is the product of a mutiny's occurring in a setting that is severely hostile to it. Think of a mutiny as a small but nimble venture, lacking many resources and having its own boundaries, subsumed by a larger organization that is fundamentally opposed to it. For such a venture to succeed in that kind of environment, a profound and deep sense of strategy is vital.

Second, a mutiny distinguishes between its members and nonmembers even though all of those individuals share membership in the larger organization. Participation in a mutiny is not open to just anyone who wishes to join, yet participants and nonparticipants do not usually regard each other as enemies. An effective mutiny's participants assume specific and complementary roles, but all subscribe to an ideology based on shared values or principles. Although a mutiny almost always relies on secrecy in its early stages, individual accountability eventually runs high because of the identifiability of specific roles. Mutinies involve more personal responsibility than revolutions do.

Third, a mutiny tends to succeed in spite of (not because of) its size. Even though a mutiny is not typically large, one person alone is not sufficient.[1] A mutiny entails a small or medium-sized group that benefits from secrecy, not a movement of hundreds or thousands driven by a public revolutionary zeal. For a mutiny, size and force do not necessarily correspond to success. Instead, as with most organizations, management decisions and smart execution by an effective team are what lead to successful results.

Fourth, a mutiny is an endogenous organizational event. It begins and usually ends with internal members of an organization. There are many kinds of organizational stakeholders, internal and external, any of whom can seek to depose an organization's leadership or authority. After all, boards of directors, customers, distributors, suppliers, shareholders, stakeholders, and other constituents have interests in an organization. Such parties sometimes can and do try to depose an organization's leadership when its actions threaten their interests. But their act is not a mutiny, because the primary actors are not internal. External constituents are neither subject to an organization's leadership or authority structure as fully as members are, nor are they as familiar with the organization's cultural values. Whereas such outsiders may support a mutiny, the force of a mutiny does not originate with them. The internalism aspect is important because mutineers and organizational leaders participate in a vital dynamic that touches the heart of an enterprise with constructive intentions. The dynamic is bipolar by nature: although members usually see mutiny as vital and ameliorative, a leader may see a frightening and dangerous lack of devotion.

The definition of mutiny is not simple, but the concept is rich. It has a long history as an implicit element of social action. Its positive aspects are embedded in the same history and derive from the goal of a mutiny: organizational improvement. Unfortunately, mutiny tends to be construed very differently today. Our work reflects the definition of mutiny delineated above and reintroduces its ameliorative aspects to contemporary enterprises.

When seen as an upward, internal, coordinated force, historical mutinies offer lessons that apply to many organizational settings. Department members removing a supervisor, an entrepreneurial firm reforming an organizational field—both instances of coordinated upward defiance can offer examples of mutiny. The historical cases provide more interesting and dramatic reading experiences, however, and they offer deep insights that are difficult to gain otherwise. If mutiny on a seafaring vessel and mutiny in a business setting stem from the same dynamics and elements of human nature, as we believe they do, then why does the former offer richer data and sharper features for building a procedural understanding?

Mutiny's conceptualization has roots in seafaring. The industry is an old one, but its legacy is hardly obscure. Indeed, historians who study its lessons and produce high-impact contributions have enjoyed mainstream assistance from powerful allies, the film industry and the popular press. Authors and filmmakers have done much to make the mutiny concept familiar to new generations. Some of these works, such as *The Caine Mutiny* and *Mutiny on the Bounty*, have captured the imagination of millions to such a degree that truth is indistinguishable from fiction. Many people today do not know which famous mutinies actually occurred and which ones are fictitious—to wit, the two just mentioned. The entertainment industry has thus generated confusion about mutiny even as it has embedded the concept in popular thought with celebrations of mutiny's dramatic aspects. For these reasons, we shall return to the film industry in Part II.

With so much attention paid to mutiny in the twentieth century, the concept is clearly part of the Western world's cultural lexicon. Mutiny is almost axiomatic when members are dissatisfied with leadership and take coordinated action to do something about it. That is not always a bad thing if leadership is poor. So where did the negative perceptions of mutiny come from?

We identify two specific sources in this book: an influential 1553 document by Sebastian Cabot, quoted in the epigraph, and a 1578 action by Francis Drake. These sources heralded a larger movement that unfolded over many years, culminating in Britain's Mutiny Acts of 1689 and 1765; the latter act was instrumental in leading to the American Revolution and was cited in the Declaration of Independence. Military regulations still reflect the tenets clearly. Throughout the sixteenth, seventeenth, and eighteenth centuries, the dominant perception of mutiny shifted, becoming ever more negative. The original notion from the Age of Discovery that a mutiny can improve an enterprise is practically gone.

Mutinies were seamlessly woven into the operations of enterprises in the Age of Discovery. A mutiny could be regarded as positive if it helped achieve the enterprise's original aims. In most business organizations, the perception is quite different. Even though a mutiny can be helpful if leadership is poor, it is almost always regarded as subversive.

Entrepreneurial firms that aim to be adaptive and perform in uncertain environments provide suitable contexts for mutiny. Knowledge-based or "learning" organizations are also highly amenable to coordinated internal action. The history of the development of Silicon Valley in the later twentieth century provides many examples. Mutiny emerged easily among empowered "knowledge workers" in nonhierarchical, egalitarian ventures. It is only natural in such contexts, from the Age of Discovery to the Age of the Silicon Chip.

In entrepreneurial settings where big discoveries are made, members are less insulated from shifts in the environment than are workers in more established, bureaucratic organizations. Where there are lower internal boundaries, flatter structures, and delegated authority, it is easier to transform authority from the bottom if necessary.

These factors do not necessarily mean that a mutiny should occur. Rather, they show by extension that if a mutiny is impossible for structural reasons, then strong leadership is probably also impossible. A degree of tension is important in adaptive firms because it drives excellent performance. At first glance, that notion may strain credulity. But on a deeper, procedural level, most business professionals have experienced it. After all, organizational climates become tense when external environments become uncertain, for the same reasons that they always have. How a leader and a membership respond to that uncertainty stems largely from their shared values. Those values were rather basic ones in the Age of Discovery (e.g., physical safety), and they are of a higher order (e.g., esteem) today. Nonetheless, what is more important to a mutiny is that all such values are shared and can be violated.

One very practical similarity between seafaring enterprises and modern firms is the nature of contact between would-be mutineers and other members. In either setting, almost everybody communicates with one another, including across functions and departments. This process reinforces shared values. On old sailing ships, even members who were locked away and shackled in irons could talk to other members through partitions and bulkheads. Open communication is clearly also a big part of entrepreneurship. It enables the leadership of a venture to harness and coordinate bottom-up forces that are transformational, but it can yield threats if those forces take certain turns.

Exit strategy is another important similarity between historical and modern contexts. Modern firms, especially entrepreneurial ones, need smart exit strategies when undertaking projects. The formulation and implementation of an exit strategy is vital to performance. It was also vital to ventures like the ones we will examine. In this respect, seafaring ventures in the Age of Discovery and modern firms have especially close parallels.

So, why not study contemporary firms, like those that make up the history of Silicon Valley, to understand mutiny better? Cases in the Age of Discovery offer better access to primary data and better quality of information. Members of modern firms are understandably unwilling to provide much quality information about mutinous activities in their departments or organizations. It is a dicey topic. Detailed personal accounts of a mutiny are usually available only long after the event anyway, by which time they are already "historical." The reasons for mutiny usually differ radically across firms, because firms themselves differ categorically at structural and technical levels. Moreover, those personal accounts are not generally agenda-free.

Most enterprises have incentives for concealing upwardly defiant behavior and reassuring internal employees, external constituents, customers, and stakeholders of internal harmony. That is especially so in public companies or ones relying heavily on investors. In fact, today's organizational leaders often treat a potential mutiny as a kind of upstairs deal. Another response from leaders is to trivialize a suspected mutiny until they cannot ignore it any longer, which is when it may also be too late for them to resist should a real mutiny take form. Companies are not forthcoming about internal struggles because they do not want negative attention. News agencies do not report mutinies because the particular contexts in which they occur lack broad relevance and interest. Business firms all have their individual strengths, weaknesses, opportunities, and threats. Idiosyncratic reality makes it hard to delineate a mutiny's constellation of elements in a reliable and valid way. At the level of the data is a thicket of antecedents and parameters that apply to a single organization. This tangled species of empiricism haunts social science research. It works well for figuring out what happened in a specific case, but is inadequate for understanding a complex phenomenon in general.

By contrast, researching mutiny in historic seafaring ventures has some big empirical advantages. Large volumes were written about cases of mutiny in the seventeenth, eighteenth, and nineteenth centuries. Many of these books offered rich historical accounts. In the early nineteenth century, newspapers and trade periodicals published hundreds of detailed secondary accounts of mutinies from varying perspectives. We have examined many of those secondary sources. When comparing divergences among them to maximize accuracy, we discovered, however, that the most valuable data come from primary sources recorded as the events occurred or shortly thereafter.

Cases of mutiny were recorded directly in logbooks, journals, and diaries maintained by people experiencing the events firsthand.[2] Importantly, these sources were not created in response to the action. Rather, they were maintained scrupulously as a formal matter of tradition and culture. For example, the January 8, 1609, contract between Henry Hudson and the Dutch East India Company specified that for him to receive compensation, "he shall obtain as much knowledge of the lands as can be done without any considerable loss of time, and if it is possible to return immediately in order to make a faithful report and relation of his voyage to the Directors, and to deliver over his journals, log-books, and charts, together with an account of everything whatsoever which shall happen to him during the voyage without keeping anything back."[3] Before, during, and after these ventures, virtually everything was recorded from multiple perspectives.

This level of detail is typical of the Age of Discovery. Qualitative researchers know that such detailed sources are a treasure trove when it comes to gaining insight into the intentions of key players. These data were compiled daily and systematically over time, giving a longitudinal basis for inferring root causes. Another important empirical difference between older and modern enterprises is that the routines and procedures that drove the former were standardized. There is more reliability; the level of contextual error in the data is low. Even better, the number of cases is very large. Not only were seafaring ventures the most advanced way to travel the world for centuries, but the volume and frequency of enterprises were quite large. In the middle of the sixteenth century Portuguese ships crossed the Tropic of Capricorn, which passes through Argentina and southern Brazil, multiple times a day.[4]

In case-study research, varying physical elements of the setting can affect the reliability of what is observed across cases. When a researcher is in situ, these effects can impair the objectivity of inferences about a construct. On seafaring vessels in the Age of Discovery, the boundaries, temporal and spatial context, and common tasks undertaken were practical constants. Taking a few days off or transferring to another department to avoid problems was impractical. There was far less venture-specific variance. What actually happened between leaders and members is thus more directly attributable to pure social and human dynamics than in the task environment of a business organization. Variance unrelated to the criteria of interest creates well-known thorny problems for business and organizational research. Consequently, much of that research employs artificial statistical corrections when comparing cases to detect the essence of a construct, and these render invisible the particular aspects of each case.

The human resources functions in a company, a college department, an entrepreneurial team, or a government organization are all quite different from those in a sixteenth-century caravel. Yet, those organizational settings are also quite different from each other. They have qualitatively different boundaries, time frames, technologies, structures, and operations. The covariates can frustrate attempts to gain a deep sense of the commonalities. True scores and errors are confounded because the settings are patently unique.

The cases we examine in this book have one final and related advantage that is familiar to all historians. Former U.S. Secretary of Health, Education, and Welfare John W. Gardner wrote in 1968, "History never looks like history when you are living through it. It always looks confusing and messy, and it always feels uncomfortable."[5] His insight highlights the principle, often overlooked, that historical distance can increase objectivity. With the benefit of hindsight, social tensions, injustice, disrespect, power, influence, and other human factors are more discernible in relation to each other. Settings in which we experience such factors are not divorced from our current attempts to understand them. Therefore, distance from the historic mutinies removes certain subjective factors that make contemporary cases harder to understand formally.

Mutinies on seafaring ventures often occurred because of threats to shared values about such basic needs as food and safety. Our research has shown that mutinies in many ventures today involve shared values in a similar way. The difference is that values in the latter context concern higher-level human needs, such as socialization or esteem, or the values of an organizational culture. In the prelude to mutiny, leadership actions and authority structures clash with these shared values. This mechanism is hard to detect without the rich hindsight provided by a deep examination of historical cases.

Mutiny and leadership can be thought of as the two edges of a sword. Our research program seeks to go beyond a declarative understanding to a delineation of this sword's blade, edges, and cutting capabilities. As part and whole, this kind of conceptualization of mutiny and leadership is clearer than one that merely considers these two constructs sui generis. The result is a procedural understanding that leadership and mutiny rest substantially on the same foundation. Understanding either construct helps one understand the other. Both mutineers and leaders can pursue virtuous ends via illicit means in the face of uncertainty. A flawed mutiny can destroy a cause it intends to promote, just as bad leadership can promote a cause it intends to destroy.

We remarked that the dominant perception of mutiny has shifted throughout history. So has the conceptualization of leadership. In the Age of Discovery, it was impossible to define or evaluate leadership without specific reference to mutiny or its potential. The quotation at the beginning of this chapter, for instance, in which Sebastian Cabot instructs members of his Company of Merchant Adventurers, is an obvious example. The passage comes from a long document that was essentially a leadership manual, one that opened with a crucial admonition about mutiny. Since those times, a somewhat dubious doctrine rooted in the nineteenth century called the "great man theory" has recast the general perception of influential historical figures, especially leaders. Its influence on the perception of leadership in the mid-twentieth century drove a search for the right traits of leaders despite the social contexts and cultures in which leaders were embedded. The logic of the theory renders it somewhat inappropriate for members to question the actions of leaders because those actions come from the "right stuff." Not so in the early Age of Discovery, when the notion of coordinated upward defiance was part of the leadership narrative. Even today's research that examines "substitutes" for leadership does not consider mutiny.[6] In the historical period that we shall examine, mutiny was the ultimate substitute for leadership.

The conceptual foundations that drive current understandings of human and social influence in organizations are incomplete. Leadership studies, which are based wholly on these foundations, are sufficiently unrealistic as to not generate a deep and practical understanding of what actually happens in organizations. The dominant conceptualization of leadership is exceedingly top-down, no matter how much it is painted as bottom-up and transformational. Something significant is lacking.

Neither mutiny nor leadership makes much practical sense without the other. Both tap into the same force. Without a formal conceptualization of how this force's potential emerges naturally from the bottom of an enterprise and endogenously among coordinated members, leadership theory is jaundiced and does not describe organizational realities very well. This is especially true in entrepreneurial ventures, where risk and uncertainty are salient, the environment can be intense, and adaptivity is vital.

The notion that mutiny can overlap with leadership may sound strange at first because the two forces are functionally opposed. But in reality, they have a certain congruence because both release a bottom-up force in an organization. Theorizing along these lines takes us out of the domain of leadership and into the domain of mutiny. Indeed, the boundary is not always clear. Mutiny was certainly not as divorced from leadership in the Age of Discovery as it is today. In Part I we will illustrate this point and delineate how leaders can even utilize mutiny as transformational force.

Part One

ROPE AND KNIFE

Who that of bees feareth the stinge,
Shal never by hony have great wonninge.
As the swete Rose bringeth forth the thorne,
So is man truely to joye and payne borne.

—Richard Eden

Richard Eden, writing in the middle of the Age of Discovery, offers a poem addressed to all those who explore "new founde lands and islands." The title of the poem makes his audience clear: "To all adventurers and such who take great enterprises in hand." He proceeds to share his thoughts about boldness, then offer admonitions.

Whoever has not experienced the bitter taste of sourness
Is not worthy to take a meal of sweetness.
Whoever would eat the kernel of a nut
Must take pains to crack open the shell.

Whoever fears the sting of bees
Will never win much honey.
As the sweet rose brings forth the thorn,
So truly is man born to joy and pain.

The bird builds her nest with hope
Where oftentimes she has but an uneasy rest,

Yet she is not thereby driven to such fear
But that she performs the same act the next year.

Casting oneself into peril comforts the noble, courageous spirit,
Yet I do not commend rashness or outrage.
What fools tell stories about, take no heed of at all,
For what they don't know, they call fantastic.

"Nothing ventured, nothing gained" is a saying of old.
"It is better to blow on a coal than to sit in the cold."
"Fortune favors the bold," the Latin proverb says,
But it fails those who faint and lack faith.

God gives all things, but not as the bull gives his horn.
The farmer by labor increases his corn.
As fortune favors, you may be rich or poor,
As rich as Croesus or as poor as Irus, who begs at the door.[1]

The poem emphasizes a natural duality that attends all risky human enterprises. Eden makes the usual comparisons—bee stings and honey, thorns and roses—and offers sententious sayings already hundreds of years old when he wrote them down: "Nothing ventured, nothing gained"; "Fortune favors the bold." Such dualities are often manifested in enterprises as the dual forces of mutiny and leadership.

At the end he refers to Croesus, a king of Lydia (where gold and silver coinage was first used) around 550 BCE who was known for his immense wealth, and Irus, an arrogant and abhorrent beggar given a name of derision. Ovid featured both individuals in a poem in his *Tristia* to illustrate that fortune comes to some, not others. In the ancient world fortune was seen as rolling on like a flood or a wheel; shifts in fortune could be swift, powerful, and unpredictable. The description can apply to mutiny situations, although knowledge of the elements that contribute to mutinies can help make them more predictable and controllable, as we shall see.

1

Columbus
"The Dawn of an Age"

The continent we shall find further ahead.

—Christopher Columbus, logbook entry,
Sunday, September 16, 1492

The Age of Discovery, the historic period in which Christopher Columbus, Ferdinand Magellan, Sebastian Cabot, and Henry Hudson led their enterprises, lasted for around 250 years. The practices of the seafaring culture that they represented originated on the Iberian Peninsula, expanded to the rest of the European continent, and eventually entered Britain and Ireland. The cases of mutiny that we explore span this period and are intricately connected with one another.

The enterprises of Columbus and Magellan were separated in time by about three decades (1492; 1519). Columbus's enterprise influenced Magellan, who went on to achieve what Columbus had actually intended: finding a route to southeastern Asia by sailing west instead of east. Later, Sebastian Cabot and Henry Hudson, informed in turn by the earlier ventures, pursued similar objectives. Contrary to great-man theory, these feats were enabled by social and cultural factors in addition to the actions of the seafarers themselves. The culture of Portuguese seafaring was a strong influence.

As was the case for many seafarers in the Age of Discovery, both

Columbus and Magellan planned and led enterprises for a country that was foreign to them. They both had to secure funding, recruit members, organize resources, and make strategic decisions while relying on fortune to favor them. In fact, they faced challenges very similar to those of modern entrepreneurs.

Mutiny and leadership are tied to the cultural context in which they occur, because values drive behaviors embedded in that context. Understanding the Age of Discovery as a period is important for making sense of the cases of mutiny. Let us examine how this culture developed on the Iberian Peninsula in the fifteenth century. Columbus's first enterprise was seminal to the age.

THE IBERIAN PENINSULA IN
THE AGE OF DISCOVERY

In the fifteenth century, the Kingdom of Castile, located on the Iberian Peninsula near the heart of modern Spain, was a superpower. The Roman Empire, which had occupied the peninsula for more than six centuries, had been extinguished in the thirteenth century with the sack of Constantinople. The mutinous army of Charles I of Spain, who had become king of Castile in 1517, sacked Rome in 1527. This king (later known as Charles V, Holy Roman Emperor), had a big influence on Spanish seafaring and made Castile inordinately important. His name crops up throughout this book.

Castile was a small geographic area in the ninth and tenth centuries. After a period of feudal vassalage, it grew dramatically. When Castile's Queen Isabella married Aragon's King Ferdinand (Charles V's grandfather) in 1469, the Castilian Empire was becoming too big to fail. Aragon, located on the Mediterranean coast of what is now Spain, had expanded into nearby territories and even into Italy. It was the last of Castile's conquests. The union of Castile and Aragon created an enormous region referred to as España. It was separated from France and the rest of Europe by the Pyrenees Mountains in the northeast. On the north and south it was bounded by the sea, a bay of the Atlantic to the north (the Bay of Biscay) and the Mediterranean to the east and south.

To the west of Castile was a much smaller and more enigmatic region. This western area had origins in the Roman province of Lusitania and a couple Germanic kingdoms. It later became a Moorish region (711–1249) referred to as Al Gharb ("the west"), but achieved independence when the Moors' power declined on the peninsula. It always had a distinct culture, mainly because the boundless ocean to its west profoundly influenced the local worldview. The societal focus in Castile, by contrast, tended to the east, toward the Mediterranean region with its centuries of commerce and trade.[1]

The Spanish capital shifted several times during the Age of Discovery with continued conquests, dynastic inheritances, intermarriages, and alliances. Eventually, in 1561, Philip II, Charles V's son, installed the royal court at Madrid. By then, Spain dominated the peninsula except for that mysterious western region along the ocean. On the peninsula, immediately to the north of that region, was a kingdom called Galicia, which had rebelled against Castile in the 1360s and almost became part of its southern neighbor. Castile reclaimed Galicia. But Galicia's southern neighbor, that smaller enigmatic region known by this point as Portugal, always resisted.[2]

Historians still marvel at Portugal's enduring sovereignty as other Iberian kingdoms fell to Castilian conquest. A small Portuguese force executed a decisive strategic victory on land over a far more powerful Castilian force in the Battle of Aljubarrota in 1385. But the Portuguese were at their best on water. Almost a century later, Portugal outmatched a much larger Spanish fleet at sea in a war over an African colony, now Guinea-Bissau. Since 1373, Portugal has maintained an alliance with England.[3] But the true source of its proud resilience derived from a culture shaped by the ocean's embrace of its coast.[4] The ocean was always part of its national identity and still is part of it today. Spain hindered Portugal's commerce with Europe over land, making those trade routes unduly expensive. Portugal's best options for all sorts of enterprise were strategic ventures by sea. Its ability to maintain its independence evolved into an orientation for exploration and conquest at sea. Portugal was the first European state to sanction seafaring and probably the first empire to gain territory at sea when it seized Ceuta, across the Strait of Gibraltar, from the Moors in 1415.[5] Portugal went on to explore the entire coastline of Africa in the fifteenth century, it found great quantities of gold, and eventually Vasco da Gama discovered a route to India that yielded rich spices. Portugal went even farther and established history's longest-running international administration, in Macau, which ended in 1999 after almost five hundred years.

Portugal's ocean coast and its contentions with its larger eastern neighbor generated an exceedingly strong seafaring culture. Its seafarers were the very best. In fact, Spain's seafaring advancements were about a century behind Portugal's, and England's trailed Spain's by another century. The port at Lisbon had been a stopping point on the coastal maritime route between southern and northern Europe since the days of the Roman Empire. It provided excellent shelter from and access to the ocean. Knowledge gained from Portuguese seafaring so fully exceeded that of other cultures during the Age of Discovery that it was kept secret as a valuable resource. An early Portuguese map called the Cantino Planisphere, smuggled into Italy in 1502, detailed the entire African coastline with amazing accuracy, charted islands in southeastern Asia, sketched a recently discovered Brazil, and showed hundreds of complicated ocean wind patterns. At the time, such knowledge was unknown to the rest of the world.[6]

The Portuguese were the most adept navigators in the Age of Discovery and among the best seafarers in world history. The early records of seafaring with references to events involving Portugal often describe Portuguese navigational actions as secret, hazardous, and entailing advanced techniques. Henry the Navigator (1394–1460), third child of a king, John I, is the one who sponsored and promoted systematic explorations of the immense coastline of Africa. But Ferdinand Magellan, a Portuguese seafarer, did more as an actual navigator. He discovered and named the Pacific Ocean for Europe, found the South American strait that bears his name today, and led (but did not survive) the first circumnavigation of the earth. The circumnavigation, which took three years, was one of the Age of Discovery's two most impressive ventures. But like Columbus, Magellan did not achieve his amazing feat for his homeland. He achieved it leading an enterprise for its rival, Spain.[7]

The culture of a social system or an organization is partially shaped by the social and physical environment. In this case, Spain's Atlantic coastline in its southwest corner is just 150 miles (241 km) long. In the early Age of Discovery, the barbarous northwest coastline in turbulent Galicia offered no safe harbor or supply route and was less important to the empire than its Mediterranean side. The Bay of Biscay, with its rugged northern coast, is shared with France. On the southwest coast, the Guadalquivir River connects the port of Seville, which lies about 40 miles (64 km) inland, to Spain's Atlantic port of San Lucar. The other ports in this small southwestern region of Spain were Palos, 30 miles (48 km) northwest of San Lucar, and Cádiz, about 20 miles (32 km) south of San Lucar. These four ports gave Spain access to the unknown.[8] However, Spain's larger interests had always been in the Mediterranean, where Castile and Aragon had 1,000 miles (1,609 km) of coastline and had traded for centuries with the Genoese, Venetians, and others.

Even though both Spain and Portugal occupy the Iberian Peninsula, Portugal's situation has been quite different from Spain's throughout both of their histories. For one thing, Portugal's ocean coastline is 500 miles (800 km) long. During its various periods of rule, by Romans, Visigoths, Moors, and Christians, Portugal has spawned generations of navigators. The ocean shaped cultural values different from those of its larger neighbor and immortalized in Fernando Pessoa's 1934 poem *Mensagem*. Its mysteries still capture the human imagination.[9]

As Eden's poem at the beginning of Part I illustrates, history assigns to the adventurer a fearless spirit that transcends time and culture. It is the spirit of self-determined human enlightenment that we see in the art of the Renaissance, the period of cultural and scientific exploration of which the Age of Discovery is a part. During the Age of Discovery, nowhere was this spirit more intense among enterprising seafarers than in Portugal.

Like today's entrepreneurs, seafarers of the age were sometimes seen as crazy. Moreover, they did not usually have the resources required to undertake their projects. They needed financing from investors, such as nobles at the court of a monarch or wealthy merchants. As with many entrepreneurial projects, rejections were common. Portugal's royalty realized early on that investing in successful seafaring ventures could generate enormous returns. When Portuguese enterprises succeeded, the rewards of spices, treasure, and land were very large. Before long, many adventurers across Europe actively sought support in various countries and courts for risky ventures at sea. As the Age of Discovery's first mover, Portugal was usually the first country to be approached. Its eastern neighbor followed its example. As a financier of ventures, Portugal was a brilliant yet arrogant patron and Spain was a generous yet fickle mistress. Both sought to support the potentially most lucrative seafaring enterprises and admired and favored only the boldest of adventurers.

One such adventurer, an Italian seafarer from Genoa named Christoforo Colombo (b. 1451), approached Portugal's John II in 1485 and then again 1488 with daring ideas for exploration to the west.[10] Genoa had a proud history in its own right, being one of the first places to support navigation out of the Mediterranean and into the Atlantic, which it did as far back as the thirteenth century, but its seafaring was not quite on a par with Portugal's. Genoese expertise and history notwithstanding, the Portuguese king rejected Columbus both times, just as his cousin King Manuel I would reject Magellan thirty years later. In the former case, the rejections were partially because Christopher Columbus was Italian and because, in 1487–1488, Portugal's own Bartholomeu Dias had discovered opportunities to the east in the first rounding of the southern tip of Africa by a European.[11] Columbus, living in Portugal when the news arrived, knew rejection well. He also realized that the wily Portuguese courtiers would send out caravels based on the plan he had presented. He needed to undertake the enterprise first. As with today's venture capital firms dealing with entrepreneurs, strategic rejections were the status quo. With help from his brother, Bartholomew, Columbus turned to England and then to Spain. After multiple attempts, further intrigues, and bureaucratic delays in the court, he finally negotiated a deal with the Castilian queen, Isabella, in April 1492.[12]

Compared to other seafarers, Columbus was an uncommonly dedicated journal keeper and strategic planner. His seafaring prowess was based on what he learned from the Portuguese and from counting and recording every single thing he could observe and research. He viewed the Italian explorer Marco Polo with cultural pride. Columbus's own copy of Polo's writings is filled with his critical marginalia.[13] For his proposed venture to the west, Columbus had "determined to keep an account of the voyage, and to write down punctually everything we perform or say from day to day." He promised Queen Isabella that he would "draw up a nautical chart, which shall contain the several parts of the land in their proper situations; and also to compose a book to represent the whole by pictures, with latitudes and longitudes, on which all accounts it behooves me to abstain from sleep and make many efforts in navigation, which things will demand much labor."[14] As a manager, his style was based on evidence and hard work. As a leader, he relied on the transformational effect of his ability to persuade others, as we shall see.

LEADERSHIP STYLE AND CULTURE

We examine Magellan in the next chapter, but a brief comparison here will help define Columbus as a leader and illustrate the age in which these two individuals lived. Columbus the Italian was just over twenty-eight years older than Magellan. Like Columbus, Magellan did not hail from the Castilian Empire that would sponsor him, although he was Portuguese. Yet Portuguese seafaring traditions guided both seafarers. Columbus developed his navigational expertise after settling in Portugal in 1479 and working on its ships for almost a decade. He learned the Portuguese way of tracking birds based on species and time of year to discover islands. He mastered the mariner's astrolabe, a Portuguese improvement upon the quadrant used elsewhere.[15] He studied the Portuguese navigational technique *volta do mar,* ignorance of which had doomed his fellow Genoese explorers Vandino and Ugolino Vivaldi, who in 1291 were the first to enter the ocean in search of the fabled Orient.[16]

Columbus had the same goal as the Vivaldi brothers, but he knew that the hulking Spanish carracks of the Mediterranean were too heavy and fragile to explore the ocean. By 1400, thanks to Henry the Navigator, the Portuguese had developed a nimbler and sturdier ship suited to ocean navigation, the caravel. The masterful construction of its lines, rigs, and hull made it the Age of Discovery's finest, most weatherly, and most maneuverable ship.

Columbus's lust for seeking and collecting external information and Magellan's instinctive tendency to impose his will made for two distinct leadership styles. Columbus worked hard; he acquired knowledge voraciously and studied it thoroughly. He sought status. Magellan had been born into privilege but was independently driven. He was educated in the world's foremost seafaring culture. Status was not as important to him as results. As with other seafarers we will examine, their backgrounds shaped their distinct leadership styles, but all had similar objectives.

The Function of Mutiny

A mutiny can begin to form when external events, including opportunities for the organization, generate internal threats to shared member values. Environmental uncertainty and leaders' actions complete the equation. Thus, in the Age of Discovery, if something that happened at sea created discontent, that is when the captain's actions could spark a mutiny. Such internal threats emerge because of a gap in values between leaders and members on the human side of the enterprise. In each case that we have examined, this gap is evident. It exists in many kinds of organizations, to be sure, but the historical seafaring cases are far easier to examine. Highly ambitious plans and events that strain or break an organizational structure test members' capacity to trust their leader. Shared values define trust. That is why low levels of trust can inspire mutiny naturally in uncertain environments.

Mutinies were so natural in the Age of Discovery that they could be reliably expected to occur in just about any bold seafaring enterprise. They were a normal part of taking risks together in organized but uncertain settings. Leaders and members abided by an authority structure, but proximity during an enterprise made for a certain sense of equality. All leaders directly experienced mutiny. Great leaders knew how to respond effectively to mutiny, often through means so artful as to transform it into success.[17] Because mutiny is a force, it ought to be possible to leverage it in creative ways to serve a human enterprise. The culture of the Age of Discovery, especially in its early years, admitted these kinds of possibilities.

Like trust, culture is defined to a large extent by a set of values that are shared. Functionally, culture moderates the relation between leadership and organizational outcomes because shared values can determine which leader actions are good and which are bad. In other words, culture has evaluative aspects. That is one reason why great-man theory does not explain very much. It is also why a given leadership style will not work equally well in all organizations, for organizations have cultures too. As noted, Magellan was different from Columbus. He was not much of a journalist or researcher. His homeland had bred generations of seafarers before him who all valued discovery. Magellan navigated and commanded, and he updated charts. He was not prone to optimism (or pessimism) or to managing impressions. His leadership reflected those values. Columbus, by contrast, learned to navigate in Portugal, but Mediterranean commerce had shaped his worldview. The values driving his leadership were more person-oriented. The relation between the values that a leadership style connotes and the shared values in a given setting is vital because mutiny can become natural when this relation turns contentious.

At this point in the book, conceptualizing mutiny as "natural" and "not so bad" may still seem strange. Accepting mutiny as natural and potentially positive requires an understanding of the complex nature of trust. The historical cases will illustrate how and where trust fits in an enterprise. Later we will examine trust more formally as a function of shared values.

A MANIAC IN PALOS

Columbus's first enterprise is an excellent illustration of how a leader can respond to subtle and underlying tension when it flashes into mutinous action. In fact, he incurred at least two mutinies during his first and most famous venture to the New World.

The boldness of Columbus's venture raised the bar for all other seafarers. At age forty, he led an enterprise comprising three ships and 120 members. The ships sailed past Palos and into the ocean on August 3, 1492.[18] But months before the departure, the atmosphere around the enterprise had been uncomfortable. Columbus noted that the crew grumbled from the start about the long distance ahead and the uncertainty. Three days after leaving port, crew on the *Pinta,* reluctant to keep sailing away from familiar territory, sabotaged its rudder. Columbus was unflappable in response to such incidents. The *Pinta*'s rudder was repaired at the Canary Islands as it was refitted with square sails.[19] Such bothersome matters as sabotage stemmed in part from the royal decree given to Columbus. It prohibited Portuguese from joining the enterprise and authorized exoneration of crimes for those Castilians who did join. The latter allowance ensured the requisite number for an enterprise that "should not proceed

The *Niña, Pinta,* and *Santa Maria.* this hand sketch of three ships is one of two such sketches found on a map of the New World in the copy of the first decade of Peter Martyr that belonged to Columbus's son, Fernando. It is likely that Christopher Columbus himself sketched them, in light of his strong tendency to fill books and charts with marginalia. (Reproduced in C. Markham, *Journal,* pp. iv–v.)

by land to the east, as is customary, but by a westerly route." It also attracted criminals while repelling good sailors, and it discouraged ship owners from lending their vessels to the ambitious project of a clever foreigner who had become known in Palos as a madman and a maniac. Yet sabotage, problems with crew membership, and unflattering perceptions of his character had no chance of breaking Columbus's spirit. To the contrary, they reinforced it.

As the *Pinta*'s rudder was being repaired and its sails were refitted on Grand Canary, the *Niña* and the *Santa Maria* sailed between Gomera and Tenerife, where they saw an enormous volcanic eruption, "a great fire," from Mount Teide. Shortly after the *Pinta* joined the other two ships on Gomera, all three ships departed the islands. On September 6 the venture formally began.

Two brothers from a Palos family, Martín Alonso Pinzón and Vicente Yañez Pinzón, captained the *Pinta* and the *Niña,* two Portuguese caravels.[20] Their middle brother, Francisco Martín, joined the *Pinta* as master. The flagship, the *Santa Maria,* was a carrack, a heavier vehicle that Columbus grudgingly accepted while pointing out that the royal decree ordered the "supply of *suitable* vessels for the expedition." Privately, he regarded the *Santa Maria* as an unsuitable hulk. He knew the value of caravels from his time in Portugal, and although the hulk was not made for the open ocean, he had to take it.

Throughout September 1492, despite uncertainty, Columbus displayed confidence. He constantly reminded the reticent crew members (and himself) of their high hopes. His journal exhibits a deeply private, gleeful optimism, with no hint of doubt. The scene, he wrote, was "wanting nothing but the melody of the nightingales," and the air was "so fragrant that it was delicious to breathe it."

As a leader, Columbus treated large problems as if they were small but interesting questions. To promote good feelings and raise morale, he promised everyone a "sure sign of land." He was wily. One of the tactics described in his journals is common among unethical accountants: he kept multiple books. His own book was accurate. The public one deceived the crew about the actual distance traveled so they "would not be so terrified and disheartened." Since most measurements and entries of position and speed were made publicly, the forged entries began to excite suspicions among experienced crew members. But Columbus deflected the suspicions with another tactic. Although he was Italian and had lived in Portugal, he often appealed to Castilian pride with eloquent addresses. Thus, he kept distrust low through skill, optimism, deceit, and invocations of a higher purpose. He persuaded the crew, largely composed of petty criminals, to support more than the putative honor among thieves and led them as a cohesive unit.

No one sailing with Columbus could reasonably distrust his prowess as a navigator. He was an expert and was quick to reprimand others for poor skill. His shrewdness combined with his optimism made for volatile but effective leadership in the face of uncertainty. Although no land had yet been sighted, he constantly alerted everyone to winds, birds, whales, seaweed, water color, salt content, and clouds as indicators of nearby land. At times his pronouncements inspired the caravels to race across the waves until excitement waned

Christopher Columbus. (From the gallery of Paolo Giovo,
reproduced in C. Markham, *Life*, frontispiece.)

into melancholy and grumbling. He repeatedly raised spirits only to
then do something to undermine the crew's survival and security.
His tactical cycle sustained the operation for about three weeks after
leaving the Canary Islands.

For a few days beginning on September 25, the venture was on
the verge of success and mutiny simultaneously. The captain of the
swift-sailing *Pinta*, Martín Pinzón, announced that land had been
spotted to the southwest. Excitement was intense as the entire crew
of younger brother Vicente's *Niña* ascended the rigging; they also
claimed to see land. The slower *Santa Maria* trailed the two caravels.
When it reached their position, Columbus and his members also saw
land. The members were ecstatic. On the *Pinta* and the *Santa Maria*
they broke into songs. Later, after a night of strategic planning and

deliberations, Columbus commanded the three ships to turn southwest. They made straight for the land as the sun rose.

The three ships sailed all day and all the next night. By the next
noon, they had covered about 64.5 miles (104 km).[21] The hours grew
longer as the excitement cooled. Once everyone realized that land
had not been sighted after all, the mood became grim. What they
had seen was a cloud bank refracted on the horizon in an illusion
called looming. Columbus retained control by setting the course due
west again. Few words were spoken for three days, but Columbus's
optimism returned. He was burning with confidence and excitement
as the members sulked and grumbled. He slowly managed to restore
morale. But a dark seed had taken root.

Mutiny on the *Niña*, the *Pinta*, and the *Santa Maria*

At midday on October 7, Martín Pinzón was certain that land had
been spotted. The members were more spirited than ever and joined
in an impromptu singing of "Gloria in Excelsis Deo." Columbus
had learned from the events of late September and quickly ordered
the three ships to close in and wait for the cooler evening air to improve visibility. Evening fell, and it was too dark to verify the sighting. The next morning, spirits turned sullen when no land was in
sight. Morale had taken a deadly blow. But Columbus's assurances
continued: they could use the Portuguese tactic of following birds.
His words of hope, more strained than before, did not cool the simmering tension.

The mutiny came on October 10. Several members told Columbus publicly that they would not follow his direction. They wanted
to turn around, not keep heading southwest. Columbus knew immediately from the coordination of the pronouncement that this
mutiny was serious. The ships were now at rest in the middle of the
ocean. He had to head back to Palos, or they would throw him into
the sea. Until this point, the members did not distrust Columbus's

ability, but the two failures to make landfall, and the subsequent false assurances, shifted the balance. Columbus was known for assurances going unfulfilled. And he was Italian. Most people in Palos knew that the Castilian court regarded him as a clever foreigner, a master seafarer but guileful, undeserving of trust. Most of the crew shared those perceptions. They accepted his expertise but not his values.

Distrust and trust are two different dimensions in organizational settings. They can vary independently. The principle holds true today as much as it did in the Age of Discovery. A leader keeps distrust low with demonstrated competence and expertise. But low distrust underpins influence only until uncertainty runs high or a leader starts making big mistakes. Once that happens, trust, which involves a deeper personal connection, is vital. Trust can prevent a mutiny from occurring and allow a leader to keep her or his position. It is earned by connecting with the shared values of members and can carry a leader through periods of high distrust.

The members knew that Columbus was a superb navigator, but he valued discovery rather than what they valued: safety, payment, and exoneration for prior offenses. They did not share the same values with him. They trusted the Pinzón brothers on the caravels as fellow Castilians far more than they trusted Columbus. The assurances that Columbus gave them, the misleading logbooks, and the Pinzóns' presence carried the enterprise farther than it would otherwise have gone. As Columbus's cleverness wore thin, it opened the way for a coordinated mutiny. The members indicated that his authority was in remittance, and he had to respond to them.

Columbus reminded them of the profits they would make if the venture succeeded and insisted that his leadership was necessary to ensure their reward. But the argument that might have been effective weeks earlier was made in vain on October 10. The members had begun to value safety more than money by this point. His argument did not quell the mutiny because it did not connect the shared values of members with his primary objective for the enterprise: finding a route to the East.

Columbus's next tactic was simple and brilliant. He recouped control of the enterprise by effectively doubling down. He first shared the plan with the Pinzóns and then proclaimed to all that if land was not discovered in three days, they would turn around and head back to Palos. That is, he framed the situation with an objective logic that transformed uncertainty into risk and took the focus off himself as the leader. The effect was aided by his ability to deliver gentle words in a sweetly calming tone. In this way he sidestepped the distrust issue generated by mistaken land sightings. He promised the return home desired deeply by the crew but also left a (narrowed) opening for the enterprise to achieve its bold objective.

Columbus thus formulated and implemented the exit strategy that heretofore had been lacking. This kind of management decision hands the success of a going concern to fate. Rather than relying further on his powerful subjective optimism, Columbus now articulated the objective conditions under which he would admit failure. He had already minimized distrust and stretched uncertainty as far as possible. Now he turned uncertainty into risk with a clever switch and, almost instantly, quelled the mutiny.

Columbus immediately returned to calling out sure signs of land. Members were encouraged again. Most entrepreneurs know that the difference between triumphant success and utter failure is often a torturously thin margin. Here, Columbus had led the enterprise for over two months to that extreme edge where mutiny and leadership intersect. That interval during which his leadership was seriously threatened afforded him three more days to achieve success.

Two more days would have been enough. As luck had it, at 2:00 a.m. on October 12, a crew member on the relatively speedy square-sailed *Pinta*, Rodrigo de Triana by name, spotted land approximately several miles away, and directly in front of them.[22] At that moment, the mutiny and recent events were forgotten. The next morning, Columbus and the two Pinzón brothers captaining the other ships landed a small boat on the beach of today's San Salvador. For the next two months Columbus and his crew explored a new world, interacted and traded with the people living there, collected spices, aloes, and other treasures, caulked and repaired the ships, and searched for gold. The potential for mutiny was still under the surface, however.

As powerful as good fortune is, it does not build trust between a leader and members. Columbus's crew did not see achieving landfall as a clear outcome of his leadership. Columbus had predicted finding land, but that is a fairly general prediction to make, and anyone could reason that land indeed existed far to the west. The more meaningful question was how far. By contrast, as we shall read in the Magellan case, when such a prediction was more highly specified and falsifiable, a prediction can build trust if it is proved correct. Therefore, despite Columbus's success in mid-October, it was not long before another mutiny emerged. This time it was among his leadership team. On November 21, Martín Pinzón and the *Pinta* deserted Columbus against his orders. According to Columbus, Martín's purpose was to discover treasures and return to Palos and even claim the discovery of the New World as his own. As night fell, Columbus shortened sail and stood for hours toward the *Pinta* with a lantern. It was still visible far off in the distance. Then it disappeared. The next day, Columbus resumed exploring the islands with two ships.

One month later, on the evening of December 25, 1492, the *Santa Maria* was wrecked and destroyed. An inexperienced crew member had been left in charge of the ship's tiller during the night. The crew, mostly northern coastal people of whom Columbus had a low opinion as sailors, had not laid out the anchor. The tide carried the carrack aground on a submerged shoal, invisible under the light of the half moon. Columbus awoke and ordered the small boat, a standard shipboard complement designed for such emergencies, to stand off the wreck, but the people who took the boat out (one of whom owned the *Santa Maria*) left for the *Niña*. The *Niña* sent them back with one of its own small boats. In the meantime, the surf pushed the hulking *Santa Maria* sideways onto the shoal, and its hull fractured. Columbus ordered the masts cut away to reduce its weight and free it from being grounded, but the move was ineffective because the ship was flooded. Left with only the *Niña,* he blamed the mutinous crew of the *Pinta* for the mishap. Thanks to native people who came out in canoes, most of the cargo was recovered and then guarded on shore.

True to form, Columbus viewed the tragedy as "great good luck, and the settled design of God," for it simplified his decision to leave members behind to search for gold, collect spices, and prepare for future arrivals. The wreck of the *Santa Maria* was used as a target for cannon fire to impress natives with a show of force and win respect for the forty-four men that Columbus would leave behind.[23] By January 4, 1493, he had formulated a return strategy. It had been six weeks since the *Pinta* mutinied and deserted, and there were still no clues about its location.

Columbus recorded the *Pinta*'s actions as mutiny and referred to Martín Pinzón and the *Pinta*'s crew as a "mutinous set." When he unexpectedly found them on January 6, navigating dangerous reefs between islands, he was not sure whether to have them arrested, for he needed cooperation to return to Spain with dignity as a leader. The *Pinta* was at the mouth of a river, and its members were bartering for gold. Sixteen days into a rich round of trade, Martín Pinzón learned from the natives that another ship was nearing. He knew whose it was. Seeing no escape, the *Pinta* sailed to meet Columbus, who had just bade farewell to the crew members left behind.

Columbus was now on the *Niña* with Vicente, the youngest Pinzón brother. The *Pinta*'s crew were loyal to their captain and middle brother Francisco. Those two led the *Pinta,* and its members were a cohesive team. They all agreed to claim that they had been lost and had been bartering for gold for just six days while waiting for Columbus. They admitted nothing, but their treachery was apparent. Columbus saw the *Pinta*'s crew as guilty of "pride, avarice, and covetousness," but he also knew that action against Martín could be disastrous. Columbus did, however, threaten him with hanging when the caravels rejoined each other and Martín boarded the *Niña.*

Martín explained that he had parted company by mistake and offered excuses in the name of the mission. Indeed, the *Pinta* had collected much gold by bartering. Columbus regarded those excuses as lies and knew the *Pinta* had rejoined the expedition because it had no option for escape. Columbus endured the mutinous act in silence, merely wanting a favorable end to a landmark voyage. His incorrigible optimism shone again when he thanked God for allowing the *Pinta*'s mutiny to occur, "causing the *Pinta* to remain here, this being the best place in the whole island to form a settlement and the nearest to the gold mines." But privately, even as he thanked God, he recorded the actions of Martín and his crew as "evil works of Satan."

The two caravels began preparing for their homeward voyage and departed together on January 10, 1493. Columbus still avoided offending Martín for the sake of a smooth trip. In the context of what they had discovered, both mutinies were inconsequential. As he explained, "I will not suffer the deeds of evil-disposed persons, with little worth, who, without respect for him to whom they owe their positions, presume to set up their own wills with little ceremony."

The journey home was initially uneventful. The travelers stopped at more islands, and Columbus reported sighting three mermaids.[24] As before, he rationalized every single event in terms of the mission. He blamed the *Pinta*'s weakened mast and its resultant inability to support a topsail in a storm, which was a common problem at this point in history, on Martín's "motives of avarice" weeks earlier, which prevented its repair. Positive developments, by contrast, he attributed to the justness of the mission.

The end of the journey was not without drama. Columbus and Martín Pinzón parted ways while trying to avoid an oncoming storm in the North Atlantic in mid-February. Columbus had ordered the *Niña*'s mainsail held close so it would coast over the waves and not get swamped as Martín ran the *Pinta* far into the distance. Columbus and the *Niña* spotted islands of the Azores and finally landed at the island of Santa Maria, 1,000 miles (1,609 km) from Portugal, on February 18. There he presented misleading charts to Portuguese mariners to conceal his discoveries. After receiving ominous threats from men claiming to be agents of the Portuguese crown, he departed and made his way through rough seas that forced a course toward Lisbon. He stopped there on March 4. His arrival was potentially dangerous. But King John II, who knew Columbus, reportedly saved him from Portuguese assassins during this stop. In a strange twist of fate, Bartholomeu Dias—whose discoveries were responsible for John II's rejection of Columbus's venture back in 1488—now asked Columbus for details of his trip. Dias was currently the master of the Portuguese sovereign's private ship.

Columbus met with John II on March 9. The meeting was layered with nuance, given the revolutionary nature of Columbus's discovery, his earlier rejection by John, and the histories of the Portuguese and Spanish empires. Columbus reported sailing west and reaching the east coast of India. The king replied that India was Portuguese territory based on a September 4, 1479, treaty signed by his father, Afonso V, and Ferdinand and Isabella at the end of the Castilian War of Succession. His assertion was correct, but that treaty was based on latitude, not longitude. It granted the "ocean sea" (except the Canary Islands) to Portugal. Of course, at this point in history it was believed that only a single ocean existed. Mapmakers and explorers knew the earth was round, which meant that India was on the other side of that single ocean. Spain dominated the Mediterranean Sea. Since the earth's size was radically underestimated, the idea of reaching India (which Portugal had already reached by rounding Africa and going east) by going west across the Atlantic was plausible. Moreover, in 1493, the terms "India" and "the Indies" were vague geographical references that described the enormous area between the east coast of Africa and the easternmost parts of China and Japan. Much has been made of Columbus's error of believing that America was India, but it was a reasonable conclusion given the state of geographical knowledge.

Before Columbus left Lisbon on March 13 and sailed for Palos, he stopped at the convent of San Antonio, outside the city, to pay respects to Queen Leonora. It is quite possible that a boy named Fernão de Magãlhaes saw him there. In any case, Magellan—to use his English name—probably learned of Columbus's feat around this time. King John and the Portuguese court were left bewildered by Columbus's alleged discovery for Castile and the new threats and opportunities it posed.

A month after the two caravels parted, on March 1, the *Pinta* landed at Bayona, in Galicia. It then ran out to sea and tacked south to arrive in Palos on March 15, on exactly the same day the *Niña* arrived from Lisbon. The two caravels thus returned to their home port together after 225 days away. Alonso Pinzón was ill and died shortly thereafter. Columbus never made big issues of the mutinies. The enterprise's success far outweighed the insurrections.

Columbus did make big issues about his records. The rich nautical charts and data from this journey heralded a paradigm shift that was quickly reflected in new maps. The ramifications became clear and inflamed jealous tensions between Spain and Portugal, which believed its territory had been coopted. The contention led to a formal division of the entire globe along a line of longitude passing through Brazil. Portugal had all territories east of the line; Spain, all territories to the west.[25] This new Treaty of Tordesillas was endorsed by Spanish-born Pope Alexander VI in 1494 and amended several more times over the years.

Despite disagreements with the Spanish court over the new territories, Columbus's legacy was intact. His feat ranks among the greatest in seafaring history. He made three more trips to the New World, leaving on September 24, 1493 (with Ponce de León), on May 30, 1498 (during that trip he first sighted the American mainland, on August 1), and finally on April 2, 1502. On May 20, 1506, Columbus died in Spain, at the age of fifty-four. By that time, Ferdinand Magellan, aged twenty-six, was fighting along the west coast of India.

2

Magellan
"Follow and Ask No Questions"

Although so many were against him, nothing was further
from his intention than to yield.

—Francis H. H. Guillemard

Fernão de Magãlhaes was born in 1480 in northern Portugal
(the precise city or parish is unclear) to a family of minor
noble status. His parents died when he was young, and he
was made a page in Queen Eleanor's court. In early 1493, when the
ships of Columbus's first enterprise returned to Castile, he was one of
many young and impressionable Portuguese inspired by the news of
Columbus's discoveries and conquests. He longed for a life at sea and,
in late 1504, enlisted as a volunteer in a Portuguese armada preparing
to sail for India. When it departed on March 25, 1505, Magellan began
his career as a seafarer. For years he traveled with hundreds of hard
fighting men on voyages to India and Africa. He thrived in harrowing conditions and witnessed deaths on land and at sea. He himself
was wounded in 1506 and again in 1509. He earned a promotion to
captain for bravery while fighting in what is now Malaysia in 1510.

As a commander, Magellan adopted the bold style favored in
Portuguese seafaring culture: his fearlessness and focus were unre-
lenting. His leadership was different from Columbus's, although both
had immense talent. Columbus was a warm consensus builder, but

he was not weak. Magellan was dictatorial but not unjust. He led by actions rather than words and, as a leader, responded boldly and intelligently when a mutiny was fierce and organized.

In August 1513 a lance pierced Magellan's leg during an attack in Morocco. The injury was serious; it severed a tendon behind his knee and made him permanently lame: he limped for the rest of his life. He sent a request for the usual recompense for such an injury. Although King Manuel received the request, he did not respond, to Magellan's disgruntlement. His falling-out with Portugal began. In the meantime, he was given the desirable position of quartermaster-major, responsible for dividing booty and the spoils of war.

The Portuguese court that denied support to both Columbus and Magellan was more intrigue-ridden and volatile than the Castilian one that supported them.[1] As a smaller kingdom but with better-organized and more profitable overseas trade than its neighbor, Portugal had a culture underpinned by pride. Indeed, Portugal had much to be proud of in the Age of Discovery. Magellan's prideful-ness did not sit well with his king, however. King Manuel had known Magellan since the latter was a boy, but he could be fickle. When Portuguese officers jealous of Magellan's promotions wanted to discredit him at court, they accused him of selling resources gained in war to enemies in Azamor (Morocco) and keeping the profits. After seven adventurous years at sea and on land, Magellan returned to Portugal. He had been away for longer than his orders specified and was accused of leaving his post in Azamor without permission. But, emboldened by his distinguished record, he not only trivialized those violations and the false reports against him but requested an increase in the stipend associated with his family's status as minor nobility. Unheeding of the tensions at court, Magellan then sought support for a venture idea he had been formulating based on his rich experiences in south and southeastern Asia.

Like many seafarers, including Columbus, Magellan wanted to find the East by sailing west. He knew better than to report his plan to the Portuguese court in a way that would make it easy to replicate, as Columbus had done. In fact, Magellan intended to circumnavigate the globe if the enterprise made it to the Spice Islands that he knew so well. These islands are today's Maluku Islands in modern Indonesia. Reaching them by traveling east would be a bold feat well suited to the Portuguese spirit. But alas, Magellan's strained relationship with Manuel ensured rejection. For Magellan, as for many entrepreneurs, rejection created an opportunity for achievement. By 1514, after a year back in his native land, assured of no support for any ventures, he left Portugal for good.[2]

Magellan knew Castile offered opportunities, as evidenced by the recent history of Columbus. He reasoned that the Spanish would be interested in a westerly route by way of their newly acquired New World territory to reach the East. In late 1517 he was a foreigner in Spain, newly married and living in Seville.[3] Magellan kept pitching his idea to multiple investors. When necessary, he kept certain parts of his plan secret, like the undiscovered passage to the East that he believed existed far at the bottom of the South American continent.

This idea was bold. The expected passage was farther south than all previous explorations of that coast had gone since Pedro Álvares Cabral discovered Brazil for Portugal almost two decades earlier. Magellan estimated that it was about 1,000 miles (1,609 km) farther south than the Portuguese seafarer Bartholomeu Dias had gone to reach the Cape of Good Hope, at the foot of Africa.[4] No European had ever ventured nearly as far south as Magellan intended to go. In terms of audacity, it was the equivalent of America's goal in the 1960s of traveling to the moon.

Fate smiled on Magellan in Spain. He described his project to the ministers of the Castilian court and convinced them to recommend the enterprise to King Charles V. Here the plan was presented fully, with maps rotated 90 degrees to put his homeland at Europe's apex and even with a portable globe, all from Portugal.[5] The case was made in very detailed terms. Even the exit strategy was specified: he named an extreme turnaround point at 75 degrees south latitude. This parallel actually passes through Antarctica, or what Magellan would have

Ferdinand Magellan. (Courtesy Library of Congress.)

called the "unknown southern land" (*terra australis incognita*) or *brasilia inferior*. His promise to relinquish his head if he failed was sincere but unnecessary. The agreement went smoothly, and a document giving him a captain's title and explicit authorization "to find the strait to the oceans" was signed on March 22, 1518.[6]

Portuguese intrigue was already a threat to Magellan's venture. The potential marriage of the daughter of King Manuel I to Charles V gave the Portuguese minister to Spain, Alvaro da Costa, a way to discourage investment in it. But Charles was young and ambitious.[7] He valued the promised rewards of Magellan's venture more than convenient dealings with Portugal.[8] And he sympathized with Magellan despite the maneuverings and intrigues.[9]

Charles exhibited the same warm manner to Magellan that his grandmother Isabella had shown Columbus twenty-six years earlier. Everyone knew the history. Many saw Spanish justice responding to Portuguese rejection. In a poetic twist, the signer of Magellan's commission was the favorite daughter of Queen Isabella, who had signed Columbus's commission. Magellan won firm backing. He was given the power of "rope and knife" over those who would venture with him.[10] The planning and development stages took almost a year. A final decree for local arrangements was sent to Palos on May 5, 1519.

LAUNCHING THE ENTERPRISE

The 1519 decree specified that Magellan would have five ships and a crew of no more than 235 members for two years. Although the king trusted Magellan and was generous in his support, the decree set bounds. It granted a well-stocked armada but also limited membership to no more than five Portuguese. Nonetheless, accounts show that Magellan had up to 268 or even 280 crew members, and we know from the record that many more than five Portuguese were among them. Some historians report that almost forty expert Portuguese joined the enterprise, several holding the most important posts as pilots and navigators.[11]

Magellan's armada, with more than the three ships led by Columbus, was a substantial Castilian enterprise, but it was still a bit conservative by Portuguese standards. Cabral, for example, was leading thirteen ships when he discovered Brazil on the way to India in 1500.[12] After dealing with locals at the port of Seville about some troubles related to his Portuguese identity, Magellan brought the five ships out of the well-appointed harbor on August 10, 1519. They traveled the 62 miles (100 km) down the Guadalquivir River to San Lucar. After refurnishing the ships there, the *San Antonio, Santiago, Concepción, Trinidad,* and *Victoria* departed in the early hours of September 21, 1519.[13] They sailed for the Canary Islands, a routine stopping point off the northwest coast of Africa. There, like Columbus, they stayed for repairs and provisioning before venturing into the open ocean.

Trouble was brewing. Before leaving the Canaries, Magellan received a letter from his father-in-law, the exiled Portuguese noble Diogo Barbosa, a warden in the castle of Seville. Magellan's marriage to Barbosa's daughter Beatriz had provided social capital for dealing with the Castilian court. The letter strongly cautioned Magellan against trusting the Castilian captains on the other ships, but Magellan was already well aware of Castilian-Portuguese ill will. Before leaving Seville, he had faced local difficulties as a Portuguese who favored having other Portuguese beyond the allotted complement join his enterprise. The *Santiago*, in particular, was manned mostly by Portuguese. According to the letter, two groups of caravels, sent by the Portuguese court of King Manuel, were cruising the Canaries and the seas toward Brazil searching for Magellan. Magellan easily outsmarted them. When departing southward on September 29, he tacked close to the African coast to elude them before heading west across the ocean on October 3. The strategy was to turn southwest immediately once Brazil was sighted, a much earlier turn than the normal course called for, and eventually fall in along the South American coast.

Magellan's problems with his members were related in part to the challenges of leading men of various cultural backgrounds.[14] Portuguese wondered why he had really left Portugal. Castilians did not fully accept him because he was Portuguese. Everyone welcomed his knowledge, and no one distrusted his competence, but few trusted his values. Magellan knew that his expertise was not sufficient to establish his authority in case of uncertain circumstances. He needed to connect with members. One of the best primary sources on the distrust that Magellan faced is the account by an Italian named Anthoyne Pigaphete, or, in modern English, Antony Pigafetta. His job was to write a firsthand chronicle of Magellan's voyage. To him, the gap between leader and members was apparent. Pigafetta writes: "The masters and captains of the other ships of his company did not love him: of this I do not know the reason, except by cause of his, the captain-general, being Portuguese, and they were Spaniards or Castilians, who for a long time have been in rivalry and ill will with one another."[15]

Magellan did not, like Columbus, create misleading logbooks. He instead declared a less ambitious version of his goal before leaving Seville so as not to dishearten potential members. At sea, one of his first acts was to establish a command system for the ships of his armada based on lantern signals. His orders were conveyed from the stern of his ship (the *Trinidad*) three times a day in coordination with the standard Castilian three-part watch schedule. The expectation was that the leaders of the other ships would follow and ask no questions. During this part of the journey Magellan did not entertain communications in response to his signaled orders unless it was absolutely necessary to do so.

In mid-October 1519, before sighting Brazil or even crossing the equator, Magellan had to respond to a mutiny. Juan de Cartagena, captain of the *San Antonio*, organized the mutiny with two other Spanish captains, Luis de Mendoza and Gaspar Quesada, during an unpleasant court-martial against Antonio Salamón, a member of the *Victoria*. Salamón was caught sodomizing a cabin boy, who later died by jumping overboard, or perhaps more sinister means brought about his death. The court-martial brought the leaders together.

Cartagena was the ringleader. He had a dotted-line relationship to the crown and positional authority as inspector for the fleet. Being inspector general made him the highest-paid member in the fleet, even above Magellan, which bolstered his confidence. As a patriotic Castilian, he certainly did not trust Magellan and indeed was openly critical of him for many things. At the court-martial he derided Magellan for sailing so close to the African coast, even though that maneuver had enabled the armada to avoid the pursuing caravels. When the fleet came together at sea for Salamón's hearing, the captains were able to communicate closely with one another. Francisco Serrão, the only Portuguese captain, was not approached to participate.

LEADERSHIP AT THE FIRST MUTINY IN OCTOBER 1519

SHIP	LEADER	BACKGROUND
Concepción	Quesada	Spanish
San Antonio	Cartagena	Spanish
	Coca	Spanish
Santiago	Serrão	Portuguese
Trinidad	Magellan	Portuguese
Victoria	Mendoza	Spanish

The court-martial offered an opportunity for the captains to question Magellan's leadership, but it was not enough. There was no clear linkage between Magellan and Salamón's crime involving the cabin boy, so Cartagena's collaborators lost their nerve. When Cartagena nonetheless openly challenged Magellan's decisions on the deck of the flagship, he called on his fellow captains to help him take command. That moment could have shifted the enterprise in favor of the mutiny. But the other captains did nothing. Magellan had Cartagena arrested.

Magellan used the quelling of this attempted mutiny to lower distrust. He removed Cartagena from command of the *San Antonio* and replaced him with the armada's Castilian purser, Antonio de Coca. He sentenced the sodomizer, Salamón, to be executed on land once they reached Brazil. Technically, Magellan had the authority to sentence Cartagena, but he did not because of the latter's status. So he ordered him jailed among the stores of the *Victoria*. These bold moves preserved trust because he was putting the organization under a rule of law and taking into account Cartagena's Castilian ties.

The armada fell along the South American coast on November

29. They were already farther south than the normal route to Brazil would have taken them. Their maps would soon become less reliable, and unfamiliarity with the new environment would complicate progress. Magellan also needed to avoid Portuguese territory. The group landed at Rio de Janeiro on December 13, right at the beginning of summer in the Southern Hemisphere. Salamón was beheaded on December 20. The ships took in supplies and were refitted before continuing south one week later. The crew had expected to spend the winter months in Rio de Janeiro and, wondering if the warm weather would sustain itself through the long journey ahead of them, grumbled about a poorly timed departure. Uncertainty was growing. The coast was indefinitely long and uneven. And the temperature was becoming colder as they headed away from the equator; it was recorded at various points, capes, and shoals in journals and on charts. But Magellan ordered further progress. He did not want idleness to allow a mutiny to be organized.

On January 10, 1520, the expedition arrived at the Cape of Santa Maria, later the site of Montevideo. They entered the large freshwater river and named it after Saint Christopher. Juan Díaz de Solís, a Portuguese venturing abroad for Spain, had entered this region five years earlier. Six years after Magellan, Sebastian Cabot would give this region its current name, Río de la Plata, for the silver he expected to procure there. Magellan knew that members of the Solís expedition had been killed and eaten by natives. When he and his crew landed to get wood, they did it on a small, uninhabited island. No seafarers had ever gone farther south than this point. Here, near the border of what are now Argentina and Uruguay, Magellan sent his ships in different directions, mindful of which captains shared proximity. After exploring the expansive inlet for almost three weeks, he concluded that it did not offer a passage to the East. Storms complicated the progress back out to the ocean. The ships finally exited and continued down the coast on February 3.

The expedition carried on methodically down the coast. They came upon shallow, rocky areas that caused leaks in the *San Antonio*

and bumped the *Victoria* several times. The cold weather was becoming unbearable. Storms were frequent, separating the ships and
forcing them back into the open ocean. They followed the coastline
as closely as they could and named and charted the geography. They
either mistook auks or other pan-alcid birds for ducks or chose to
refer to them as such (*patos*) even though they had no feathers and
had to be skinned before being cooked and eaten. They named one
inlet about 400 miles (643 km) south of the Saint Christopher the
Bay of Ducks. They referred to sea lions as sea "wolves" and feared
them as man-eaters on a par with sharks, marveling at how fierce
they would be if they only had legs to run.

Several times the ships entered bays and inlets only to find dead
ends. Near the end of February, as they tacked into winds out of an
inlet they were forced to moor and wait out the storm. All the *Trinidad*'s moorings but one snapped, and the ship was almost wrecked
on a shoal. Finding a route to the East seemed more and more unlikely, but Magellan's leadership was solid. All previous expeditions
had turned back long before coming so far.[16] Still, deep problems had
been brewing for weeks. Magellan was aware of the crew's lack of
trust in him.

On March 31 they discovered another inlet. At first, they believed
it to be a long strait that perhaps offered a passage through the continent. After discovering that it was merely a bay and full of shoals,
Magellan named it Saint Julian. All members of the crew were growing more and more anxious about the uncertainty of their voyage.
Their latitude estimates showed that they were, unbelievably, about
860 miles (1,384 km) farther south than the Cape of Good Hope.
(They were in what is now Argentina.) They had been at sea for eight
months, and a harsh, cold winter was closing in.

This bay was suitable for sheltering the fleet during the coming
storms and rough seas. Although they found themselves unexpectedly low on supplies, the land was not rugged and fish were plentiful.
Portuguese sabotage back at Seville before departure had resulted in
an undersupply of stores. This shortage was not noticed until well

into the voyage. So Magellan reduced the rations. They could stop here and hunker down for the winter weather, when sailing was dangerous, or turn around now for Spain. Once the members considered the prospect of staying put for five months, many concluded that the land stretched uninterruptedly to the south with no passage through and defiantly wished to go home. Magellan rejected their views and recognized the seeds of mutiny.

Whereas Columbus had been a communicator, Magellan was a man of few words. We translate from a celebrated account, based on primary sources, of Magellan's initial response to mutiny:

> They definitely recognized the coast was still headed south as they traced its primary capes and bays. On March 31 the armada entered the Bay of San Julian, where Magellan proposed to spend the winter and ordered the rations fixed and reduced. The ruling, along with the sterility of the country, coldness of temperature, and unsuccessful surveys to find the strait, began to exasperate the members, who expressed their general desire to return to Spain. Magellan negotiated with their demand, urging them to steadfastness in their works to conclude with honor what they had begun, comforting them with the hope that soon the rigor of winter would cease and they may continue with better weather and more navigational temperance. In the meantime, they had much firewood for heating, a variety of delicious seafood and fishes, clean water, and other things in abundance. They did not even lack bread and wine as long as they remained faithful to the rate that was set. Finally, the enterprise was sanctioned by the emperor, and thus Magellan was determined to die before returning to Spain because of weak discipline and in disgrace.[17]

After Magellan cited Charles V's order to discover the strait, he marveled that these Castilians, who had expelled the Moors and discovered America, could show such cowardice. When he said he would die before going home as a coward, he was appealing to Castilian valor.

Order was restored, but it was short-lived. Despite Magellan's assurances, the crew felt that the enterprise was risking their safety and security. Worse, despite his overtures, their leader was clearly non-Castilian and did not share their Castilian cultural values. His talent for communication did not measure up to Columbus's. In this uncertain environment, unable to appeal to the shared values of the members of his enterprise, he was beginning to lose control as its leader.

A few days later, Magellan learned that several Spanish members were proposing certain elaborate theories based on his Portuguese nativity. The first theory was that he intended to destroy them all on a suicidal voyage for the glory of his homeland, whose inhabitants would rejoice to see the demise of a venture supported by the Castilian king. The second was that Magellan's real intention was to bide his time, waiting until Castile forgot about them or assumed they were lost. Having presumably relaxed the search for a clear route to the East for that significant period of time, Castile would allow Portugal that much more time to enrich itself with Asian spices.[18]

When Maximilianus Transylvanus, noted in the previous chapter, interviewed survivors of the trip a few years later, he found that "Magellan, very much enraged by these sayings, punished the men, but rather more harshly than was proper for a foreigner, especially when commanding in a distant country." Indeed, Magellan's initial response involved threats. The result was a clear affront to the members' shared values.

Here is where mutiny and leadership began to overlap. Either Magellan's actions or those of the mutineers were about to transform the enterprise. The leader and the members were reorienting against each other. Shortly before the confrontation, Magellan replaced Coca as captain of the *San Antonio* with his own cousin, a Portuguese, Álvaro de Mesquita, hoping to build bonds of trust among the leaders.[19] But Mesquita was not the most experienced or qualified person for this position, and the replacement not only heightened tensions but stoked the passions of Cartagena, who was no longer in command of a ship and who was no longer under arrest, either. Gaspar Quesada (captain of the *Concepción*) and Luis de Mendoza (captain of the *Victoria* and treasurer of the fleet) shared Cartagena's values and had special influence over the Castilian members. Again we translate from Martín Navarrette's account:

> Although Magellan believed that he had calmed the agitation among the Castilians he was carrying [on his ship], a few days later he noticed new hatreds and resentments between them and the Portuguese, a renewal of hate and rancor and vulgar preoccupations, which are always fatal to peace and happiness among nations. They murmured about Magellan for being Portuguese, supposing sinister ideas about his service to the emperor; and taking advantage of this discontent, Captains Mendoza, Quesada, and Cartagena conjured against the Captain-General, with whom they had already had some quarrels during the voyage.

Accounts in primary sources give further specifics. Like the first attempted mutiny, this second one was born in the context of an event that brought everyone together. On Sunday, April 1, 1520, Easter mass was held on shore for everyone. The three Spanish captains did not attend. Magellan had invited all of the captains to dine with him on the *Trinidad* later that evening. His cousin Mesquita was the only one who showed up. A line had been crossed as clearly as if it had been drawn in the snow on the banks of the Bay of Saint Julian.

Juan Sebastián Elcano, master of the *Concepción,* joined with Cartagena, Mendoza, and Quesada. They finalized their plan and put a mutiny into action that Sunday night. First, a small boat of thirty men took control of the nearby *San Antonio.* Mesquita was the easiest target because his ship had seen the most instability in authority. The boatswain, Juan de Lorriaga, received multiple dagger stabs from Quesada when he resisted. The attack shocked the members of the *San Antonio* into submission. Temporary command of the ship was given to Elcano. Quesada comforted the crew by opening the stores and distributing all of the food and wine with the help of his assistant, Luis del Molino, and Coca, the former captain. Quesada then told everyone that they were headed for home. A Castilian captain, he said, would take proper control of the armada. This was all it took for the largely Castilian crew to join the mutiny. The appalled Mesquita refused to join, so he was locked away belowdecks. All arms were put into Coca's cabin, for he had joined the mutiny. Cartagena, the original captain, stayed on the *Concepción*.

In a flash, the mutineers took command of the *Concepción*, the *Victoria*, and the *San Antonio*. Magellan, on the *Trinidad*, was still unaware of the situation. His countryman Serrão, also unaware, was in command of the *Santiago*. The next morning, the *San Antonio* would not acknowledge a skiff that Magellan sent to pick up four men to go ashore for fresh water. Guessing what was going on, he sent the skiff to the *Santiago* to affirm Serrão's allegiance. Confused, Serrão nonetheless pledged loyalty to Magellan, who had known Francisco Serrão and his older brother João since all three fought the Zamorins and Arabs at sea near Calicut (modern Kozhikode) in 1505. Later, in 1509, Magellan and Francisco barely escaped death together in an ambush in the Maluku Islands.

Magellan's quelling of this mutiny, though violent, was strategic and brilliant.[20] It epitomizes a basic rule for dealing with a mutiny: the leader's cunning must outmatch the mutineers'. Otherwise, that leader is liable to be deposed or lose authority. Effective action is more important in a mutiny than during normal operations, and mistakes can have grave effects. The advantage does not necessarily go to the first mover. Moreover, mutiny is outside the authority structure that gives a leader power. From the perspective of participants, the old rules do not apply anymore. Thus, it is not generally useful for a leader to make lawful arguments to quell a mutiny. As one historian wrote, in situations of mutiny "right is no longer might," "legal measures are occasionally impossible," and "fairness is worse than a mistake."[21]

Quelling the Mutiny

Multiple members of the enterprise documented Magellan's actions. These primary sources include Pigafetta's journal, a Genoese pilot's account, logbooks kept by Francisco Álvaro (or Albo), and the narrative of an anonymous Portuguese crew member. Maximilianus Transylvanus's writings based on interviews with surviving members also provide details.[22]

A chess match of epic proportions played out on the Bay of Saint Julian. Magellan did not immediately recognize just how serious the situation was. When Quesada sent a list of formal demands, Magellan merely suggested meeting on the *Trinidad*, a halfhearted response not unlike Columbus's first response to mutiny. The mutineers, unmoved, sent a counterinvitation to meet on the *San Antonio*. Magellan then knew that this mutiny was far more dangerous than the one he had quelled the previous October. They were trying to get rid of him. So he kept the boat by which Quesada had sent the note. That was his second move.

Magellan's first move—establishing the allegiance of the *Santiago*—had been more proactive. He knew that the mutineers did not regard the smallest caravel, with thirty-two members, as necessary to their cause. But Magellan had other plans for it. His third move was to ignore the request to meet on the *San Antonio*. Responding would have acknowledged Cartagena's framing of the situation. Not responding also gave Magellan time to prepare a strategy. But he would need to act quickly and decisively when the time came.

Magellan understood that a mutiny does not generally weaken over time. On the contrary, it can strengthen. In a mutiny, the status quo is that time becomes an enemy to the leader. For mutineers, by contrast, it is the opposite: time is an ally. Yet, over the course of the action, the tables can turn and time can become a resource for either side based on strategic actions and cunning. Magellan was nothing if not cunning. He had two ships loyal to him (*Santiago, Trinidad*); his opponents had three ships (*Concepción, San Antonio, Victoria*). Of the three ships opposed to him, Magellan knew that the *San Antonio* was most attuned to the situation, given the multiple changes of its leader. He also thought (incorrectly) that Cartagena was still there. So he decided not to deal with the *San Antonio* directly. All five ships stood in a bay that had one exit to the sea. Magellan intended to change the strategic balance to his advantage. He could afford to wait for dusk.

Magellan turned to Mendoza because the *Victoria*'s crew was second only to the *Santiago*'s in its proportion of non-Castilian foreigners, making it a less cohesive group than the groups on the other ships. Thus, those members were less likely to share the values that underpinned the mutiny. On April 2 he sent the *Trinidad*'s master-at-arms, Gonzalo Espinosa, and five men to the *Victoria* by the light of the moon. They carried a brief note from Magellan asking Mendoza to negotiate. Mendoza would not let the messengers board at first. He was confused because Magellan was ignoring Cartagena and Quesada on the *San Antonio,* but he was finally convinced that the messengers were harmless. He did not know that these men had daggers concealed in their coats. Mendoza met with Espinosa and another of the messengers on the *Victoria*'s deck. Magellan had given Espinosa a simple order: "Cut Mendoza's throat as he reads my words." Espinosa carried out the order with assistance from the other member. Mendoza died immediately.

Magellan had also sent his brother-in-law Duarte Barbosa to the *Victoria* in a small boat, this one with fifteen men. Once the men in the first small boat had killed Mendoza, Barbosa's men boarded the *Victoria* to carry out Magellan's order to kill anyone who resisted. But there was no need. In an instant, mutiny was quelled on the *Victoria.* With Mendoza's death, the entire crew switched allegiance back to Magellan on the spot. Barbosa took command of the *Victoria* around ten that evening and waited for Magellan's orders. These orders included hanging six mutinous members from the yardarm. Mendoza's dead body was strung up by its feet alongside them to send a message to the mutineers on the other ships, and especially to the primary ringleader, Cartagena.[23] The balance was shifting; it was now three ships to two, but the mutiny was far from over.

Magellan responded. He put the *Trinidad* in front of the bay's exit and ordered the *Victoria* to stand off the *Trinidad*'s stern and the *Santiago* to stand off its bow. With the three ships now in formation across the exit from the bay into the ocean, small boats went to the *San Antonio* and *Concepción* to summon them to surrender. They refused. On the *San Antonio*, Elcano asked Mesquita if he would plead their case to Magellan. Mesquita responded that the attempt would be useless. Magellan knew that the destruction of the ships was not part of the mutiny's strategy because the mutineers wanted to return to Spain. Their best option was to slip past the blockade to the exit. As midnight approached, Magellan organized the *Victoria*, the *Trinidad*, and the *Santiago*. They were to fire on the *San Antonio* or the *Concepción* and do whatever became necessary to prevent their escape.

Shortly after midnight, the *San Antonio* approached the blockade slowly. The historical record is unclear about this move. One account says the *San Antonio* was trying to depart but dragging its anchor. Pigafetta tells of Magellan sending a Castilian to the *San Antonio* on a skiff during the night, falsely claiming to have escaped from Magellan and asking to join the mutiny against the Portuguese captain-general. That sailor, as the account goes, later cut the moorings of the *San Antonio*, setting it adrift. Yet another account describes a desperate Quesada, not supported by the other members, standing on deck alone in battle dress as the ship neared the blockade under his solitary charge. In any case, there was no way the *San Antonio* could remain undetected given the light of the moon and the three ships blocking the exit. It seems likely, based on the evidence, that Quesada surmised the fate of the *Victoria*'s captain and was engaging in a last act of desperation. The *Trinidad* fired a round of cannon into the hull of the *San Antonio*, and men on a small boat flung aboard grappling hooks extending from the *Trinidad*. One of the cannonballs passed through the hull and flew right between the legs of the Portuguese cosmographer João Rodriguez de Mafra, who had declined to join the mutiny.

These final events took less than an hour. Only Mendoza and the hanged members had been killed so far. Members of the *Trinidad* boarded on the port side of the *San Antonio,* those of the *Victoria* on the starboard side. Again, in an instant, all the mutineers present switched allegiance back to Magellan. The count was now four ships for him to one against. The mastermind Cartagena, still out on the *Concepción,* knew what had happened. He was asked again from a small boat to surrender and readily obeyed. He was arrested and brought to the *Trinidad,* and the *Concepción* was brought back under normal command. Magellan had extinguished the mutiny.[24] He may have lowered the level of distrust, but he had not yet earned trust; still, nobody would dare to doubt his competence or effectiveness.

The next morning, Mendoza's dead body was brought to shore. An address was read that decried him as traitor to the Castilian crown. The body was beheaded, then drawn and quartered. Next, a pole was driven into the ground, and the remains were hung up in view of all five ships. This act served as another illustration, far beyond words, of Magellan's resolve.

Magellan and a few leaders whom he trusted then held a formal inquiry into the circumstances surrounding the mutiny. Every single member of the enterprise was examined and judged. The process took three days to complete. Not many details about the proceedings are available. There are suggestions that the strappado, a cruel method of interrogation with a long history in the Medieval Inquisition, was used in the trials. Strappado involves suspending a person in the air by the hands, which are tied behind the person's back. A total of forty crew members were found guilty and sentenced to death during the inquiry. The problem was that forty amounted to 20 percent of the crew; the voyage could not continue without them. So after consigning them to death, Magellan pardoned them all but had some put in chains for several weeks.

The two mutinous captains, Quesada and Cartagena, were a different matter. Quesada was the simpler case. He was guilty not just of mutiny but of attempted murder, for stabbing Lorriaga six times on the *San Antonio*. We know that Lorriaga's injuries proved fatal a few months later.[25] Quesada was taken ashore on April 7 to where the body of Mendoza had been four days earlier. In this case, Magellan's shrewd style of justice resulted in Quesada's assistant, Molino, being given an opportunity to execute his own master. Molino had helped in the mutiny. In return for serving as executioner, Molino would keep his life. He resisted at first but gave in. After Quesada was beheaded, his body was drawn and quartered. The limbs were hung on gallows poles not far from Mendoza's. The grisly monument stood as a message to all even after the armada departed.[26]

Cartagena's was a more complicated case because of his position. He had a royal appointment as fleet inspector, so Magellan spared him a violent death. But Cartagena was venomous. He was sentenced to remain under arrest until the armada left the bay. At that point, he would be left behind. Marooning Cartagena avoided a formal record of the direct execution of a Castilian royal appointee by a Portuguese, which even his power of rope and knife might not have allowed.[27] A Castilian religious cleric with French ancestry named Pero Sanchez de Reina was sentenced along with Cartagena. This passionate and reckless priest tried to re-incite the mutiny repeatedly even after Quesada was executed. Not one member of the crew would even listen to him. Since sentencing a priest to a violent execution would have been questionable, the two men shared the same fate.[28]

One more dramatic event occurred before the end of winter. The local area appeared to be navigable to only one of the five ships. The *Santiago*, a tough Portuguese caravel, was Magellan's most maneuverable ship and had the smallest draft. Near the end of April he ordered the *Santiago*, still under the command of Serrão, to explore to the south and seek evidence of a passage through the continent. The other four ships would wait for them to return. By May 3, the *Santiago* had gone about 60 miles (96.6 km) south and discovered a large river, which Serrão called the Río de Santa Cruz. The name remains today. There they refurnished the ship and hunted the curious sea wolves. Once they had explored the river and discovered no passage, they continued southward down the barren coast. On May 22, after sailing only about 11 miles (17.7 km) farther, they encountered a storm that pushed the *Santiago* toward the rocky shore, grounding it there. Fortunately, the members could jump to shore before the ship was smashed to pieces. Only one member (of thirty-seven) was lost.

The members stayed in the wreck's vicinity for a week looking for anything of use that might wash ashore. They procured only wooden planks, which they surmised could help them cross the Río de Santa Cruz when they trekked back north. The weather was cold, the terrain was rough, and the load of wood was too heavy to carry for long. They left many of the planks behind as they progressed. After four days they reached the river. Three went ahead to seek rescue. Altogether, their journey took almost two weeks. Those waiting at the bay almost failed to recognize the first two members who came out of the forest wearing animal skins. The larger ships at the bay, however, could not make the voyage to rescue the remaining thirty-four members on the southern banks of the Río de la Santa Cruz, so Magellan sent a party of twenty-four members overland. At the wide Santa Cruz a raft had to go back and forth a number of times with only two or three men on it each time. When all returned to the armada, the *Santiago*'s members were distributed across the other ships, and Serrão was given command of the *Concepción*.

Magellan sent a small party of four armed men to explore inland, and natives appeared over the coming days to trade and interact with the foreigners on their shore. In the first contact a single native danced on the beach to greet them, and one of Magellan's crew returned the greeting. Natives eventually boarded the *Trinidad* in peace. Magellan noted that their clothing was made skillfully from the hide of the guanaco, an animal similar to a llama. The boots made from the hide looked like large paws, which inspired Magellan to refer to these people as "Pataghom," or "great paw." It is the original source of the term *Patagonia*.

As a Portuguese seafarer, Magellan knew the value of taking on natives and teaching them the language used aboard ship to promote smoother interactions with local populations. The practice had already been a Portuguese tradition for over a century, but it often led to regrettable outcomes. Indeed, in a few weeks, Magellan's taking two Patagonians as prisoners led to altercations. In one instance, the reckless invasion of a native settlement led to death of the *Trinidad*'s man-at-arms after a poisoned arrow penetrated his thigh.

By August, the hint of temperate weather was palpable, and Magellan was intent on proceeding with the voyage. He still did not have the trust of most of the members, but at least the leadership team was cohesive. The trust that Magellan shared with his Portuguese crew was deeper than the trust he shared with the Castilians. Although Portuguese were minorities in this Castilian enterprise, all the captains were now Portuguese and had common values. Magellan reinforced trust on his management team in this way. The *Santiago* disaster and the mutiny in the Bay of Saint Julian had offered opportunities to strengthen the leadership structure, resulting in smoother operations.

Magellan resolved to move the fleet to the Río de la Santa Cruz, which the *Santiago* had discovered, before winter passed. The action would lift members' spirits, helping to put the memory of mutiny behind them. It would also allow the sentences of Cartagena and the intransigent priest to be carried out. Those two were put on shore on August 11, 1520, with an abundance of food and wine, even though the ships did not move away until August 24. Given that the explorers had soured the relations with the natives by taking prisoners, marooning was now almost as terrifying as drawing and quartering.

Two days after departure, and after navigating through a violent squall on the coast, the armada anchored in the Santa Cruz river. Here they stayed for two more months, building up their stores for the next big push. On October 18, the weather was perfect for departure. They proceeded down the long and uneven coast toward the bottom of the world, maintaining the systematic tactics they had used before entering the Bay of Saint Julian the previous March. It was only several days later that someone aboard the *Victoria* sighted

Leadership at the Second Mutiny in April 1520

SHIP	CAPTAIN	BACKGROUND
Concepción	Quesada (moved to San Antonio on April 2, executed on April 7)	Castilian
	Cartagena (took command, arrested on April 2)	Castilian
	Serrão (took command in June)	Portuguese
San Antonio	Cartagena (replaced in October 1519)	Castilian
	Coca (replaced in March 1520)	Castilian
	Mesquita (deposed by mutineers on April 1)	Portuguese
	Elcano (temporary command on April 1)	Castilian
	Quesada (took command/deposed on April 2, executed on April 7)	Castilian
	Mesquita (retook command on April 2)	Portuguese
Santiago	Serrão (shipwrecked on May 22)	Portuguese
Trinidad	Magellan	Portuguese
Victoria	Mendoza (executed on April 1)	Castilian
	Barbosa	Portuguese

a large inlet of the sea that seemed to continue deep into the land. Unbeknownst to them, this inlet was the "strait to the oceans" that was the objective of their enterprise. They named it after the *Victoria* because someone aboard that ship saw it first.

Any possible foreknowledge Magellan may have had of this passage was inexact at best. In those days, cosmologists and diviners were very active in cartography. Maps were badly drawn because the true magnitude of the earth's size was unknown, and methods of determining longitude had not yet been ascertained. There were merely rumors and speculations about a passage. Wildly inaccurate charts showed that one existed, but they were largely the product of soothsayers. Magellan's reasoning had also been influenced by Portuguese experiences along the African continent. In South America's case, the continuous coastal trend to the west insinuated an eventual passage through it. Yet the slow pace of the trip and the uncertainty felt by its experienced members made exploration and hope the important elements at this point. Now the whole venture seemed to be paying off, and the leadership was solid. How could there be another mutiny?

The armada entered the strait on October 21, 1520. Magellan immediately sent Serrão's *Concepción* and Mesquita's *San Antonio* ahead as scouts. Magellan's *Trinidad* and Barbosa's *Victoria* would wait five days on the southern side of the strait for their return. There they endured storms for the next day and a half. After seeing smoke from beyond the horizon, Magellan and Barbosa feared that the reconnaissance mission had ended in a wreck of the two ships. Instead the smoke signaled the scout ships' position. Upon their return, cannon were fired and shouts rang out that the passage offered evidence, such as bottom soundings and tide patterns, of a great ocean beyond.

In a few weeks the armada was deep in the tortuous labyrinth of the strait, and Magellan began to sense a new unrest. His response was action: a push ever farther to the northwest. Although many bays and inlets proved to be dead ends, the main channel continued to carry them. Still, by November 21 the tension was palpable. Members had begun grumbling that it would be wise to return to Castile now because they had achieved success. Returning would allow them to report all their discoveries and prepare a new armada to finish the job. After all, that was what Dias had done when he first rounded the southern tip of Africa. Some Portuguese members, even Magellan's brother-in-law Barbosa, were beginning to support the idea.

Magellan disagreed but he thought better of a bold attempt to prevent another mutiny on the brink of success, as it were, and instead he sought counsel. He called all members to give their opinion on whether to proceed. This was his famous order of the day for November 21. Here is an excerpt:

> I, Fernão de Magãlhaes, Knight of the Order of St. James, and captain-general of this fleet, which his majesty sent for the discovery of the spices, etc. I make known to you, Duarte Barbosa, captain of the ship Victoria, and to the pilots, masters, and quarter-masters of that ship, as I have understood that it seems to you all a serious matter, that I am determined to go forward, because it seems to you that the weather is little fitted for this voyage on which we are going; and inasmuch as I am a man who never rejected the opinion or counsel of any one, but rather all my affairs are discussed and communicated generally to all, without any person being affronted by me; and since, because of that which happened in the port of S. Julian with respect to the death of Luis de Mendoza, Gaspar de Quesada, and the banishment of Juan de Cartagena and Pero Sanches de Reina, the priest, you, from fear, desist from telling me, and counselling all that may appear to you to be for the service of his majesty, and the safe conduct of this fleet, and you have not told it me nor counselled it: you err in the service of the emperor and king our sovereign, and go against the oath and plighted homage which you have made to me; for which I command you on the part of the said sovereign, and on my part beseech you and charge you, that with respect to all that you think is fitting for our voyage, both as to going forward, and as to turning back, that you give me your opinions in writing each one for himself: declaring the circumstances and reasons why we ought to go forward or turn back, not having respect to anything for which you should omit to tell the truth. With which reasons and opinions, I will say mine, and my decision for coming to a conclusion as to what we have to do. Done in the Channel of All Saints, opposite the river of the islet, on Wednesday, twenty-first of November, in

fifty-three degrees, of the year one thousand five hundred and twenty.[29]

His order was personalized and delivered to each ship. It did not take long to receive responses. The leadership indicated cautiously that the voyage should continue. However, many members favored a return home. Andrés de San Martín, a famed cosmographer, responded with doubts about an opening to the East, but he publicly suggested going forward while summer lasted.[30] The response of San Martín, who was famed for his knowledge and was something of a charismatic mystic, resonated with all.

To build confidence during the discussion, Magellan referred to a spherical chart of the world, sometimes known as an apple.[31] A similar globe had been used as a prop when presenting his enterprise to the Castilian court. Magellan and the members already knew that the earth was round. A portable globe that showed the ocean beyond western lands had made the idea of crossing the ocean and arriving in the East seem feasible. The newest globes reflected the latest knowledge of world geography and hinted at a passage where they were now situated. On these grounds, Magellan explained to the Castilians, they must have hope. Fortune had favored them. His message was powerful and transformational. The next day they forged ahead.

The Castilians still did not connect with Magellan, but none could make a strong argument against following him. None, that is, except for a certain brilliant Portuguese crew member. Esteban Gómez was the expert pilot of the *San Antonio*. Back when Magellan was seeking funding for his enterprise in Castile, Gómez, a celebrated seafarer, had proposed a similar but less developed plan, only to lose out to Magellan. Now Gómez's dark sentiments had been reawakened by Magellan's success at finding the promising passage. The neutrality of the November 21 order of the day gave him the perfect opportunity to make a strategic move. Magellan was very much aware of Gómez's record and his rejection and knew that Gómez was a risk to his authority. That is part of the reason why Magellan had given command of the *San Antonio* to Mesquita, a less capable seafarer than Gómez, after the mutiny in the Bay of Saint Julian the previous April.[32] Now the expedition was on the brink of success, but that also brought certain new threats to his leadership.

Gómez brilliantly championed the idea of returning later with another armada, and he illustrated the risks they were now facing given the state of their provisions. Magellan had a unilateral response: Gómez was to stand down. The hardest parts were over, he declared. No one was to talk any further of the difficulties of their mission.

Around November 21, the armada reached a spot where three smaller channels diverged from the main channel. Again, Magellan ordered Mesquita and Serrão to explore smaller channels on both sides and then return and report. In the meantime, his *Trinidad* and Barbosa's *Victoria* would move slowly along the larger middle channel. Pigafetta recounts that the two ships progressed in this way for one day and covered about 40 miles (64 km) before anchoring and taking in provisions. They settled in to wait for the scout ships to catch up with them, and the *Trinidad* sent a small boat to do further scouting ahead. The small boat was gone for three days. When it returned, it brought the news that everyone wanted to hear. There was no longer any question: its crew had found a cape at the end of the strait and had clearly seen the ocean beyond. Magellan's men responded with cannon fire and tears. Now they just needed to wait for the *Concepción* and the *San Antonio* to rejoin them.

After another day passed, Magellan turned back to search for the two scout vessels. Serrão, found with the *Concepción* in the main channel, reported no outlets to the ocean. Nor could he report further contact with the *San Antonio* since they had parted to explore. So the *Trinidad,* the *Victoria,* and the *Concepción* traveled back east through the strait; the *Victoria* even went most of the way back to the Atlantic entrance. They now had some familiarity with the region and could look around with less anxiety than before. According to several journals, the scenery was breathtaking. They marveled at the glacial walls, snowy peaks, and evergreen forests. Everything was new and strange. The original accounts show that Pigafetta wrote, "I think that there is not in the world a more beautiful country, or better strait than this one."[33] But the *San Antonio* was nowhere to be seen. After waiting four–six days, Magellan ordered Barbosa to write out their intended course, put the document in a clay jar, and bury it at the foot of a cross on a high peak near the strait for the *San Antonio* to find. Three such monuments were left before the fleet turned back to find what might await them.

Magellan reasoned that if the *San Antonio* had been wrecked, there would have been signals and crew members somewhere along the route. Since there was no such evidence, it must have been lost completely—either by accident or on purpose. In this case, Gómez had mutinied against Mesquita and thus against Magellan's leadership.[34] The two older Pinzón brothers had mutinied on the *Pinta* on almost the exact same date in 1492 (November 21) on Columbus's first voyage.

Magellan's first mutiny had occurred in October 1519 during normal operations. The second mutiny, in the Bay of Saint Julian, occurred at one of the darkest points of the voyage. Now a third mutiny had occurred at the pinnacle of their success. What was the common element? Magellan again consulted San Martín, who had filled many pages with notes during the voyage. San Martín was an astrologer, and Magellan wanted a reading of his horoscope. He had no intention of turning back, but the reading would carry weight with many of the crew. An ocean had been sighted at the end of the strait, and they knew how to get there. Many were now wondering, Was it better to turn around? The cunning San Martín had a rich political sense of context. He knew what Magellan wanted to hear and confirmed that the ships should not turn around.

By this point, Mesquita was in irons in the *San Antonio*'s hold, not far away from the dead body of a Patagonian prisoner.[35] He was tortured to make him swear that the mutineers, led by Gómez, were justified. Gómez gave command of the *San Antonio* to a clerk named Geronimo Guerra, who was also a talented pilot. They navigated back

Seville, where they arrived on May 6, 1521.[36] The fleet's largest ship, it carried most of the stores. Magellan knew that the loss of the *San Antonio* would affect the crew on the other ships, and he wished to avoid any perception that the enterprise was weakened. With Martín's horoscope in hand, he ordered that the three-ship armada set sail for the west.

Westward they went. Along the way they sighted hundreds of small fires made by indigenous people—the Yaghan—on the southern side of the strait and called the area the "land of fire," a name it bears to this day.[37] Tierra del Fuego consisted of many islands, between which the natives traveled in canoes. Thirty-eight days after entering the strait, on November 28, 1520, the trio of ships passed Cape Deseado, the "longed-for" cape, and sailed into the South Pacific. Pigafetta estimated that the strait through which they traveled was between 350 and 400 miles (563 and 643 km) long. He was close: it stretches about 348 miles (560 km).

The first and original European name for the strait is somewhat unclear. One fifteenth-century cartographer had projected a smoothly curving coastline for the continent down to its "dragon's tail" tip, and one name came from that shape.[38] The primary account of the anonymous Portuguese crew member called it the Victoria Strait after Magellan's ship. The journal maintained by Pigafetta referred to it as the Streto Patagonica after Magellan's name for the land's inhabitants. Magellan did not name the strait. As in his November 21 order of the day, he called it the Channel of All Saints because the armada entered it on All Saints' Day (November 1, 1520).

Yet some proud members of Magellan's landmark enterprise assigned it the name of their captain-general, giving it the name we use today: Strait of Magellan. Magellan had finally earned the trust of his crew by making a very specific prediction that was realized. The trip had taken them through some of the most dangerous waters in the known world. He had endured difficulties together with his members. He was active, could be ferocious, was never distant. His way was to quell mutiny on rational grounds based on the original mission objective. His actions reflected his own values. Magellan realized success by all these means. Some very dire days would come as they crossed the Pacific Ocean, but even then, Magellan did not face another mutiny.

The ships took three months and twenty days to cross the ocean. The members spotted what are today known as the Magellanic Clouds and the Southern Cross. They called the ocean "pacific" (*mare pacificum*) for its calmness, lack of storms, and warmer climate. They badly underestimated the distance across it, however. After all, the west coast of South America is east of the east coast of North America, allowing a profoundly wrong assumption about geography. Existing models of the round earth were also scaled exceedingly conservatively, implying much shorter overall distances between bodies of land. Like other seafarers of the age, Magellan and his navigators struggled with calculations of the correct longitude and were baffled by the need for a dateline. The small fleet sailed with good speed, but the long journey with no land in sight, plus the scarcity of food and an intense outbreak of scurvy, almost killed them all.

They finally sighted what are now the Mariana Islands on March 6, 1521. As they explored farther west, Magellan and his crew saw familiar territory and islands and knew they were indeed on track to becoming the earth's first circumnavigators. The adventures continued, and the full story is worth reading. Serrão died, Magellan was killed by natives (in the Philippines in April 1521), and the shipmates had many varied interactions with natives, shipwrecks, and another mutiny (after Magellan's death) before rounding the Cape of Good Hope on the return to Spain.

The *Victoria*, whose members first sighted the strait, was the only ship to make the entire trip around the world. On September 6, 1522, it arrived at San Lucar, where it had been three years earlier. Elcano, a participant in the mutiny against Magellan in the Bay of Saint Julian, was its captain.[39] Thirty-one crew members out of more than 235 completed the trip.[40] Two days later, the *Victoria* moored in the harbor of Seville and fired all of its cannons at once. News of the arrival quickly spread across the entire Iberian Peninsula. The enterprise significantly changed the course of world history.

MAGELLAN'S LEGACY

Even today, for reasons related to Magellan's Portuguese birth and his allegiance to Castile, the assessment of his legacy varies based on culture and historical perspective. But whatever the viewpoint, this case shows how shared values are integral to bold leadership and monumental achievement in uncertain environments. Uncertainty wins committed allies based on trust just as it generates enemies who do not share in that trust. Environmental uncertainty creates sharp boundaries that, when crossed, are germane to mutiny. Trust, as the values that leaders and members share, makes it possible for such boundaries to be expanded and for an enterprise to achieve outcomes that would be otherwise impossible.

Then as now, mutiny can and does bring forth extreme feelings and acts, both compassionate and treacherous. But from the perspective of successful leaders like Magellan, mutiny brought short-term difficulties but added positive value over the longer term.

Beyond achieving the first circumnavigation of the globe, Magellan offers a specific legacy for leaders by illustrating the true worth of unflagging determination and obstinate leadership through uncertainty. Just like Columbus's enterprise a generation earlier, his enterprise achieved a landmark objective because of leadership tempered by mutiny. Indeed, both leaders leveraged mutiny into a force instrumental to venture performance. The styles and limits of both leaders fit the challenges facing their enterprises.

3

Cabot
"Nobody Knows Who He Is"

In so much that all with great admiration affirmed it to be a thing more divine than human, to sail by the west into the east where spices grow, by a way that was never known before. By which fame and report there increased in my heart a great flame of desire to attempt some notable thing.

—Sebastian Cabot, describing his reaction
to Columbus's 1492 voyage

The English seafaring tradition matured later than the Portuguese and Spanish traditions, primarily between 1485 and 1550 and mainly during the reigns of Henry VII and Henry VIII. Its initial development was driven largely by commerce and trade with nearby European neighbors. When Portuguese and Spanish seafaring achievements became impossible to ignore, England looked to the ocean beyond it. But the English seafaring culture was different from the Iberian one, driven to a greater extent by company rule rather than royal decree, and there was much catching up to do. By the mid-sixteenth century, England's commercial organizations had become active as financiers of ever-bolder enterprises. English seafaring continued to develop significantly, eventually producing seafarers like Henry Hudson.

England's procurement of the Portuguese caravel in the early sixteenth century was a catalyst for its development of seafaring. This small but sturdy and maneuverable vehicle from Portugal opened up new possibilities for English exploration and discovery.[1] This period saw many English developments in the arts and sciences, supported by relative peace between Protestants and Catholics. The complications of the union between Spain and Portugal (1580–1640) had made Spain less of a threat to England and encouraged greater English commerce on the world's oceans. As English seafaring became bolder, an empire began that would become, in a few hundred years, the most powerful the world had ever seen. But back in the sixteenth century, its development was limited to two simple fronts.

English seafarers faced Portuguese seafarers to the southwest and in India and Spanish seafarers to the southeast and in the Americas. Moreover, instead of navigating, English sailors were accustomed to following the shores of Europe. When John Cabot landed on the faraway transatlantic coast in 1497, that worldview was upended in more ways than one. Whereas Columbus had bumped into islands in the Caribbean, Cabot actually came to the coast of today's Newfoundland and Labrador and thus discovered the North American mainland. His achievement promoted England's "age of discovery" (1485–1550), which led to its own golden age. It was presided over by Elizabeth I (reigned 1558–1603) and populated by William Shakespeare, Christopher Marlowe, Sir Walter Raleigh, and Nicholas Hilliard, and many others.

The two preceding centuries of the Italian Renaissance (the era of Michelangelo Buonarroti and Leonardo da Vinci) inspired England's golden age. During those same two centuries, Iberian seafaring and the Age of Discovery (the era of Columbus and Magellan) inspired England's seafaring. Yet England extended all such traditions. England was a world power by the 1500s, but that status was based on manufactured goods and exports and a commercial empire. Its development followed the logic of commerce rather than the spirit of conquest. England's commercial activities were far less developed than what was common on the Italian Peninsula, with its ancient

Mediterranean trade network—but that was changing as England began to enjoy its geographic maritime advantages. Moreover, unlike what was common on the Iberian Peninsula, England's seafaring enterprises were often sponsored by large commercial organizations, which had vital operational aspects and took equity stakes in its ventures. As a result, British expansion entailed a distinct and continuous spread of infrastructure and supply chains across its territories.

Company rule was different from the support of a royal court in other ways, too. The company's existence often depended largely on the success of the venture. English seafaring was thus more careful and deliberate than Spanish or Portuguese seafaring. Its orientation was based more on commercial profits and less on bold discoveries. The early English seafarers were less daring than the Portuguese or Spanish ones because their values were different.

English seafaring might have developed differently without the mercurial Cabots. The elder, John Cabot (Giovanni Caboto), had much in common with Christopher Columbus (Christoforo Colombo) and was similarly inspired by Marco Polo. Cabot's birthplace is unclear, but he became a Venetian citizen (Zuan Chabotto) in the mid-1470s. From Venice, he visited Mecca disguised as a Muslim to research spice caravans. By the late 1480s, debt-laden from failed construction projects, Cabot fled to Spain. There he claimed expertise in construction on water (learned in Venice). In the early 1490s, he proposed harbor redesigns in Valencia and a stone bridge across the Guadalquivir River in Seville to replace a 700-year-old floating one. In 1494, the bridge project's funding was withdrawn. Cabot then went to England, where he sensed quickly that the English wanted from him what Columbus had done for Spain.[2]

King Henry VII sponsored the elder Cabot's landmark venture, hoping he would exceed the achievements of navigators sailing for Portugal and Spain. Cabot commanded a small crew on a ship called the *Matthew* in a strategic replication of Columbus's venture. His was riskier, though, entailing one ship, not three, and 18 members, not 120.

Fortune favored John Cabot on this enterprise. He was well prepared, having studied everything available about current English sea-faring. The English now tentatively sought "the islands of Brasil and the Seven Cities" believed to exist in the middle of the great ocean.³ Belief in these destinations was supported by English and Italian sightings of the Azorean archipelago, which includes nine islands. Small communities of Portuguese had already been living there for the better part of a century.⁴ Yet Columbus's trips to the Caribbean changed everything. Cabot eventually set sail from Bristol on May 2, 1497. He sailed straight west and landed on the North American coast near modern-day Newfoundland on June 24. His ship returned to Bristol on August 6. England celebrated. Cabot, dressed in silk, soon feasted at the English court, bearing the title of admiral. In May 1498 he set sail again.

Given the excitement surrounding Cabot's initial success, his second enterprise back to the "new found land" was of unprecedented size. It included a ship sponsored by Henry VII and four other ships sponsored by powerful merchants. Foreshadowing future English sea-faring ventures, this one met with disappointment. Newfoundland was a cold and barren land, nothing like China or India. There were no payloads of spices nor discoveries that would translate into riches. The merchants who invested in that enterprise saw their investments vanish, and John Cabot himself disappeared from the historical record in 1499. Some historians believe that he died during the trip. Other historians think that he perished through more scandalous means. His fate remains a mystery.⁵

Most English seafaring voyages at the time were smaller commercial ones to the European continent. Like the Portuguese and Spanish ventures, a few were intended to discover resources, but the English ones were not nearly as sophisticated. Many such English ventures brought nothing but loss to their sponsors. The ships often experienced mutinies, some of which saved the enterprise, others of which hampered its success. For example, a mutiny was undertaken against a Bristol merchant named Hugh Elyot, who had sailed with John Cabot. It happened during a 1502 voyage in search of a northwest passage through or around North America from the North Atlantic. Nicholas Thorne, who had also sailed with John Cabot, was a member of Elyot's crew. A letter from Thorne's son Robert offered a 1527 declaration to Henry VIII through his ambassador: "Of which there is no doubt (as now plainly appeareth), if the mariners would then have been ruled and followed their pilot's mind, the lands of the West Indies (from whence all the gold cometh) had been ours, for all is one coast."[6] Elyot made multiple attempts from 1502 to 1505 to find a northwest passage, but his sponsors finally cut their losses. Finding a passage to the East was a long-running dream of English seafarers. Thorne himself, along with others, sought sponsorship for a trip to the North Pole to find one. A century later, Henry Hudson would attempt the same thing, for most explorers still believed that the North Pole was the location of a warm and gentle sea. But back in the early 1500s, England was just making its acquaintance with oceanic navigation, and it had much to learn.

The Uncanny Sebastian Cabot

John Cabot's sons Ludovicus (Lewis), Sebastian, and Sanctus (Sancio) probably accompanied their father on the 1497 venture.[7] Sailing to the north was natural for England, for Portugal and Spain dominated everywhere to the south. England was not yet ready to compete directly with those two empires at sea. In fact, just weeks after word got out that the elder Cabot had made landfall on the northeastern American coast, Portuguese caravels were there. The Portuguese quickly determined that the land offered little in the way of resources. The Cantino Planisphere, cited in chapter 1, shows John Cabot's "Newfoundland" marked with the name "Terra del Rey de portuguall."[8] Sebastian Cabot's small 1508 group explored the same area inconclusively. Sebastian went farther than his father, however, and charted today's Prince Edward island along with the entrance to the enormous bay that Henry Hudson later gave his name to.

It is not exactly clear when or where Sebastian Cabot was born (circa 1475, probably in Venice) or when he died. What is clear is that he was a strategic, passionate explorer with a worldly, entrepreneurial spirit. His character reflected the intensity of Magellan and the cleverness of Columbus. He often acted with multiple intentions that seemed conflicting but would prove congruent. His actions could be mysterious, and he had an uncanny and unerring capacity for achieving simultaneously positive and negative results. Cabot was a master at turning utter failures into successes. He was also a rebel. For example, Cabot turned south during his 1508 trip to the northwest Atlantic and traced the North American coast almost all the way to Florida—a sidetrip beyond the scope of his contract. He did not stop until mutiny compelled him to head back to England.[9]

When Cabot returned to England from his Florida excursion, it was early 1509, and a new king, Henry VIII, was on the throne. Cabot's venture had generated nothing other than a rough survey of the American coastline that offered no new information. He lost some credibility as a navigator, but his carefully engineered reputation for world-class cartography skills won him a royal commission to make maps and charts. This career move took him away from his more entrepreneurial aspirations as a navigator. A map he made in May 1512 guided the English army to Spain as part of a campaign against Aquitaine in southern France. Cabot joined that expedition secretly hoping to find Spanish employment as a seafarer in a culture that valued discovery and exploration more strongly.

When the English army mutinied and the whole expedition dissolved, Cabot snatched his opportunity. A few months later, he secured a meeting with the secretary of the Spanish princess Juana Loca (Joanna the Mad) at Burgos, which was instrumental in gaining an audience with her father, Ferdinand II of Aragon. Many people in Spain had heard of Cabot's father, and he freely used his father's name when it helped his cause. Moreover, Ferdinand's other daughter, Catherine of Aragon, had recently become Henry VIII's first queen. Henry eventually banished her and married Anne Boleyn, but at this early point Ferdinand welcomed this "Englishman" who had served his admirable English son-in-law. Cabot's clever presentation of ability and knowledge was met with favor.

Ferdinand remembered how his wife had warmly supported Columbus, a contemporary of Cabot's father, in the early 1490s. Columbus's enterprise had brought great value to his large kingdom. Queen Isabella had died in 1504, so it was the elderly Ferdinand who now appointed Cabot as sea captain on October 20, 1512. Cabot's charge was to go to Seville and wait for orders.

Cabot allowed the Spanish to regard him as English. The English, however, had thought of him as Italian. When he later returned to England, he was practically thought of as Spanish.[10] In any case, he was a foreigner. All was initially promising and even joyful for the clever foreigner in Seville. But his wait for an enterprise turned into a long one owing to unfortunate events. First, the aging Ferdinand became indisposed and then died, on January 23, 1516. Charles I, son of Juana, became the new ruler of Spain. Charles I became Holy Roman Emperor Charles V three years later. He might have supported Cabot's ideas for enterprise, but the new emperor had not yet been to Spain. Originally from the Netherlands, he would not arrive at his new kingdoms until late 1517.

In the complicated interim after Ferdinand's death, Cabot's opportunity disappeared. The entrenched Castilian enemies of all clever foreign explorers could now align against Cabot. These enemies sought to advance their own fortunes as complexities unfolded into dissension in the royal system.[11] Cabot's cunning could not help him because he lacked the position to utilize it. He knew it was best to return to England.

The historical record is unclear about Cabot's next English enterprise. Some sources report that he never left Spain at all, whereas others show that he undertook an English venture with Vice Admiral Thomas Spert in 1516–1517, with Spert in charge.[12] He won sponsorship from Henry VIII, whose interest in seafaring was to bolster British commerce. For this voyage he had two ships, and his mission was to find a passage to the East by taking a northwestern course.

But here again Cabot ventured south after reaching the Americas. He believed there might be a passage through the middle of the continent. This time, he traveled so far down with Spert that they passed Florida. This unauthorized move reflected Cabot's life goal to do something notable. The ships finally turned back to the north and ended up where Columbus's armada had made landfall a generation earlier. There, they ran into trouble. Although Portugal and Spain both secretly violated the Treaty of Tordesillas dividing the globe between them, for England to do so was a risky business: the treaty gave Portugal the hemisphere to the east of a north-south line through Brazil, and Spain the hemisphere to the west. Nor did Cabot and Spert have the navigational skills to violate the treaty with impunity. Nonetheless, they entered Spanish territory under English colors.

Some historians find what happened next at odds with Cabot's character, whereas others find it perfectly sensible. The event is described from various biased points of view. It is clear that Cabot and Spert landed and attempted to undertake trade with local people, perhaps out of necessity after the long journey down the coast. Such activity in Spanish territory was foolhardy. Not surprisingly, a Spanish armada found them and fired cannon at their ships, and they frantically retreated. Cabot publicly regarded Spert poorly but admitted that the failure of the voyage was not entirely Spert's fault.[13] The disappointing enterprise was another turning point in Cabot's career. He was back in England because he loved exploration but had found barriers in Spain. Now he was reacquainted with the incongruity between his grand aspirations and the modest worldviews of the sponsors of English seafaring ventures.

The Spanish court decided to promote Cabot from sea captain to pilot major on February 5, 1518. He married a very ambitious Spanish woman named Catherine Medrano. His new post, entrusted to him by Charles V, entailed teaching cosmography, examining and licensing pilots, maintaining maps and instruments, approving all seafaring ventures, and updating the register of geographic discoveries. It was a desirable position and the perfect stepping stone to winning a large-scale enterprise and achieving fame. His appointment must have incensed Castilian navigators, most of whom had superior experience, for Cabot was not Spanish but now had much authority over Spanish seafaring. Many in Seville regarded Cabot as a foreign impostor and a charlatan, reflecting the same impression that Columbus had made in Castile. Cabot's career now had impetus. He was masterful at turning the mystery around him into a source of opportunity, even though most experienced seafarers saw him as vain and posturing.

In 1521, Cabot found one more potential opportunity for a new venture in England. Henry VIII and twelve major livery companies planned to finance the launch of five ships seeking a northwest passage. Such a route was badly desired, and venture success promised vast riches. The deliberations for this venture illustrate a bureaucratic process that eventually generated strongly expressed doubts about Cabot. Since Cabot had not been born in England, they wondered about his true allegiance. The merchants also cited a twenty-year chasm in the history of Cabot's transactions. His reputation was celebrated, but they did not trust him. Records show that the merchants declined the "sore adventure" based on the "singular trust of one man" who "made a report of many things, only as he had heard his father and other men speak in times past."[14] So Cabot continued his activities in Spain while pitching for an opportunity in England.

Cabot was reckless and had an uncanny ability to turn mistakes into advantages. He displayed this oddly complex style in Seville, often playing scandalous games. He had pledged his soul to Spain in 1518 and denied any intention to serve England even as he was secretly angling for an English enterprise in 1521. He was lucky that the English livery-merchant sponsors withdrew, for Spain would have exacted a price for disloyalty. Misleading two nations at once was risky, but it paled in comparison to some of Cabot's other gambles.

Cabot was actually misleading three nations at once. In addition to his dealings with Spain and England, he undertook shockingly brazen intrigue via an intermediary named Don Hironimo de Marin de Bucignolo. This man was from Ragusa, in the southern part of modern Croatia. On behalf of Cabot, Hironimo sent a request to a powerful group of Venetian political leaders called the Council of Ten. The Ten had originally maintained the security of the Venetian government but expanded their power by clever designs. Cabot requested a meeting with them and reported that he had knowledge of a northwest passage to the Indies. He wanted to lead a venture and claim this passage for Venice. Dealing with them while serving Charles V could have cost Cabot his livelihood or his life. His correspondence with them displays his patriotism for an Italian homeland he barely knew, for which they expressed appreciation, and his intended treason against Spain. If the Spanish had discovered his disloyalty, Cabot would have been finished.

Cabot was clever, but as diplomats in a venerated tradition, the Ten were cleverer. For more than two hundred years they had developed a facility with the spirals of intrigue. They were more sophisticated intriguers than the kinds of individuals in England whom Cabot was accustomed to outsmarting. The Ten intended to draw him out and capture information for their own records, playing along even as Cabot urged them to send a false letter inviting him to Venice to reclaim his mother's dowry and family property before an ailing aunt died.

Cabot met with Venetian ambassador Caspar Contarini many times, and asked to sail for Venice. There were obvious problems. For instance, such an enterprise, if not stopped by the Turks, could not hope to escape the Portuguese or the Spanish at the Strait of Gibraltar. Cabot displayed navigational knowledge persuasively, even claiming an ability to measure longitude, a task that had routinely frustrated navigators.[15] He excited distrust with his idle treatment of serious but simple and practical questions, such as where to get the ships. He claimed falsely that he had already spoken to other Venetian ambassadors. He was pilot major of Spain, but he expressed a readiness to deceive Charles V. The 1522–1523 correspondence concerning Cabot between Contarini and the Ten is well documented but brought neither reward nor punishment because it was not discovered until many years later. In any case, all was forgotten by all sides when another, larger-than-life event occurred: Magellan's circumnavigation of the globe.

Magellan's achievement caused a shift in social consciousness and generated new opportunities and threats. Portugal and Spain's famous treaty was now overturned because of the newly discovered underestimates of the earth's size. It was not clear anymore who had the rights to the Spice Islands, which traditionally belonged to the Portuguese. Councils were held to handle the territorial disputes. The opening up of the world to exploration and travel stoked Cabot's passionate desire "to do some notable thing."

In April 1524, Cabot, as pilot major, attended a council of geographers and cosmographers that met at Badajos. Cabot met Fernando Columbus, son of Christopher, there. This council intended to create new chartings of the meridian that divided the globe and put boundaries on Portuguese and Spanish interests. Basically, it needed to make sense out of the fact that rounding Africa was not the only route from Europe to the East. The Portuguese, feeling threatened, demanded that Spain stay out of the Spice Islands. But they also wanted to keep what they could of Brazil. Pushing the meridian dividing line west to gain more of Brazil balanced a loss of Spice Island territory by pushing it west on the other side of the globe. Despite many Portuguese protests, the new charts drafted at the council seemed to favor Spanish demands.

The Portuguese were outraged at the potential loss of the Spice Islands. One of Portugal's native sons—Magellan—had dishonored the kingdom by sailing for Spain. Now the ramifications of his enterprise disfavored it further. The council adjourned in stalemate. Portugal still kept some of Brazil (a larger area than the Spanish believed it was) but was in danger of losing much of its spice trade. Portuguese wrangling turned into threats. Spain offered to launch a new enterprise to chart the disputed region directly. The Portuguese responded with wrath, swearing to attack Spanish ships. Magellan's treachery and his achievement had shattered their pride. Indeed, only an expert and daring navigator (or a very foolish one) would be able to lead a Spanish expedition in such an environment.

Here was Cabot's big opportunity. His life's ambition was to establish a new route to Asia. He claimed knowledge of a shorter route than Magellan's based on his maps and charts. His first voyages for England had targeted the northwest. Now he could sail southwest for Spain and improve upon Magellan's achievement. Did Cabot ever meet Magellan or know of his true plan? The two undoubtedly had met in Seville in 1519 as Magellan was outfitting his armada.[16] That Cabot knew of his plan at that point is unlikely, because Magellan was careful about discussing it with others before departing. Once news spread of the *Victoria*'s return three years later, Cabot's aspirations intensified. The reputation he had engineered, combined with the crown's esteem, sealed the deal. In September 1524, he received authorization to lead the enterprise, with at least three vessels and 150 crew members. The contract was signed in Madrid on March 4, 1525.[17] Cabot managed to keep his role as pilot major and chose temporary appointees to serve in his absence.[18]

The official terms of the contract specified that Cabot would "sail by Magellan's Strait to the Moluccas and other spice islands of the Orient."[19] After retracing Magellan's route to the Spice Islands, he was supposed to turn around, recross the Pacific, and explore the western coast of South America before returning to Seville. The plan was large in scale and exceeded even Magellan's original plan, for it involved crossing the Pacific not once but twice. Cabot had seen thousands of maps and enterprise plans but had never led a successful enterprise at sea.[20] Given the circumstances and what we know about the uncanny Cabot from so many primary sources, it is not surprising that this 1526 voyage makes for a complex illustration of the dynamics of mutiny.

Cabot built trust with the Spanish court in ways that Columbus and Magellan never could. He embodied aspects of both of his forerunners. He could make people believe in him by playing to his strengths and concealing his limitations, or even vice versa. He did not mind suspicions of his incompetence because he used them to exceed expectations. Columbus persuaded others through sustained communication. Cabot achieved the same effect with brevity. Cabot was worse than Magellan as a navigator but better at handling trust issues with crew. He could also be as severe as Magellan when it came to darker forms of justice. Indeed, Cabot's disastrous four-year voyage brought out the best and the worst of human nature.

Cabot's Leadership

Cabot's unusual yet substantial leadership became apparent as he took command of this important Spanish venture. Almost every general description of him in the original records indicates a gentle man able to create attachments to others. But as a leader, his chaotic actions produced good and bad outcomes at once and often yielded a middling final result.[21] Cabot could profit from his own mistakes through seemingly odd actions. He was extremely bold in situations that did not seem to call for boldness. For instance, he hired one of his patrons, Michael de Rifas, as lieutenant general while planning the venture in Seville.[22] Everyone else preferred the experienced Martin Méndez, an attendee of the Council at Badajos in 1524 and a respected survivor of the Magellan trip.[23] But Cabot did not want someone who had served with another renowned navigator to impede his journey. His obstinacy was absolute. He was thinking several steps ahead, but his resolution led to contention, leading some sponsors to send a letter to Charles V detailing faults and defects in Cabot's character. Not until the king ordered the inclusion of Méndez and Miguel de Rodas from Magellan's *Victoria* was the matter resolved. Méndez was made lieutenant general of Cabot's flagship under the agreement that he never undertake actions that Cabot did not expressly commit to him. Nonetheless, Cabot largely ignored Méndez and seemed to detest him, giving many of his responsibili-

Sebastian Cabot. (Reproduced from J. Sparks, frontispiece.)

ties to Rifas. The highly recommended Rodas was similarly assigned as pilot major of the armada.[24]

As preparations were made to depart, some sponsors suggested an auxiliary objective: to find Cartagena and de Reina. Those were the two members whom Magellan had marooned at the Bay of Saint Julian five years earlier. Cabot was not interested.

Although the plan was to launch in August 1525, another seven months of preparation were required. The infamous Portuguese tendency to intrigue now delayed arrangements with merchants just as it had led to a reduction in Magellan's supplies. Because Cabot was provisioning ships only six years after Magellan did, some of the same local individuals were probably involved.

The challenges of the enterprise outran Cabot's true skill at ocean navigation but not his talents at political navigation. The impressions of the king had been managed skillfully; he obviously held Cabot and the enterprise in high esteem. The merchants who invested in it shared that view initially, but they grew anxious about Cabot's leadership. They would have preferred Francisco de Rojas or Méndez, who had sailed with Magellan. Although these discussions excited Cabot's jealousies, he refrained from expressing them in order to maintain balance in the organization. As it turned out, neither Columbus nor Magellan faced such a carefully planned mutiny as Cabot did. Entrenched members in leadership roles surreptitiously plotted even before departure. Méndez was so affronted by Cabot's appointment and his enforced subordination to him that he took all his property off the ship and resigned, but the Council of the Indies refused to accept his resignation and ordered Cabot and Méndez to collaborate. Méndez even met with Rojas, Rodas, and other members to discuss a plan for mutiny at Saint Paul's Church in Seville in the days before Cabot's armada left the harbor.[25]

Cabot's armada, which included four ships and more than two hundred men, set sail on April 3, 1526. Cabot commanded the flagship, the *Capitana*. Gregory Caro, nephew of the bishop of the Canary Islands (who later became bishop of Salamanca), commanded the *Santa Maria del Espinar*. Francisco de Rojas commanded the *Trinidad*. Rifas commanded his own caravel, included mostly at his own expense. Many members were spirited volunteers from respected backgrounds, eager to join a high-profile venture. Like Magellan, Cabot also hired additional crew beyond the number specified by the royal decree.

An additional royal directive, sealed, was to be opened only after the venture had launched. It specified who should be in command, in sequence, in the event of the death of Cabot or others. Eleven names were listed, beginning with Rojas on the *Trinidad*. The experienced Rodas was second. Méndez was third. If the list was exhausted, then members were to draw lots for leadership positions. The arrangement set the stage for mutiny and even treachery.

Some of the members regarded the venture as cursed from the

outset. The more experienced ones did not trust either Cabot's character or his ability. Most others were inexperienced or participating for payment because of relationships with supporters in Seville. Eleven joined merely because the royal decree listed them.[26] Two English members recommended by Robert Thorne, whose father had sailed with Elyot and who had advised English seafarers to sail through the North Pole to find another passage to the East before the Spanish or Portuguese did, were along to "learn the navigation of those regions."[27]

Cabot's initial genius in leading this fraught trip was detachment punctuated by an intense but mercurial spirit of purpose. He avoided public interactions. He knew many crew were disaffected. To draw them out, Cabot described a strategy for success that none could understand, and he remained unflappable when asked about it. It was hard for someone like Rodas to challenge Cabot because he never brought the decision makers together. Indeed, Cabot was at his very best when dealing with people individually. That is when the gentle force of his personality was irresistible. The effect was different from that induced by Columbus's perpetual optimism and constant engagement—he created a shipboard mood out of sheer energy— and from Magellan's thundering will and his impulse to act. Cabot was opaque. When Méndez, who learned about leadership by serving with Magellan, wrote a damning letter reporting Cabot's conduct to the king before the fleet left the Canaries, Cabot, who checked all outgoing communication, intercepted the letter and burned it. Méndez received no punishment. Cabot never mentioned it.

The mutiny began to form early. Méndez, Rojas, and Rodas had conspired before departure, and now Méndez was close to Rodas on the flagship. The record shows that Cabot had a sense of what was happening but did nothing, directing his energy elsewhere. The crew granted Cabot nominal trust because no one could figure him out or detect his limits. He made sure members knew his celebrated reputation but not his ability. As a result, Rojas, Rodas, and Méndez could find absolutely no opportunity or pretext to initiate a mutiny. But such a delicate dance is not liable to last very long, and Cabot soon made mistakes.

Cabot left behind four men when he stopped in the Canary Islands and let eight more join the expedition, starting a common practice of his. He consistently provided exit options, a rare practice in the Age of Discovery, when members were often coerced to serve and often not permitted to leave at will. Cabot hoped that exit options would reduce the threat of discontent and mutiny. He also reclassified and moved many members to new positions regularly. Once on the ocean, he formally replaced Méndez with Rifas as lieutenant general. The replacement was no surprise, given the increasing shifting of Méndez's responsibilities to Rifas that started in Seville. Méndez already hated Cabot, and this act excited his passions. Yet all such moves frustrated the coordination that was vital to any mutiny.

Méndez, Rodas, and Rojas thought mutiny would be easy. They met again to finalize their plan during the seventeen-day stopover in the Canaries. If they could depose Cabot and assign the leadership to Rojas as they crossed the ocean, they believed they would double the odds of not only surviving but succeeding in accomplishing the venture's mission.

Once the fleet was halfway across the ocean, Cabot's lack of navigational expertise began to reveal itself. He went against Rojas's public advice and led the ships into a huge region near the equator described commonly in terms of its "calms and baffling winds." Experienced navigators avoided this dead zone. With no wind, they floated for weeks and supplies ran low. The crossing normally took less than two months, but this time it took a full three months to reach South America. During the passage, Cabot ignored Rojas and Méndez and interacted with many crew directly, winning the admiration of many and mollifying their personal frustrations. He quelled mutiny before it happened because the potential mutineers could not organize against him. Individual and interpersonal actions against Cabot did not amount to mutiny, and such interactions were coins of the realm of which Cabot was master. Rodas, Rojas, and Méndez did not know *how* to depose Cabot in a coordinated way.

Cabot knew how to use distance to maintain control despite the close quarters aboard ship. His style is a study in contrasts. He rarely initiated communication without good reason. His decisions were authoritative and often wrong but never crippled the fleet or compromised the mission. Members interacted with him individually rather than in groups. Méndez sulked in silence on the *Capitana* while Rojas grumbled on the *Trinidad*. Nothing changed with Rodas; he knew Cabot was a hopeless navigator but could not find a way to make a serious issue of it. Cabot, surrounded by ill will, made for Brazil as fast as possible.

At the end of June they finally moored in Pernambuco, on the point of the continental horn. This bulge of South America extends far into the ocean and is only about 1,780 miles (2,865 km) from the coast of Africa.[28] Pernambuco was not the planned arrival point, but the unduly long crossing made them desperate for supplies and fresh water and, after sighting manatees, prone to fanciful musings about mermen.[29] They quickly restocked, but a new problem emerged: they could not navigate out of the harbor. In summer, winds blow directly onto the coast and make exiting the harbor an exercise in tricky tacking. Unable to leave after three or four attempts, they had to wait. Stuck in Pernambuco, the members developed a sense of aimlessness. Not sure of the details of departure himself, Cabot communicated no public information about how or when they would leave. Rodas told stories about Magellan's voyage, with its dangers and mutinies. It was a humbling comparison that irritated Cabot.

Pernambuco was Portuguese territory and the site of a large spice warehouse whose overseers made friends with Cabot's crew.[30] Soon there were rumors of treasure in a large river to the south. The possibility of riches excited the crew, and Rojas and Méndez sensed a new opportunity for mutiny. Having sensed it long before it emerged, Cabot was two steps ahead of them.

On July 2, Cabot ordered Rojas on the *Trinidad* and Méndez on the flagship arrested. He charged them with mutiny, citing their earlier conspiracy, and ordered them put under the watch of Caro on the *Santa Maria del Espinar*. Cabot then patiently questioned each crew member individually to learn about Rojas's and Méndez's intentions to mutiny. Although Cabot's suspicions were correct, he found no evidence. Rojas and Méndez had been discreet enough before sailing and during the ocean crossing. Rodas, with his close proximity to Méndez on the flagship, was also involved, but he had not compromised himself.

Cabot knew what was going on but could do nothing to Rojas and Méndez without documentable evidence. He put Rojas back in charge of the *Trinidad,* pledged his confidence in Rojas as captain, and gave him extensive public compliments. Several days later he freed Méndez. Rojas hated Cabot and found the ingratiation unsettling. Yet because the reinstatement was done publicly, members now perceived less of a difference between Rojas and Cabot. Cabot used this dynamic to protect his leadership.

People are less prepared to repay benefit than injury, so ingratiation is a dubious way to build trust with others. It creates a kind of obligation between two individuals that is uncomfortable if their values are not shared. The result can be feelings of humiliation. If trust does not exist between the parties, then obligation highlights its absence. For a cunning person like Rojas, repaying an injury through revenge was a pleasure. Cabot operated on this level with Rojas but outclassed him. Cabot's public compliments were a means to draw out Rojas's true feelings so he could address them. When Rojas did not express appreciation for Cabot's compliments, it defined a trust gap that had been concealed in the intent to mutiny. Indeed, Rojas fumed and Cabot grew wiser by his mistake. Just as Cabot artfully navigated his own mistakes, he navigated Rojas's. Cabot "soon found out his error, and later profited by it."[31]

A few weeks later, Cabot made a decision that dramatically changed the entire strategic plan. The overseers of the spice warehouse had now become friendly companions. They shared more information about the region to the south called La Plata, with its great river rich in silver. Given the new and detailed information, Cabot saw an opportunity to decrease the uncertainty of the venture and even turn it into a success that would be recognized in Seville.

According to the Portuguese, many survivors of the doomed Solís venture eleven years earlier were still living along the river. Now, taking information from the Portuguese overseers to pursue a new venture and forgo the sponsored Spanish venture would be treasonous, and Cabot eventually had to defend himself against that charge. However, continuing 3,700 miles (5,939 km) down the coast all the way to Magellan's strait seemed suicidal. Cabot did not reveal his change in plans yet. He figured a rationale for the change would emerge, ideally one that would bring crew members together, especially if he could find some of the Solís expedition's survivors and perhaps learn exact locations of the rich resources.

Before he could proceed south, as he would do in either case, he had to navigate out of the harbor. The fleet was not able to exit until September 29, 1526, when the winds shifted with the season. Upon exiting, the four ships steered south down the coast toward La Plata. Along the way they encountered a French ship of spice merchants, rivals to the Portuguese they had just left at Pernambuco. The weather was stormy as they passed a series of rivers over the next two weeks, and once they almost collided with another French ship. By October 19 they had traveled about 425 miles (683 km) and arrived at All Saints Bay.[32] Continuing on, they recorded ten more rivers and various islands. After traveling another 725 (1,165 km) miles, they approached Rio de Janeiro.

Despite a smooth transit thus far, several members begged to stay in Brazil. Then, after rounding the point at Cabo Frio, they were hit by a storm that knocked the small boat off the back of the *Capitana*. That small boat was vital; the ships were too big to land. Now they needed to find a place for the carpenters to build another small boat to travel between ships and shore. Before they could, another, even fiercer storm hit. The limits of Cabot's navigation skills were again revealed as the storm forced them toward a few islands near the entrance to the Rio de Janeiro harbor. They took shelter by the islands, which were uninhabited by humans but populated by birds, which they called *tabiahoreados*. When the weather cleared, they sailed the 200 miles (322 km) to the port at São Vicente. By this point, many members had no interest in continuing. Cabot granted permission to fifteen sick and disaffected members to leave the ships at São Vicente. Today this city is a large port on the coast, not far from São Paulo. In those days, it was a very small village inhabited by Portuguese.

From São Vicente, it was a long, straight shot of almost 2,500 miles (4,023 km) to Magellan's strait. Cabot had definitely given up this objective. But he still needed an undeniable rationale for publicly implementing a new plan. They sighted the pan-alcid birds Magellan had called *patos* (ducks) north of La Plata. Cabot named an island where thousands of them gathered Tierra de los Patos, just as Magellan had named a bay after them. They considered landing there, but the coast was not suitable. They still needed to build a small boat. Finally they arrived at a very large island near the coast that concealed a gentle bay. Cabot called both island and bay Santa Catalina after his wife.[33]

The journey from Pernambuco to Santa Catalina had worn down many of the members. Most of them were merchants, not seafarers, and an increasing number were becoming sick. The large island offered the timber required for building a boat. There was also a mountain, which could mean fresh water. Cabot opted to land, build a new boat, and let the members have a long rest. His decision restored confidence, but it would soon be shattered.

As they approached the bay, a few members thought the entrance might have dangerous underwater shoals near three very small islands. Cabot ordered the depth sounded. Rodas disagreed, pledging that there was no need to worry about the depth. He glibly offered his own head if there was any danger. Cabot asked Rodas and a member named Grajeda to sound the depth anyway. Just as both reported it safe to proceed, and even as Grajeda held the sounding line in his hands, the *Capitana* jolted. It ran aground on a submerged bank of sharp rocks that shattered part of the hull. The current rolled it onto the obstruction and then onto its side. The *Capitana* started sinking fast.

One member said that "the ship was lost owing to carelessness on the part of Sebastian Gaboto, for when the ship struck [the rock], he should have cast anchor from the stern, to draw her off the rock, which he failed to do." In fact, Cabot did not stay aboard. He was the first one to run, leap over the side into the water, and swim toward shore. The experienced Caro, who was generally favorable toward Cabot, reported: "Immediately upon the ship's striking [the rock], Sebastian Gabota left and abandoned her. The ship was lost because, upon seeing that Captain Gabota had left, all the people who were on board tried to escape, while some went in search of something to steal from the vessel. And if the captain had not run away from the ship, nothing on board would have been submerged, although the ship could not be saved. His want of courage is the cause of all being lost." The episode earned Cabot much disrespect and distrust. It negated his public outsmarting of Rodas and Grajeda when they sounded the depths. Rodas had been embarrassed, but now he was emboldened. The *Capitana* sank so quickly that everyone was soon in the water and swimming to shore and the other ships. Cabot was the leader of this mad rush.[34]

Half of the armada's supplies, including provisions, ammunition, sails, and anchors, were now gone. The resources carried by the *Capitana* were more valuable than the combination of those carried by all the other ships. As the ship sank at Santa Catalina on October 28, Cabot finally gained his opportunity to shift the mission. But what sealed the decision was a mutiny.

The purpose in landing on Santa Catalina was originally just to build a new small boat, but now they had to try to recoup the loss of the *Capitana*. The land was inhabited by a tribe of cannibals who were friendly and peaceful. They helped Cabot and his crew reclaim some of the lost supplies and gather new provisions. Cannibals were terrifying to seafarers in the Age of Discovery, but it was understood that they ate their enemies only if they succeeded in killing them in a fight. At this point in history, peoples that Europeans encountered in newly discovered lands were usually known in Portugal and Spain as "Indians." Cabot's members were very friendly to these Indians, who graciously returned the courtesy.

A plan was made to build a medium-sized ship called a galiot with what could be salvaged from the *Capitana* and procured from the forest. As ever, Rojas was a voice of dissent. Like Rodas, he had become emboldened by Cabot's huge blunder. He had been fuming ever since Cabot announced his trust in him. Cabot viewed Rojas as a particular threat now and arrested him again. After speaking with a few crew members, he then arrested Méndez, Rodas, and several others. This time Cabot had evidence that treasonous language was being used on the *Trinidad*. As before, the arrestees were put under the command of Caro on the *Santa Maria del Espinar*.

In the meantime, about twenty marooned or castaway members of other Spanish and Portuguese ships excitedly came to meet Cabot once he landed at Santa Catalina. Some were survivors of Solís's tragic 1515 venture and had made new lives with friendly natives.[35] Like the Portuguese spice merchants in Pernambuco, they told Cabot about treasure in the La Plata region—riches enough to make all of them wealthy. After interviewing some of these strangers, most of whom were criminals or fugitives, Cabot invited them to join his enterprise. As he had planned at Pernambuco, he wanted them to show the locations of the silver and help interact with natives.

Cabot then dealt decisively with the mutinous designs that he had been tolerating since April. He had the master-at-arms of the *Trinidad*, Gaspar de Ribas, bring forth Méndez, Rodas, Rojas, and others who had stood against his authority and coolly informed them that he was going to maroon them on Santa Catalina. Rojas and Méndez had thought Cabot was spineless and would release them as he had

done after arresting them at Pernambuco. But now Cabot calmly reduced them to tearful begging. Cabot ordered Ribas to use the new
small boat to deliver them to the shore and leave them there.[36]

Cabot was ready to use this mutiny to his advantage, which he
did by announcing the new strategic objective for the enterprise: to
fill the ships with silver and any other discovered resources from the
La Plata river and inform Seville of the location of these resources.
The empire would send a fleet to mine them and enrich itself. The
members unanimously and wholeheartedly agreed. Cabot had tempered the mood before members made any coordinated attempt to
usurp his authority. He sensed a rising excitement because their objective was less dangerous now, although he realized that he himself
would have a lot of explaining to do back in Spain. His only hope
now was to reap riches in La Plata.

On February 17, 1527, after more than four months at Santa Catalina, the ships weighed anchor and left. Following a short stop for
repairs on a small uninhabited island a few miles south, they carried
on for about 600 miles (966 km) to the enormous mouth of the river
in La Plata. On the course to La Plata, they noted smaller rivers, large
rocks, and many people along the coast. They enjoyed a surprisingly fast six-day transit. Upon arriving at the enormous river mouth
around February 23, they passed today's Isla de Flores, which they
called Isla de las Palmas, and saw a nearby island with many seals,
which they called Isla de Lobos. The La Plata region was as far south
as the fleet would travel. The original course to Magellan's strait was
still another 1,300 miles (2,092 km) to the south.

The armada now consisted of the *Santa Maria del Espinar,* the
Trinidad, and Rifas's caravel, which all traveled under sail. The company had built a row-galley with twenty oars during the months at
Santa Catalina with help from the natives, and it was under tow. With
its smaller draft, it would be useful for exploring the islands and
smaller passages that striated the La Plata river. Cabot still had hopes
of finding a passage to the Pacific there even though he had heard the
stories told by new members from Santa Catalina. One recounted

the ambush of an unsuspecting landing party from Solís's enterprise. Volleys of arrows came from two directions before the natives rushed in to kill any wounded men who had not made it to the boat. Those members who did escape watched from the water with terror as the natives, screaming, stripped the dead and roasted them on a great fire.[37] The macabre actions occurred in the very region they were now entering. Solís's enterprise had departed that place as quickly as possible, and without Solís. Undeterred, Cabot was now more motivated than before. He expected a very different fortune from Solís's.

Madness and Genius

Cabot had no idea that the barely charted La Plata region was an insanely complex but also beautiful labyrinth of navigational puzzles.[38] Years later Cabot would describe the convolution of the river with many tributaries running into it as incredible and the land as very fair.[39] But at the moment he had no illusions about its dangers. Cabot ordered all members never to go far away. Immediately after entering the large estuary, the armada followed the north bank all the way around to Isla Martín García, an island named after a steward of Solís's who had died there.[40] Just behind that island is the mouth of a large river. On April 7, 1527, on the north bank across from the island, they set up camp near a stream and called their layover spot Sanct (San) Lazaro. They stayed there for a few days before moving to the other side of the river, where they constructed a storehouse for provisions and cargo.

La Plata was a haunting place. The infinite tributaries and channels were a maddening maze of false starts and dead ends. The first sightings of natives were unsettling. Cabot felt the menace and maintained a cohesive enterprise by communicating to everyone the nature of the threats they now shared. Now that Cabot did not have to navigate the ocean, he became more tactical. At San Lazaro on May 8, he divided the members into two teams. One team took Rifas's caravel and the row-galley, and the other team took the *Santa Maria del Espinar* and the *Trinidad*. While several crew members who had become sick stayed behind, the remainder moved up the river together. In a couple of days they reached another large tributary, where they separated.

As soon as they split up, both teams faced surprise attacks by natives. Arrows killed two crew members. Cabot's men responded with guns and cannon, terrifying the natives. Then and there they decided to build a fort, which Cabot called Sanct (San) Salvador.[41] It took three months to build. Once this new position was established, Cabot sent the row-galley back to Sanct Lazaro to pick up the members who had regained their health. It returned in three days, on August 28, 1527. Now they were ready for another push inland.

Cabot put Grajeda in charge of Sanct Salvador and allotted several more members to stay behind. He also left the two ships there, for their drafts were too deep for the river. Cabot commanded the row-galley and the caravel up the river until they reached a delta, where at least ten rivers seemed to converge. Amazingly, they encountered a Spanish man on an island at this delta. Francisco del Puerto had been a member of Solís's doomed enterprise over a decade earlier. Cabot recognized the value of Puerto's knowledge of the local geography and languages. Although Puerto had somehow settled into a life there and was more like a local than a Spaniard, he joined Cabot. Puerto even recognized some of the members that Cabot had brought with him from Santa Catalina.

At the delta, the two boats entered one of the larger rivers, today's Paraguay River. They charted many small tributaries and more rivers, including the Carcarana (today's Cuarto River). Eventually they found a remote spot that seemed safe, where they landed and built a third fort, which they called Sancti Spiritus.[42] Caro was put in charge of this fort, which was approximately 180 miles (290 km) up the river from Sanct Lazaro. When construction was finished, the main group departed, leaving more members behind. It was Christmas Eve, 1527.

The group was seemingly making progress, although the objective was uncertain. They continued up the Paraguay River, passing six more tributaries. Their boldness increased along the way. Cabot sent thirty-five members ashore under the command of Rifas to chastise a small group of natives whom he thought had threatened them. They merely fired their guns, which again had a terrifying effect and emboldened Cabot's team further. Even though no trace of valuable resources had been found, and a former member of Solís's enterprise had only heard rumors of silver in the region, internal operations went smoothly.

Natives of the La Plata varied widely in terms of their friendliness to foreigners. Some looked upon the armada with admiration. Others stared from a distance. Cabot's members were developing a less rosy perspective. The maze of rivers was maddening to negotiate. Safe exit options were absent. Although Cabot always maintained complete control, mutinous feelings again began to take shape.

On March 31, they arrived at a large river flowing from the northwest. Cabot believed this channel came from the magnificent Incan country that Pascual de Andagoya had discovered six years earlier in Peru. That region of South America had captured the imagination of Spain as the supposed location of innumerable treasures. Tales of conquistadors like Andagoya and Francisco Pizarro had revived legends like that of the fabled golden city of El Dorado. Cabot never planned to arrive at the region through the course they had taken, but now he wanted to head northwest and discover riches while avoiding Portuguese territory in Brazil. But the winding, multiplying rivers continued to frustrate them. When food ran low, a few members were ready to risk death rather than continue. Two were especially desperate.

During a stop to gather provisions, two members named Vizcaino and Orosco deserted. They stole a canoe from a village, treated some villagers badly, and then compelled two natives to row them south, toward their point of origin. They intended to regroup with members at Sanct Lazaro or Sanct Salvador and use one of the ships to return to Spain. How did Cabot respond? He was a warmer version of Columbus and a colder version of Magellan. Unlike both of them, he was not a very good strategist but a brilliant tactician and organizer. Part of his power came from a capacity for brutality and coldness that balanced his gentleness and warmth. In this instance, he had Puerto use his language skill to ask natives to catch Vizcaino and Orosco and bring them back. Upon their return, Cabot charged them with mutiny and sentenced Vizcaino to death by hanging. Vizcaino's head slipped out of the noose, so Cabot just had him strung up again. But Cabot then reversed his decision to hang a horrified Orosco, a skilled carpenter, who now swore his loyalty.

Other extreme events occurred. A member named Lorenzo de la Palma was caught stealing provisions. He was whipped. One of Cabot's trusted men, Hernando de Calderon, had both of Palma's ears cut off before the poor man fled into the jungle. When two other crew members named Corço and Aguirre were caught stealing provisions, Cabot ordered them to be whipped as well but also had their hands nailed to a wooden board.[43]

All individual actions against Cabot's authority proved ineffective because they were neither organized nor reflective of the values that united the crew. Individual actions are almost never sufficient to depose a leader if they do not touch the values that unite members of the organization. Cabot's punishments also coerced members into submission, but they varied and generally did not help achieve loyalty or trust. It was not long before Cabot had to deal with more serious mutiny attempts.

CABOT'S INVISIBLE HAND

Cabot was an expert at identifying critical incidents and smoothing things over. But as mutinous feelings jelled and the forces against him became coordinated, other members were influenced despite his best efforts. Two members who had joined the group at Santa Catalina, Francisco de Lepe and Martín of Biscay, became ringleaders. They started to actively seek an opportunity for mutiny. The environment was uncertain, and Cabot's actions were beginning to seem dangerously counterproductive. Lepe cautiously approached those he knew and trusted from Santa Catalina. Before long, about thirty members assented to the idea of mutiny in principle. They would participate if the mutiny became public and had a plan.

The plan that Lepe and Martín devised was a simple one, based on the existence of the larger external threats—the native populations—surrounding them. A few natives were traveling with Cabot's team at this point. Provisions were scarce and the ever careful Cabot was slow to trust the natives to help find them. The plan was for Lepe or Martín to challenge Cabot's resistance to cooperating with the natives. The participating crew would take Rifas's caravel, arrest or kill Cabot, and then give all nonessential supplies, such as weapons, tools, and other cargo, to the natives in exchange for full loads of food and water. The successful mutineers would leave the row-galley behind and depart.

Cabot was one step ahead of Lepe and Martín. He always maintained close and secret loyalties with one or two members who were also sufficiently close to the rest of the crew. Calderon and Caro, mentioned earlier, were two who functioned as Cabot's secret agents. They would not discourage discontented men from planning mutiny but would certainly inform Cabot of any hint of one, as he had specifically instructed them to do.

Luis de Leon, who had also joined Cabot's expedition at Santa Catalina, was not opposed to Lepe's request to participate in the mutiny, but he was not wholly persuaded either. Lepe made the mistake of sharing too many details of the plan with him before Leon agreed to participate. Leon relayed some of the details to a chaplain who was Cabot's agent, who informed Cabot in secret. Knowing that there was disaffection among crew members gave Cabot a way to quell the mutiny before it emerged by snaring a ringleader. Cabot approached Leon without threatening him and acquired more information. Then he seized Lepe and Martín.

After holding an inquiry, Cabot had Lepe hanged from a tree. Lepe was so apathetic about the enterprise by this point that he was unafraid of death. His last words were "As I pay for all, my friends, I wish you all a good voyage. Adios!" Martín was executed similarly, and several other mutineers were arrested and put in irons or given other punishments. Cabot realized that quelling the mutiny ran the risk of not having enough men to operate the ships.

The level of coordination in this mutiny had an effect on the enterprise. People have certain limits that, if crossed, make them desperate enough to make sacrifices. Lepe and Martín sacrificed their lives; today's mutineers may sacrifice their careers. When such actions reflect a deeper problem in the fabric of an enterprise, they send a powerful message to the leader. Cabot received it. Now that he realized that his actions had violated the shared values of the members to the extent that many shared the notion of deposing him, he reconsidered what he was doing in La Plata and took action to ameliorate the situation.

Immediately, Cabot halted the group's progress. He sent Rifas's caravel south to barter for food at a village they had passed. The rowgalley waited. When the caravel returned loaded with provisions, the vigor of all was renewed. The vessels traveled north together. In a few days they arrived at a large village ruled by Yaguaron, one of the region's most powerful chiefs, who treated Cabot and his men with generosity.[44] Food was plentiful, and entertainment and leisure were comforting. Cabot noted that the concept of personal ownership seemed foreign to these natives, who regarded their food and supplies as freely available to these strange visitors. The travelers stayed at this village for several days. This stopping place was happened upon so providentially that Cabot gave it a name: Santa Ana. They were now deep in the middle of the South American continent, 400 miles (635 km) north of their first position at Sanct Lazaro.

THE BEGINNING OF THE END

Caro had stayed at Sancti Spiritus while Cabot and Rifas continued exploring the rivers. In April 1528, a small expedition commanded by a Portuguese named Diego Garcia arrived from Seville, which it had left in August 1526, four months after Cabot's expedition. Garcia's mission was to explore this region; Cabot's was not. Before meeting Caro, Garcia had met awkwardly with Grajeda at Sanct Salvador. Grajeda had mistaken Garcia's ship to be commanded by the mutinous Rojas and Méndez and had prepared canoes and an armed boat to capture them.[45] Now at Sancti Spiritus, Caro and Garcia must have also had a strange interaction. For one thing, Garcia was in a caravel that had belonged to the Cabot fleet, which Grajeda had traded him for a larger ship. Garcia had wanted a smaller ship, more suitable for exploration. Now, when Garcia met Caro, he realized that Cabot's group was not following the authorized plan. Garcia calmly and confidently ordered Caro to relinquish command of his post. Caro refused, citing loyalty to Cabot and to Spain. Garcia, with no interest in using force, dropped the demand, and got what information he could about the region from Caro.

Just before Garcia arrived, Caro received some terrible news from natives. Rifas and his companions had been massacred. In fact, Cabot had sent them north from Santa Ana, where they unknowingly entered a region of hostile tribes. Rifas put several members ashore for provisions only to helplessly watch as they were attacked and killed. A horrified Rifas managed to make peace with the attackers through hand signs and was allowed to bury the dead. Then Rifas and nineteen members were welcomed to the village, where he and seventeen others were massacred. Only two escaped, and they barely managed to row the caravel back to Santa Ana.

Hearing of the massacre, Caro mistakenly thought Cabot had been killed. Garcia later reported to Charles V the conversation in which Caro "begged of me if in the course of the discoveries I was about to undertake, I happened to find any of his men, to ransom them, and he would pay me back. He also appealed to my pity that if his captain had been killed, not to leave his body on the banks of the river, but bring it back with me, and that by complying with this request, I should be doing a thing agreeable to God and to Your Majesty."[46]

An unimpressed Garcia left Caro at Sancti Spiritus on April 9, 1528. His already-low opinion of Cabot, formed during his time in Seville, was now lower, and he was intent on finding what was left of Cabot's expedition.

Cabot heard about Garcia's arrival in the region from natives at Santa Ana around the same time he learned of Rifas's fate. He for a moment believed the approaching visitors were Portuguese enemies pursuing him. Cabot was initially relieved when he met Garcia, a Portuguese commanding a caravel for Spain. They met near the intersection of the Paraguay and Parana rivers in early May. But then Garcia ordered Cabot to surrender his fort, repeating the demand he had made of Caro at Sancti Spiritus. Cabot, still reeling from the news of Rifas's tragedy, suggested a mutually beneficial alliance instead, but Garcia disagreed, and he left Santa Ana the next morning without bidding farewell.[47] Cabot retreated south and arrived at Sanct Salvador on June 23, 1528.

There, Cabot completed the formal business of a trial against Rojas, Méndez, and Rodas, marooned on Santa Catalina Island two years earlier. He drafted a judgment against them for delivery to the Council of the Indies in Seville. Calderon was put in charge of the *Trinidad* and was then ordered to take it back to Seville with a few dozen crew members who were sick or indisposed.[48] Calderon exited the La Plata river in July and landed the *Trinidad* at Lisbon just over six weeks later. Why Calderon landed in Portugal is a bit of a mystery, but weather combined with the convenient location of Lisbon's port probably explain it.

In Lisbon at the time, there on behalf of Charles V, was a Castilian named Lope Hurtado de Mendoza who witnessed the *Trinidad*'s arrival. Mendoza was trying to sell Spain's Spice Islands to Portugal on behalf of Charles V. Portugal was enjoying enormously profitable trade with India and would open trade with Macau seven years later, in 1535. In a letter to Charles V dated October 19, 1528, Mendoza describes Calderon's arrival. He also relays a promising but misleading message from Cabot, which Mendoza used in the context of the sale he was trying to make to King John III of Portugal. Mendoza's letter read, "One of the caravels that went under Sebastian Cavocto, Pilot-Major of his Majesty, has arrived at this port. On board her is an accountant and treasurer of the said fleet, whom Sebastian now sends with news of wonderful discoveries made by him and his people. Indeed, if what the messenger states be true, His Imperial Majesty will no longer want either cinnamon or pepper, for he will have more gold and silver than he requires."[49]

Calderon left Lisbon for Spain after a couple of days, carrying two letters from Cabot. The letter to Charles V was delivered at Toledo the last week in October. It is the proper source of the name Río de La Plata for the La Plata region and its river. Cabot gave an elegant rationale for abandoning the original mission, citing the gold and silver procured from natives, even though he had only a few pieces of jewelry. He described the healthy climate, fertile soil, and suitability of the land for colonization. Charles V and his court were impressed and fooled. Cabot's other letter was a request for resources from merchants in Seville who had sponsored him. The merchants were neither impressed nor fooled. Cabot waited for word during the long winter months of 1528–1529. Nothing from Spain was forthcoming. Cabot tentatively explored the region and sent another smaller team to explore as far north as Sancti Spiritus.

In September 1529, the inhabitants of the Río de La Plata reached the limits of their toleration and exploded. Thousands of them destroyed Sancti Spiritus. Those of Cabot's crew who were there had no chance of surviving. Cabot, not realizing the scope of the threat, went to the fort to recover whatever was left. He found only one large cannon that the natives could not carry away. The victims were mutilated in ways suggesting attempts to ascertain their fitness for eating. Some cannibals had already told Cabot and members that the taste of foreigners was not pleasant. Horrified, Cabot and his men retreated to Sanct Salvador. They were attacked along the way, and once there, any man who strayed was likely to be killed. The situation was terrifying. Twenty more members of the expedition perished, including Grajeda.

THE VOYAGE HOME

Since no ship arrived from Spain, Cabot implemented the exit strategy he had formulated. He held a small meeting on October 6, 1529, in which he formally announced his decision to leave the Río de La Plata. He and his men had explored the region since February 1527 and had nothing to show for it except a rough survey of the geography and a few pieces of jewelry.

His enterprise needed provisions if they were going to make it back to Seville. He put the caravel and thirty-four men under the command of a member named Montoya and directed them back to the Isla de Lobos, near the entrance to the region's river, to hunt seals. Cabot was to wait for Montoya to return. Becoming impatient or fearful, however, he left Sanct Salvador in the *Santa Maria del Espinar* in early November. In the meantime, Montoya found a Portuguese settlement near Isla de Lobos and left most of the members there by their choice. He, too, had lost his faith in Cabot and chose not to wait for him. Instead, he continued back to Seville, where he would reappear in the trial against Cabot one year later. The venture was disintegrating.

Cabot exited the Río de La Plata in January 1530, after being in the region for almost three years. The progress back to Seville was slow. In fact, it was Caro, not Cabot, who now navigated the *Santa Maria del Espinar.* They passed the Tierra de los Patos around January 19. After a stop there, Cabot took four natives on board to assist with working the ship. The ship arrived at São Vicente, where Cabot had left fifteen members on the outward leg of the journey, around March 22. Two more members requested permission to leave the ship at this point, saying they were afraid of crossing the ocean. Cabot agreed but asked that they put the request in writing. He was thinking carefully about the judgment to come in Seville and wanted to be able to justify his actions.

Several matters came to light during this stop. Cabot learned that Rojas, whom he had marooned at Santa Catalina, had made his own way to São Vicente on a ship, and that Méndez and Rodas had drowned in a canoe accident at Santa Catalina in connection with a dispute with Rojas. Cabot summoned Rojas to meet with him, explain himself, and be taken to Spain as a culprit. Rojas refused on the grounds that Cabot had forfeited his authority over him by marooning him in a hostile land, among cannibals. Now, given the sad state of Cabot's enterprise, Rojas argued, Cabot was an enemy of Spain.

Rojas warned Cabot further that serious trouble awaited him, for several of the members whom he had marooned in Santa Catalina had made it back to Seville after being picked up by a Portuguese caravel. Rojas issued a counterorder to Cabot. He had begun construction of a vessel that required decking and caulking and now demanded resources and specific members to help finish the construction. After that, he would soon arrive and retrieve any Spanish members that Cabot had left behind. Rojas also wanted to restore the four natives from Tierra de los Patos now traveling with Cabot back to their homes, to avoid destabilizing relations with natives there. In fact, however, Garcia's expedition had already soured relations on a considerably larger scale in the Río de La Plata region. Regardless, Cabot ignored Rojas's demands.

Garcia had departed the Río de La Plata region for Spain not long after meeting Cabot. Unfortunately, he had left behind several members who mistreated some native women. The natives were already upset by Cabot's actions: he had killed some of their people, and his men had forced two natives to row them south. Angered by further abuse, the natives resolved to kill all foreigners or expel them from the country. The destruction of Cabot's fort at Sancti Spiritus was a result of the actions of Garcia's members.

Now Garcia, also en route to Spain, met Cabot at São Vicente, and soon Rojas was on Garcia's caravel and headed to Seville. Both

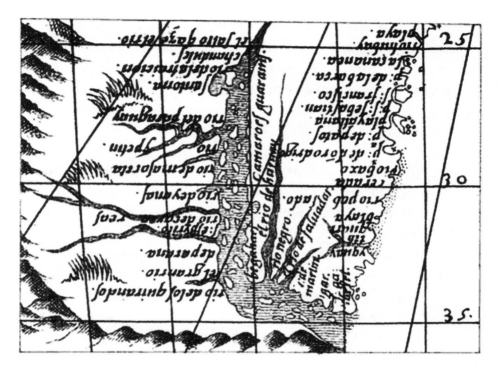

The Río de La Plata region as it appears on a largely erroneous map
drawn during Sebastian Cabot's 1526–1530 enterprise.
(Reproduced from Harrisse, pp. 262–263.)

men allied against Cabot. Before departing from São Vicente, Cabot
engaged in a deplorable round of slave trading. With a cargo of fifty
slaves bought on credit, he departed. He took four months to reach
Seville, arriving in July 1530.

Cabot had been away for almost four and a half years. His expedition returned with only twenty to twenty-four of its two hundred–plus crew members, having left the ship acquired in trade with
Garcia and at least twenty crew at various stopping points along the
long and complicated course. Cabot landed at Seville with one ship,
no discoveries of treasure, and a few members. His geographical and
nautical discoveries were insignificant. An original chart shows that
his map of the region was highly inaccurate, which is peculiar in light
of his purported talent for cartography. The merchants and the royal

court took an inventory of every item the enterprise carried. The precious metals brought back by Cabot amounted to an ounce of silver from a few earrings. The only other items of value on the ships were furs and hides belonging to members.[50]

Aftermath

The merchants who had invested in Cabot's venture lost their investment and had no return from the enterprise. They refused to support any further ventures connected with Cabot because he had failed so extremely. One wonders if these merchants in Seville knew the history of John Cabot in Spain or with merchants in England during his failed 1499 enterprise.

Charles V still trusted Cabot, however. He was impressed by his descriptions and intended to support a follow-up mission. But Spain was at war with the Ottoman Empire, Charles V was at odds with the pope, and there were problems with Venice, all of which required expensive campaigns. The royal coffers needed an infusion of cash and treasure, which is why Charles V had been pushing the unpopular decision to sell the Spice Islands to Portugal. Mendoza was still in Lisbon for that purpose, but the deal was not finalized.

When the *Santa Maria del Espinar* arrived in Seville with Cabot in late July 1530, it made for a dramatic spectacle. As Rojas had warned, Cabot had many enemies waiting, some of whom gathered at the docks even as they moored the ship. A Portuguese in Seville named Affonso Simão described the arrival:

> This week there arrived here a pilot and captain who was sent to discover land. His name is Gaboto, he is the chief pilot of these kingdoms, and is the same person that sent the ship that touched at Lisbon two years ago and brought news of the land discovered on the river Pereuai [Paraguay], which they said abounded in gold and silver. I find him very wretched and poor, for they say he brought no gold or silver, nor anything of profit to those

that fitted out the vessels, and of 200 men that he took with him he brings back less than 20; for they say all the rest were left there dead, some from fatigue and hunger, others killed in war; for they say the arrow-wounds killed many of them, and the wooden fort they built was destroyed; so that they are very ill satisfied and the pilot is a prisoner; and they say they will send him to court to see what they order done with him. What I could learn, and what is said here publicly, though in a low voice, is that in the land they say they discovered they left no guard but their dead and deserters. But notwithstanding this, these men tell me that the land possessed much gold and silver, and the reason they brought none is, as they say, because the captain would not allow them to bargain for it, and also because the natives deceived and rebelled against them. Your Highness will believe what you think best of this; but it is certain that the land is abandoned. The river, they say, is very long and deep, and very wide at its mouth. If your Highness shall find it in your interest to send there now, you could do so, for these people [the Spanish] fly from a place where they see no money for themselves."[51]

Rojas and Garcia were already in Seville. So was Montoya, along with some of the members who had been left at Santa Catalina and São Vicente. Within a day, Cabot was arrested for disobeying his official orders.

Cabot was formally accused by Rojas and the Méndez brothers' mother, Catalina Vasquez.[52] She even claimed that Cabot's wife had hired an assassin to kill one of her sons and that Cabot had tried to poison the other. Many others spoke against Cabot and accused him of being negligent, losing resources for the empire and his merchant sponsors, and causing the meaningless deaths of members of his expedition. Cabot was allowed to leave jail but ordered to stay in Seville.

Cabot filed his own case against Méndez and Rodas for mutiny, even though he had marooned them. The fact that he was not Castilian, which he had used to his advantage heretofore, had the opposite effect now. A lengthy trial ensued. Rojas delivered a damning indictment of Cabot, especially given the years they had worked closely together on the enterprise; his words appear in the title of this chapter: he was "a foreigner and nobody knows who he is." Arguments both far-fetched and valid were leveled against Cabot by almost every officer who had served on his ships. Even Calderon and Caro, who had both enjoyed Cabot's trust, spoke against him. Calderon recalled that Cabot's "management was bad, and he was not competent for the position of Captain-General." Most of the nonranking members of the expedition, by contrast, admired Cabot. They had many fond memories of individual interactions with him.[53]

The trial began in November. Cabot responded to testimonies and asserted his point of view with simple arguments. For instance, the wars with the natives were for defense of the enterprise. The violence against his men was no different from that by other Spanish sea captains facing mutinies. These members, after all, had conspired against his life. The change to the original destination from the Spice Islands to the Río de La Plata and the loss of the flagship were made in pursuit of riches in an untapped region. The undiscovered treasures outmatched anything in the Spice Islands, which were now a disputed resource anyway. By speaking along these lines, the glib Cabot outdebated most of his accusers.

According to a report by the Council of the Indies, Cabot was free on bail in May 1531. The verdict came on July 4. He was fined and sentenced to two years at the penal colony at Oran, in what is now Algeria, for excesses committed during the voyage.[54] Charles V may have distrusted Cabot, but Cabot's report so greatly impressed him that he sponsored another expedition to the Río de La Plata in 1534, four years after Cabot's return. That expedition was one of the most regrettable failures of the entire Age of Discovery.[55]

Amazingly, Cabot's position of pilot major was returned to him around 1533–1534, despite a reenacted 1527 law that prevented foreigners from serving as pilots. Nonetheless, life was no longer so easy for him in Spain. Still, Cabot, who boasted (falsely) about numerous voyages and exploits, retained an ability to impress those in positions of power that benefited him for his entire life.

Many of Cabot's actions seemed contradictory, subsuming good and bad at once. Sometimes they enabled him to escape from predicaments. At other times they led to tragic results. One of the last things that Cabot did in Spain, as part of his exit strategy in the late 1540s, was to entrust his pilot major post to Diego Gutierrez, whom he had publicly derided as incompetent in 1545. The Council of the Indies examined Gutierrez and removed him for incompetence on September 22, 1549. Yet by that point, Cabot had been back in England for two years after more than three decades in Spain. Before long he would meet the grandfather of Henry Hudson, whom we examine in the next chapter. Cabot never returned to Spain.

4

Hudson
"The Death of Discovery"

A worthy merchant is the heire of adventure, whose hopes hang much upon winde. Upon a wodden horse he rides through the world, and in a merry gale, makes a path through the seas.

—Nicholas Breton

Toward the end of the Age of Discovery a shift in the dominant perception of mutiny took place. The famous mutiny during Henry Hudson's 1610–1611 enterprise is a case in point. Unlike Columbus, who quelled mutiny by inspiring hope, Magellan, who suppressed it by exercising authority and brutality, and Sebastian Cabot, who brilliantly gauged mutineers' intentions ahead of time, Hudson was a masterful tactician but an ambivalent strategist. Mutiny evolved aboard his ship as a natural human force, and he was deposed.

Although Hudson was not the greatest navigator, he was a distinctive, influential leader for whom the Hudson Bay and the Hudson River are named. His life's goal was to find a northwest passage for ships sailing from Europe to the Spice Islands, India, and other points in the East. Mutiny saved his enterprise in at least one instance, but it was also his final undoing.

To understand Hudson and his mutinies, it is useful to examine what happened in England after Cabot returned there in 1547. His influence on English seafaring culture shaped how English ventures were led. Indeed, just as today's industries vary in terms of their cultural norms and practices, so, too, did English seafaring vary from Portuguese and Spanish seafaring. To illustrate the complexities of the events in Hudson's case, then, entails going back forty years before Hudson's time to John Hawkins and Francis Drake.

Hawkins and Drake

Some sixteenth-century English seafarers rivaled the best that even Portugal or Spain had to offer. Sir Francis Drake (1540–1596), a self-made man, embraced life on the open ocean at an early age and eventually completed history's third circumnavigation of the globe in 1577–1580. He was in fact the first leader of a round-the-world trip to return alive, despite having begun with a crew of 164 and returned with 59. Before Drake, the second circumnavigation after Magellan's was launched in 1525 by Garcia de Loaysa and Juan Sebastián Elcano, who both perished while crossing the Pacific.[1] Elcano, who had sailed with Magellan, was the one who brought the *Victoria* back into Seville. Drake and his mentor and second cousin, John Hawkins (1532–1592), were a new breed of English seafarer, ready and willing to compete with Spanish and Portuguese rivals. England rose as a sea power all the more easily because seafaring in Spain and Portugal waned during the period of the Iberian Union (1580–1640).

Drake's and Hawkins's ventures were part of the tradition that spawned many popular perceptions of pirates. In the mid-1560s, while still in his twenties, Drake undertook with Hawkins a series of profitable voyages to the northern coast of South America. At this time, the entire Caribbean region was known as the Spanish Main. "Main" was a corruption of the Anglo-French word *mesne,* meaning "intermediate, intervening," and it referred to the loose mechanisms by which Spain held the South American territories. "Loose" translated into lawlessness. Many seafarers who had been marooned by or cast away from Portuguese, Spanish, French, and English ships now cruised the Caribbean Sea and its adjacent waters in ships they had captured.[2] But the English had become better sailors in the years since Sebastian Cabot sailed. Drake and Hawkins knew how to handle the pirates of the Spanish Main.

Surviving among the pirates of the Caribbean called for Magellan's boldness and Sebastian Cabot's guile. Hawkins masterfully misled the Spanish regarding English intentions to trade in the Spanish Main as he forged agreements with local governors, his diplomacy in striking contrast to Cabot's and Spert's bumbling attempts to trade there fifty years earlier. In the meantime he advised the undercover development of a large English expedition to further explore the whole region. When the Spanish ambassador, Guzmán de Silva, discovered the plan, Hawkins duped him into believing that the expedition was actually to help Spain go to war with the Turks. When Guzmán de Silva grasped the duplicity, he was so enraged that he demanded a meeting with Queen Elizabeth I, whom he convinced to limit Hawkins's activity to non-Spanish territories. As a consequence, the young Drake led a successful expedition to the Spanish Main in 1566–1567 by himself. Exploits like Hawkins's and Drake's gave English seafaring a new bold, even brazen character.

In 1568, Hawkins and Drake led an English armada to the Spanish Main, where they lost three hundred members in a Spanish attack. They separated in the resulting confusion and even were temporarily at odds, for Hawkins claimed that Drake "forsook us in our great misery." A small war of reprisal unfolded during the 1570s, rendering the Spanish Main a maritime Wild West. Hawkins left the action and went on to serve in more administrative roles. Besides benefiting English seafaring with his useful innovations, he famously saved Queen Elizabeth I from assassination.[3]

The daring Drake continued to lead new ventures at sea. He once landed on the strip of land connecting North and South America (the Isthmus of Panama) and climbed a tree to view the Atlantic and the Pacific oceans at once. Spain had found Peru in the 1520s after traveling there overland from the isthmus. By the early 1570s, mule-drawn carts full of Peruvian gold and silver constantly traveled to the isthmus, where their cargo was loaded onto ships bound for Seville. Drake raided the caravans and returned to England in ships ballasted low with treasure. Partly with this Spanish gold, England was growing richer and closing the still-considerable gap with Spain.

Once the English learned how thin the American isthmus actually was, they pondered using it as a route to reach the East. But that would have meant confrontation with Spain over its exercise of sovereignty there. Indeed, such a confrontation finally occurred in the 1690s, when the Darien Company of Scotland (in personal union with England) sought to establish a trading center on the isthmus. The English need for a passage was a long and lasting problem. Where could they turn? Portugal owned the route that looped around the Cape of Good Hope at the foot of Africa, Spain the route that looped through the Strait of Magellan at the foot of South America. Magellan's route was too difficult and dangerous for regular passage anyway; only three European fleets passed through the strait in nearly sixty years. England's answer to the question of a route was to commission Drake to tackle the Spanish on America's Pacific coast as he sought a better passage to the East.

Drake set out, following Magellan's route. Drake's journal shows that he found the skeletons of Cartagena and Mendoza right where Magellan had executed them at the Bay of Saint Julian sixty years earlier. Drake wintered in the same spot and even executed one Thomas Doughty there, on July 2, 1578, for sorcery. The accusation was unfounded and stemmed from their intense mutual dislike. This execution played a part in transforming the general perception of mutiny. It was reported widely once Drake returned. Drake got away with it because of the magnitude of his achievement: circumnavigating the globe. The new popular perception of leaders of seafaring ventures, promoted by his act, was that they were almost infallible. In Drake's case, members had disagreed with the action, and there had not even been a proper trial. Drake had agreed to spare Doughty if those who were against it forfeited their share of treasure when they returned to England. Although the execution was questionable, remuneration lay squarely within his authority. Gaining wealth from the venture was a strong desire shared by the crew, and Drake's position gave them all something to agree about. Doughty was beheaded.

Drake forged on. Unlike Magellan, he navigated due north after entering the Pacific Ocean and followed land all the way to the northwest coast of America. In the second half of the sixteenth century, the quested northern passage from the Atlantic to the Pacific was widely called the Strait of Anián and was the subject of much fabulous speculation. Drake's venture missed today's Strait of Juan de Fuca, a discovery that might have initially fooled him into thinking he had found the passage through the continent because of its considerable width and its latitude, which lined up nicely with what England knew of America's east coast. About fifteen years later, a Greek pilot (Ioannis Fokas), the strait's namesake, made a dubious claim to its discovery while exploring the coast on a modest venture for Spain, which was still mired in the Iberian Union.

Instead of finding and entering the Strait of Juan de Fuca, Drake tacked due west and crossed the Pacific. His circumnavigation of the globe became the stuff of legend. It reportedly paid off England's national debt. Nor was it the last of his achievements. He defeated the Spanish at several of their territories in the Caribbean in the mid-1580s in the course of an Anglo-Spanish war. Soon thereafter, in 1587, he led an armada into the heart of Spanish territory at Cádiz and sank thirty-seven vessels with fire ship attacks—an astonishing victory. The strategy was a brainchild of Hawkins, inspired by sea battles of ancient Greece in which burning ships containing explosives were sent into enemy armadas. Spain retaliated by sending more than 125 ships against England—the famous Spanish Armada that failed. England, enjoying a run of luck, sent Drake back to invade Spain in 1589. This time he met with total disaster.

English seafarers were better at commerce than at conquest. Drake failed in 1598 because his fleet could not navigate effectively through storms. Moreover, England had assumed that Portugal and Spain's union under Philip II would hinder enemy response—a gross underestimation. The Spanish decimated the English. Drake witnessed the loss of approximately thirty English ships. Spain now began to focus on its defense as the Anglo-Spanish war intensified. Drake died before the end of the war during another failed English invasion in the Spanish Main. Two years later, in 1598, King Philip II died. Philip III was far more interested in compromise than fighting. England's tension with Spain eventually subsided with the Treaty of London in 1604.

These successive events pushed England's seafaring into fuller alignment with mercantilism. And Drake, despite his failures, has legendary status as a seafarer for queen and country in the Age of Discovery. Indeed, his infamy was so great during his lifetime that Philip II put a price on his head and Spanish seafarers called him El Draque (The Dragon), which was a play on his surname as well as a testament to his expertise.

Seafarers like Hawkins and Drake rank among the boldest in history, although they did prove that heavy reliance on conquest rather than commerce was problematic, at least in the English cultural context. The culture of discovery and exploration that they championed was later expanded by another seafarer. Sebastian Cabot's talent for rebounding from failure and recognizing new opportunities was redoubtable, and now he was back in England. Along with Drake's famous execution of Doughty, Cabot's actions in England would reframe the popular perception of mutiny fundamentally and permanently.

THE RETURN OF CABOT

Although Cabot retained Charles V's confidence after the debacle in the Río de la Plata back in 1530, his reputation had suffered an immense blow, and it was hard to find new venture opportunities in Spain. Few would support or join a venture if he was leading it.

By November 1538, he was using his network to make clandestine pledges to Henry VIII via Thomas Wyatt, the English ambassador to Spain. It took almost ten years of surreptitious dealings to find an opportunity in England. But, true to form, Cabot found a good one. It arose from the ever-attractive idea of finding an easier route to the East, a goal shared by many European merchants and sovereigns.

Cabot knew that England could establish a reliable route only in the north because of Spain's and Portugal's influence in the south. He pitched his idea to the English king. Henry VIII had been on the throne for almost fifty years at this point, however, and knew Cabot's history and had heard hundreds of pitches. Still, finding a new passage to the East had become a quiet English objective as its empire developed. England needed to expand beyond local trade with Europe to maintain its status as an emerging world power. Cabot, despite his reputation and mysterious history, was one of very few navigators in Spain with experience in the northern realms. He also had English experience stretching back to his famous Genoese father's arrival in England from Venice and his voyages with his father in the 1490s. Although, in retrospect, it seems that Sebastian Cabot associated his career with his father's, even confusing the two, his purported knowledge and experience were attractive to England in the mid-sixteenth century. In the end, as in Spain in 1516–1517, the death of a king was pivotal. In the English case, it was Henry VIII dying in January 1547 and the succession of Edward VI that cleared Cabot's way. On September 29, 1547, Edward VI's Privy Council accepted Cabot's offer of imperial service and seafaring expertise, and Cabot secretly went to England in October. It was a calculated move that eventually generated national attention in both countries.

In November 1549, Charles V sent a message from Spain through Antoine Perrenot (bishop of Arras and Spanish envoy in Flanders) expressing concern over Cabot's absence. Perrenot delivered it to Thomas Cheney, British minister in Brussels. It called for Cabot's return on the grounds that he "is a verie necessary man for the emperour whose servaunt he is hath a pension of hym." On January

29, 1550, the English responded that "the Lords would deliberate and make him answer with convenjant spede." But Spain's desire for Cabot made him seem more valuable to England, a dynamic that Cabot navigated brilliantly. He refused to return to Spain, as the next carefully worded message from England, dated April 21, 1550, stated: "And as for Sebastian Cabot, answer was made to the said Ambassador that he was not deteined heere by us, but that he of himself refused to go either into Spayne or to the emperor, and that he being of that mind and the Kinges subjecte, no reason, nor equite wolde that he shulde be forced or compelled to go against his will." He was unwilling to go back, and England would not force him go back.[4]

Cabot was not made the pilot major of England to match his position in Spain. The seafaring society was less mature and did not have such a position, despite his interest in creating one. Edward VI was gracious nonetheless and granted him an annual pension and an authoritative voice over seafaring activities.[5]

Despite this warm and formal English reception, Cabot had other designs. In August and September of 1551, he secretly offered his services to Venice and described himself yet again to the Council of Ten as someone who had been born in Venice and ready to serve. It is hard to imagine why Cabot would correspond with the Ten again, as he had done in 1522 shortly after arriving in Spain. This time he communicated through Giacomo Soranzo, Venetian ambassador to England, the way he had thirty years earlier through Caspar Contarini, Venetian ambassador to Spain. A need to recover an ancestral estate was the ruse. This time, however, Cabot was more careful about what he put in writing. The original exchanges show that the intrigue cooled more quickly this time too, with a ciphered letter from the Ten stating that "no one in Venice knows Cabot" but still making a secret request to the envoy "to endeavor to obtain from Cabot as many particulars as he can respecting this navigation, giving the chiefs especial notice of the whole."[6]

Cabot's proposal to the members of the Council of Ten, now known as the "Chiefs," seems to have been the same as before. He promised to lead a Venetian fleet to the East via a northwest passage of which he claimed to have knowledge. He did not know of any such passage, and their response effectively poured cold water on his idea. For the second time in his life, he had undertaken dangerous liaisons shortly after arriving in a new land and managed to avoid detection or punishment.

What was most consistent about Cabot, even outrunning his ability to influence individuals, was his intense desire to discover a westward route to the East. The aspiration to do something notable was part of his character, and it was seared into the culture of an English merchant organization that he refounded with Henry Hudson's grandfather and others. Sixty years later, this organization sponsored Henry Hudson's venture to find the same, elusive northwestern passage.

The Company of Merchant Adventurers

Formal mercantile bodies in English society have been recorded as early as 1216 and as late as 1406, when a charter from Henry IV to the "Brotherhood of Saint Thomas Becket of Canterbury" inaugurated a merchant's trade organization. This organization was reconfirmed by Henry VI in 1430. English seafaring developed with mercantile traditions. Indeed, formal English commerce preceded seafaring. This brotherhood became a standard-bearer for commerce when it used a new kind of sea channel that spurred the development of the empire. In 1505 under Henry VII, the brotherhood became known by its new name, the Company of Merchant Adventurers. Part of Cabot's intention was to create a position in this company similar to his as pilot major in Spain. A memorial drafted by a member named Stephen Burrough cited the need for a great pilot, as "allowed and esteemed in Spain, Portugal, and other places where navigation flourisheth."[7] England's traditions would not allow such a new position with the inordinately high level of authority it entailed. Nonetheless, Cabot was shifting the English culture by creating a new spirit for seafaring and the discovery of unknown regions.

Exactly when Henry Hudson's grandfather, a London alderman, first met Sebastian Cabot is not clear. Records show that both of them joined the Company of Merchant Adventurers as charter members. When the body was refounded, and renamed by adding "to New Lands" to the existing name, on December 18, 1551, Cabot was made its founding governor. Since English seafaring was probably a century behind Spain's and even further behind Portugal's, Cabot's reputation as former pilot major of Spain impressed those without clear information about his past. Cabot was able to establish himself in England as an eminent authority even though his accomplishments did not measure up to the status.

There was already another major, but more informal, mercantile organization in England: the Merchants of the Steelyard (or Stilliarde). It was not an English organization, nor was it allied with the king, but it did present a threat to Cabot's new company. Most of its members were central and eastern Europeans, working in London at the local seat of the Hanseatic League. "Merchants of the Steelyard" was the English name given to these London-based league members. Since the eighth century, the secretive Hanseatic League had conducted trade at Billingsgate, London, with suppliers coming in from the eastern regions of the Baltic Sea, hailing from what became Germany, Russia, and the countries of Scandinavia.[8]

The term "Hanseatic" comes from the German word for "association" (*hanse*). Indeed, the league was an economic association. Its network was a great, decentralized supply chain that covered much of Europe, from today's Estonia in the east all the way to Amsterdam to the west. In the course of its long history, the league crossed the English Channel and acquired a plot of land on the Thames River. Here, the league built a warehouse and followed its peculiar creed. It was widely known, for instance, that women were not allowed in the warehouse and that members almost never married. The English referred to league members as "easterlings" because of their geographic origins.

These easterlings sold woolen cloth, boards, tilings, thatch, and many other products in greater quantity (and at much better prices) than the English merchants did.[9] The enormous volume of their imports drove prices extremely low, and they were excused from paying taxes because their manufactured goods were made abroad. They even had their own ambassador through whom to interface with the English. They had generous equal rights in Britain and enjoyed the advantages of a unique business model that extended to other countries. They also had a reputation for carrying their privileges further than their charter allowed. Most English merchants resented them.

The existence of the Hanseatic League may explain why English seafaring developed so cautiously. When the easterlings entered England in the 1250s, they found a huge market for their wares and came to dominate national trade by underselling, thus reducing the need for English merchants to look abroad for goods—or for exploration or discovery. They fortified their status by lending money to the government, which earned them the favor of many London officials.

This long-standing and complex situation changed with Cabot's return. One of his early actions, on December 29, 1551, eleven days after taking office as company governor, was to take steps to eliminate the easterlings, who were a threat to his new company as it began to expand its explorations and its commercial activities. Cabot persuaded Edward VI to ban the Steelyard Merchants, making the point in a formal dispute on February 24, 1552. The ban was a shrewd move, and English society welcomed it. Some historians see the ban, and Cabot's role in enacting it, as putting England on a more self-reliant course toward becoming the richest empire in world history by the seventeenth century.

The Steelyard Merchants rose again, as they had before.[10] For the time being, the reversal of their privileges was made formal on March 25, making Cabot's reputation sterling in the commercial realm. During the same month he received a financial reward of

two hundred pounds from the royal court. There were some domes-
tic solicitations for reinstatement of the Steelyard Merchants from
city-level officials, given the political alliances the merchants had created, but those were minor. Historic accounts show Cabot's influence
on this affair clearly and report that the royal decree stated of the
Steelyard Merchants that "neither their number, names, and nation
were sufficiently known or ascertained," and they were "no sufficient
corporation."[11]

With the Steelyard Merchants deposed, Cabot could now promote his ideas for seafaring based on his experiences in Spain and the
promise of commerce. The crux of his view was that England needed
to trade directly with the East and not rely on the easterlings or the
Portuguese, despite England and Portugal's commercial exchange
agreements and long-running alliance. By 1553, English seafaring was
making positive gains. Unfortunately, the well-liked Edward VI died
in July of that year, possibly of tuberculosis. Before Edward's death,
the merchant adventurers' first enterprise was launched. Three new
ships sailed from Radcliffe and out the Thames River around May
10 to great fanfare. The flagship, *Bona Esperanza,* and the other two
ships, *Bona Confidentia* and *Edward Bonaventure,* fired their cannon
in honor of their indisposed king as they passed Greenwich. Cabot
stayed behind; he was too old to go along.

Commander Hugh Willoughby and the pilot, Richard Chancellor, were under orders to follow Cabot's detailed "ordinances,
instructions, and advertisements," which he had written as thirty-
three paragraphs in a long document dated May 9, 1553. He signed
it: "the right worshipfull M. Sebastian Cabota Esquier governous of
the mysterie and companie of the Marchants adventurers for the discoverie of Regions, Dominions, Islands, and places unknowen." The
first item is an explicit admonition to avoid dissension (mutiny) as
hostile to the enterprise; his exact words appear in the epigraph to
the introduction to this book. In the document Cabot defines trust
as unity and conformity and warns repeatedly against "conspiracies,
partakings, factions, false tales, and untrue reports toward the com-

mon wealth of this noble realm and the advancement of you the tra-vailers in this voyage, your wives and children." He implores members "to be prompt, ready, and obedient" as he describes external dangers in foreign lands. His intensity is palpable as he advises frequent refer-ence to the document: "It is convenient that this present booke shall once every weeke (by the discretion of the Captaine) be read to the said companie, to the intent that every man may the better remember his othe [oath], conscience, dutie, and charge."[12]

Chancellor and Willoughby's mission was to head northeast and sail over the top of Russia to reach the Far East. They failed to reach China, but they did make England's first major seafaring discovery since John Cabot's voyage to "new found land" fifty years earlier. Chancellor fared excellently. Willoughby, on the other hand, met with a horrendous end. Here we see Cabot's uncanny influence gen-erate positive and negative outcomes simultaneously. In late July, the ships were separated in a storm near the northern part of the Lofo-ten Islands, off the coast of Norway. In case of separation, they had already planned to rendezvous at the "Wardhouse" (today's Vardø, at the northern tip of Norway). Chancellor and his ship's master, Ste-phen Burrough, sailed there and waited for one week. Willoughby, however, kept pushing northeast into the tricky winds of the Barents Sea until the end of August. He was trying to round the northern point of the long arc of Novaya Zemlya, unaware that it was an ar-chipelago and not part of the Russian mainland.[13] Willoughby finally doubled back southwest in September and found a bay in which to spend the 1553–1554 winter. He was east of the rendezvous point, in Lapland and near today's Murmansk, on the Russian side of today's Finland.

Willoughby was no seafarer. He was a veteran of land wars on the Scottish border. In selecting him to lead the expedition, the Com-pany of Merchant Adventurers had remarked glowingly on the tall and impressive Willoughby's "goodly personage as also for his singu-lar skille in the services of warre."[14] Notwithstanding his good looks, Willoughby was a woefully inexperienced navigator. He managed to trap the *Bona Esparanza* and the *Bona Confidentia* solidly in ice on the coast. Every single member, all seventy of them, froze to death. They were not found until the following summer, ships wholly intact and all members dead, their bodies undisturbed.[15]

Chancellor was much luckier. When he and Burrough doubled back in the *Edward Bonaventure* from the point at which the ships lost contact with one another to rendezvous with Willoughby in early August, they stayed closer to the coast of Russia than Willoughby had done. That is how they discovered the entrance to the White Sea while Willoughby was still trying to round Novaya Zemlya. Ironically, Willoughby sailed past the same entrance twice, but he was too far north to realize that the Barents Sea had an inlet—the White Sea— that gave access to the Russian interior. The entire region was generally unknown to western Europeans, and Chancellor's discovery was a huge one. According to his journal, Chancellor thought it was the fabled passage to Marco Polo's Cathay (China). The *Edward Bonaventure* came upon a small fishing boat. Its occupants "trembled in great fear, as men half dead," at the sight of the large ships with copper-sheathed hulls. Once they earned the trust of these oddly fearful Vikings, they were conducted to the mouth of today's Northern Dvina River, to a village in Bjarmaland near today's Arkhangelsk. Chancellor had not realized it yet, but he had found the easternmost point of the great supply chain that the easterlings, now expelled from England, had managed for centuries.[16]

As winter approached, Chancellor explored further, traveling by land to Moscow. There he met Ivan the Terrible, long-reigning Grand Prince of Moscow, who held a lavish welcome ceremony in which Chancellor presented letters from Edward VI in multiple languages. Latin was the most useful one. It seems that Russia had been seeking a way to subvert problematic trade routes through what are now Lithuania, Poland, and Sweden. Now Chancellor had brought an opportunity to do so. He returned to England with a written invitation from the tsar for the English to trade throughout Russia.

The success of this enterprise revolutionized English exploration, even more than John Cabot's had done, and it bolstered Sebastian Cabot's reputation. Willoughby's fate remained a mystery until Chancellor returned to the White Sea in 1555. Chancellor, now famous in England, died in a storm during a third enterprise in 1556. Because of his discovery of the White Sea route, commerce and trade intensified between England and Russia. As a result, the Company of Merchant Adventurers became known as the Muscovy (or Russia) Company in 1555, although it also developed an interest in exploration in other directions. Sebastian Cabot was now serving as the company's "governor for life."

REDEFINING MUTINY

Chancellor's and Willoughby's enterprises prompted a change in the popular perception of mutiny. Cabot's May 9, 1553, document, with its grandiose damnation of all activities that can generate mutiny, was instrumental because it was associated at the outset with the transformational success of the expedition. Heretofore, mutiny had been regarded as a natural phenomenon, as a force that could balance boldness with the realities of a venture. It was regarded as a positive act if it helped an enterprise. Now the values in Cabot's document were embedded in the culture of the growing Muscovy Company. Eventually they were part of the much larger culture that drove English expansion. Twenty-five years later, as we saw, Drake put those values into practice with his unilateral execution of Doughty. His quelling a mutiny that way on his enormously successful venture promoted a shift in the perception of mutiny that was commensurate with the Age of Discovery's decline.

Before Cabot's and Drake's actions to quell mutinies, both made during landmark enterprises, leaders did not have such unilateral authority when faced with group opposition. It was acceptable for a mutiny to run its course if it had a clear and defensible purpose that reflected the dominant shared values of the crew members. The leader's power to quell it came with sufficient support of members or from an ability to reframe the situation so that the shared values aligned with the leadership's. Mutiny was a potentially positive force in adaptable and nimble ventures; dealt with in a spirit of compromise, it could correct venture operations.

With the shift in the perception of mutiny, dissension between leaders and members was regarded as always negative: opposition was to be minimized without consideration of the values or arguments being defended or put forth. Mutiny no longer reflected the functional will of the group; leaders had the sole right and responsibility to destroy it. Popular perceptions evolved along such lines and turned wholly against mutiny as the British Empire expanded. Unlike martyrdom or revolution, which could be seen as righteous, mutiny was always cowardly subversion. Ilya Tolstoy's words quoted in the epigraph to Part II capture the sentiment perfectly: "When mutiny feels strong it is wild and cruel. But this same mutiny, when power is not on its side, is infinitely base and cowardly. And no one can so easily change from arrogant pose to humble slavishness as mutiny."[17] This new, powerful paradigm was extended further, into the industrial revolution, and onward, into the present day. It still accounts for mutiny's taboo overtones.

The Death of Cabot

Because of Cabot's influence and the Muscovy Company's activities, the drive to reach the East by sea had been a widespread pursuit in England. But sailing up and over Russia began to seem impossible, and trade on the White Sea was becoming very profitable. Attention shifted toward such options as sailing over the North Pole or to the northwest. Meanwhile, thanks to Chancellor's success, Cabot's fame grew. His spirit was exuberant as he entered old age. Stephen Burrough, who had sailed with Chancellor in 1553, recorded excitedly that Cabot had banqueted at a hall in Gravesend and "entered into the dance himself with the rest of the young and lusty company." The celebration that night was for Burrough's own yearlong enterprise to the northeast the night before it departed on April 27, 1556. Cabot was more than eighty years of age.[18]

Cabot's past caught up with him soon afterward. When Edward VI died in mid-1553, his half-sister Mary I, the only daughter of Catherine of Aragon, Henry VIII's first queen consort, became queen. On July 25, 1554, she married Philip II of Spain, the son of Charles V. Philip II was Mary I's second cousin, and this Charles V was the same king whom Cabot had slighted by fleeing Spain. Mary's brief reign brought sweeping changes that did not favor Cabot, who had enjoyed a very favorable reputation with the young Edward VI and in English culture writ large. Indeed, most historic references to him during this period include adjectives such as "celebrated," "right worshipful," "veteran," and "most worthy and excellent."

Philip II arrived in England on May 20, 1557. Just one week later, Cabot was made to split his pension with William Worthington, one of Mary I's royal pensioners, with the directive that Worthington would participate in all of Cabot's activities. Another dark development concerned the resurgence of the Merchants of the Steelyard, who saw their own opportunity in the royal succession. They were an enemy of Cabot's, too, since he had strategically curtailed them six years earlier. By 1557, the easterlings were again receiving favorable allowances in England.

Cabot died in London soon after these changes put him in a difficult position, but the exact date of his death is unknown. It seems to have occurred within a three-month period in 1557, sometime between his last pension payment of September 29 and the assignment of his full pension to Worthington on December 25. There are many unanswered questions about him. His and others' letters refer to his commissioned maps and works, but aside from a few charts (like the one in chapter 3), very few of his works exist. A 1544 map of the world is attributed to him, but he probably did not draw much of it.[19] When Cabot died, his property probably passed to Worthington. Because Charles V attempted to retrieve Cabot, this property was apparently valuable to Spain. Worthington delivered it there at a price. Where it is now is no less of a mystery than Cabot himself.[20]

Throughout this early period of English seafaring, a distinct Hudson contingent was almost always part of Muscovy Company activities. The elder Henry Hudson had been a founding member of the company, and the Hudson name was a frequent feature of voyage rosters. The Hudsons listed were all relatives of the most famous Henry Hudson, the grandson of the company cofounder. They joined ventures to the northeast, due north, and to the northwest, always seeking a passage to the East Indies or the vaguer East. Henry Hudson the grandson was born into this seafaring tradition in the latter half of the sixteenth century. During these years, seafaring and especially trade benefited England greatly. Finding a reliable passage to the East was becoming as important to England as it had been to Spain and Portugal one hundred years earlier.

HUDSON AND HIS VENTURES

Although English logbooks and journals recorded many details, other kinds of record keeping in England were not so reliable during the sixteenth and seventeenth centuries. Literacy was not common outside the educated upper classes. The year of Hudson's birth was a victim of the times. The date is uncertain, although he was definitely born in the mid-1560s. Because his grandfather was a London alderman and many of his uncles and cousins occupied powerful positions in the burgeoning Muscovy Company, he came from a relatively privileged background. The Hudsons helped manage the company as England entered into more prosperous times. Booms and busts in commercial exports, English divisions between Protestants and Catholics, and the Burgundian alliance with England had all become tamer by the end of the sixteenth century as the company continued to grow.

By the first decade of the seventeenth century, the company had undertaken ventures to the White Sea and to Spitsbergen, Norway, and had explored the Barents Sea toward Novaya Zemlya, the long Arctic archipelago that had stymied Willoughby. These operations generated many commercial successes, many of which were based on fishing and whaling. But the desire to find a route to the East was always present. By the time Henry Hudson came of age, that desire filled his imagination. This idea of finding a new passage excited him as much as it had excited Columbus, Magellan, and both Cabots before him.

The Muscovy Company was becoming more open to a broader range of ventures—a promising development for the young Hudson. It did not intend merely to fish in the northeast or to trade on the White Sea. Meanwhile, Spain was forcing many non-Christians and foreigners out of its territories, causing the loss of many educated and talented people, compounding the deleterious effects on Iberian seafaring already complicated by the Iberian Union. The spirit of sea-faring, it seemed, had followed Cabot out of Iberia and was slowly traveling up the peninsula and closer to England. Hudson worked on ventures with the company during this period. He was not trusted with leadership at his young age. In fact, he did not get the opportunity to truly lead until he was over forty.

The First Enterprise

The first voyage with Hudson at the helm was undertaken with one ship, the *Hopewell,* and only twelve members, including his young son John. The ship departed on May 1, 1607. The Muscovy Company, which sponsored the venture, had recommended that Henry Hudson lead it. The record shows that Hudson possessed private information of benefit to the enterprise and that he used it to improve his contract. The private information may well have been Robert Thorne's lengthy declaration to Henry VIII in 1527. His father Nicholas Thorne had sailed with John Cabot in 1497 and with Hugh Elyot in 1502. Thorne's letter, cited in chapter 3, was still not widely known at this point. The document was originally passed to Henry VIII's ambassador to

Spain, also his chaplain, and went through several more hands before Richard Hakluyt procured it circa 1580. Thorne's "booke" came with a "carde" (i.e., map) that contained "information of the parts of the world discovered by him [Henry VIII] and the King of Portingale [Portugal]." Its postscript requested that its map be closely protected from discovery by foreigners.[21]

Hudson's first mission was not unduly difficult. The plan was to head as far north as possible and seek evidence of a northern passage to the East Indies. The *Hopewell* sailed due north from England in early May, after weather delayed departure from the Thames for a week. By mid-June it had passed the coasts of Iceland and Greenland and then Svalbard, an island group halfway between Norway and the North Pole. Seafarers still did not know that the polar region was an ice cap. In fact, Hudson believed, as many did, that the many months of sunshine each year at the poles created a warm and passive sea that could be crossed easily—a belief partially based on a strained interpretation of the Bible. An ambitious first-time leader, he sailed farther north than anyone before him. The weather was freezing. Hudson concluded that it was impossible for a warm sea to exist anywhere in the northern polar realm.

Journals and notes from this venture show a mostly uneventful but interesting voyage filled with many sightings of whales, grampuses (various species of porpoise) and "morses" ("whale-horses," or walruses) and marked by navigation through very thick fog. The crew also recorded sighting "many birds with blacke backes and white bellies, in forme much like a ducke."[22] Even though Columbus had written about the declination of the compass needle with northward travel, and even though it was common knowledge in Portugal and Spain, Hudson's crew were confused by it and mistook the alteration as supernatural. Spooked by orca sightings, some believed the venture was cursed, but the overall easiness of the voyage made the idea of mutiny far-fetched.

There were a few moments of excitement. Once, they had to

tow the *Hopewell* out of danger's way by rowing the small boat away from an ice floe—an early example of clever tactical maneuvering on Hudson's part. On another occasion, a crew member who was fishing hooked with heavy tackle a whale that had swum under the keel. Indeed, reports from this enterprise alerted England and Holland to the locations of large populations of whales and walruses and gave rise to an industry that severely reduced the populations of those animals. Overall, however, the voyage was a failure in that no passage to the East was discovered by sailing due north. The *Hopewell* returned to London on September 15, after four months at sea.

Some of Hudson's actions were hard to explain at the time but are illuminating in retrospect. For instance, the record shows that he twice turned the *Hopewell* sharply toward the west and proceeded in that direction, seemingly unnecessarily. These detours occurred in July and in August on the return to London. The record does not explain why he covered considerable distances each time before bringing the *Hopewell* back on course. The members would not have responded well to such changes in course. These moves were an early hint of the obsession with finding a northwest passage that members of Hudson's future enterprises would encounter.

Shortly after this first voyage, Hudson was offered an opportunity to lead a whaling venture to Spitzbergen, in the Svalbard Islands. Although the enterprise would have been lucrative, he declined. He hoped instead to try to find a northeast passage. It was hard for Hudson to gain sponsorship this time, but the company agreed to fund one more venture to the unpromising northeast, past the White Sea.

The last attempt at a northeastern passage had been Burrough's in 1556. Sebastian Cabot had danced at the departure party. Although Ivan the Terrible, who had welcomed English trade, had died in 1584, trade, political and societal exchanges, and alliances all remained strong. Venturing beyond the White Sea was thus a lower priority than it had been. The company approved Hudson's venture anyway, but Hudson knew that this trip might be the last opportunity he would get to find a new route. This trip would also be a tougher one

to lead because the ship had to enter harsher seas. And this time
Hudson would face a brilliantly executed mutiny.

The Second Enterprise

Once again aboard the *Hopewell,* Hudson left Gravesend with fifteen
members, including his son John, on April 22, 1608. The roster shows
Robert Juet as second in command. As we shall see, Juet was a pivotal
character at several points in Hudson's career. The formal objective
was a route to southeastern Asia. The voyage took them far over the
top of Russia. The *Hopewell* was an old ship whose hull had been reinforced with wood planks for the ice-laden Arctic waters.

An odd friction between Hudson and Juet was apparent even before the ship was launched. Juet ignored Hudson's authority; he even
visited with acquaintances in his quarters during the departure cer-
emonies. Hudson objected, but Juet ignored him. Hudson thought
Juet was bad-tempered, and Juet did not respect Hudson. The tension between them would simmer steadily for three months.

The ship's journals show that the voyagers had clear skies and
calm seas for the first few months. But near the end of May, as they
passed beyond the northern coast of Norway and entered the Barents
Sea, the cold grew fierce. On the way to Novaya Zemlya, five members became so ill that they were unable to get out of their bunks.
Large ice chunks knocked against the reinforced hull. All knew that a
large iceberg or ice floe could crush the *Hopewell.* Hudson monitored
the tactical environment closely. His ability to maneuver skillfully in
these close quarters, like a small-boat man, was phenomenal.

The journal for June 15 contains detailed descriptions of mermaids. Just as Columbus had mistaken dugongs for mermaids, 120
years later, crewmen aboard Hudson's ship did the same thing with
walruses or Risso's dolphins. "This morning, one of our companie
looking over boord saw a Mermaid, and calling up some of the companie to see her, one more came up, and by that time shee was come
close to the ships side, looking earnestly on the men: a little after, a
Sea came and overturned her: from the Navill upward, her backe and

breasts were like a womans, (as they say that saw her) her body as big as one of us; her skin very white; and long haire hanging down behind, of colour blacke: in her going downe they saw her tayle, which was like the tayle of a Porposse, and speckled like a Macrell [mackerel]. The names that saw her, were Thomas Hilles and Robert Rayner."[23]

Almost a week later, the *Hopewell* cruised among small glaciers. At night they heard the fizzling of melting ice and the roaring of polar bears. During the day they saw thousands of seals. When they reached the coast of Novaya Zemlya's islands, Hudson decided to track walruses to find an anchorage for the small boat. His tactic worked, and he sent parties ashore many times during the following days. They returned with antlers, deerskins, whale fins (presumably from beached whales), eggs, and many geese and ducks that they had hunted and killed. They tracked bear and fox and even found a wooden cross at a place where fires had been made by earlier explorers.

As the promise of discovery of a northeast passage ran thin, Hudson sensed another company loss looming. He could not tolerate another failure. It was early July, which meant that the southern route around Novaya Zemlya was frozen and impassable for another month, or so he thought. It was in fact open for travel for one or two months each year.[24] The ship did not venture far enough south to explore a southern passage anyway. At this time of year, bergs and floes were very dangerous. On July 2, the crew spent a full day using beams to push and navigate around them. In one close call they used the anchor and cables to angle the *Hopewell* away and barely escaped being crushed. Two days later they found safety in an inlet along southwestern Novaya Zemlya. They progressed 12 miles (19 km) into it and then entered a large river, which they followed for about 10 miles (16 km) until it was too shallow for the *Hopewell*. Once at anchor, Hudson sent Juet and five others in the ship's boat to follow the river, which they did for 20 more miles (32 km), until it was too shallow for that vessel. Once that group returned, all hope of a passage through to China vanished.

Juet had communicated with the small contingent in the ship's boat, reinforcing a common desire to return home. Before long, members were united around Juet's idea of going back. So when Hudson decided that the *Hopewell* would turn around, their spirits were raised immediately. However, it was not long before Hudson changed his mind, and that change sparked a mutiny.

The *Hopewell* headed southwest on July 7, 1608. Hudson had secretly planned to hunt walruses and seek the fabled Willoughby's Island.[25] Hudson laid out his reasoning in his journal. The ice at this time of year would direct them toward the island. A large stock of walruses would give him something to bring home to England, and finding the island would calm the crew. The ship faced stormy weather for a week, which gave him a chance to conceal the *Hopewell*'s true heading. Eventually Juet and a few others realized that they seemed to be exploring aimlessly. They objected. Hudson reassured them but persisted with his plan. Without discovering the elusive island or taking walruses, this trip would be another failure.

Hudson's plan placated the crew. For most of July, he led the *Hopewell* around the Barents Sea searching for a mythical island. He did not possess Columbus's ability to sustain his crew's spirits with optimism and communication, but he managed to extend the operation for three weeks. He also lacked Columbus's good fortune. Columbus had communicated his objective to members, then let the discovery of land quell a mutiny. By contrast, Hudson neither communicated much about what he was seeking, nor did he discover it. The members felt affronted by his failure to recognize their values. A critical incident was all that was needed. They already had a ringleader in Juet.

Juet did not act immediately. At the outset, mutiny is always a delicate and strategic affair. The best-executed mutinies helped a venture even while allowing mutineers to avoid punishment. By this point, in 1608, mutinies were judged with extreme prejudice. Mutineers like Juet could now easily be sentenced to death if convicted. But even an increased threat of punishment was not an adequate deterrent. In fact, this new view probably forced mutineers to be more ingenious and cunning. Juet's mutiny strategy benefited from the same elements that make leadership effective. It was, much like the leadership strategy Columbus used to quell mutiny on his 1492 voyage, simple and brilliant.

As Hudson fumbled around in the Barents Sea, many incidents offered an opportunity to put the mutiny plans into action. Juet eventually reacted to one of those incidents, a disagreement over the heading. He told Hudson, on behalf of everyone, to head back to England or else they would remove him as captain. But he cast the demand in more agreeable and subtle terms. Juet and the mutineers asked Hudson to draft an official certificate in his own hand, sign it, and circulate it. Hudson would, in his own words, write that he was stopping the venture under no compulsion from anyone. They would follow Hudson, to be sure, but only if he agreed to lead in the direction they wanted to go. With such a document in the members' hands, Hudson would find it almost impossible to take recourse against them. If he were to redact the decree or deny its veracity, trust in his ability to lead an enterprise would be destroyed in England.

Hudson's authority was thus completely subverted in a well-designed mutiny. The ship returned to England safely, and nobody was punished. His personal journal includes a long gap between July 27 and August 7, which includes the interval during which the mutiny was undertaken. The *Hopewell* arrived at Gravesend on August 26, 1608, after four months at sea. Hudson's last entry conveys the mutiny's actions.

> The seventh of August, I used all diligence to arrive at London, and therefore now I gave my companie a certificate under my hand, of my free and willing returne, without perswasion or force of any one or more of them: for at my being at Nova Zembla, the sixt of July, voide of hope of a north-east passage (except by the Waygats, for which I was not fitted to trie or prove), I therefore resolved to use all meanes I could to sayle

to the north-west; considering the time and meanes we had, if the wind should friend us, as in the first part of our voyage it had done, and to make trial of that place called Lumley's Inlet, and the furious over-fall by Captain Davis, hoping to runne into it an hundred leagues, and to return as God should enable mee. But now having spent more than halfe the time I had, and gone but the shortest part of the way, by means of contrary winds, I thought it my duty to save victual, wages, and tackle, by my speedy returne, and not by foolish rashenesse, the time being wasted, to lay more charge upon the action than necessitie should compel, I arrived at Gravesend the sixe and twentieth of August.[26]

Aside from giving rise to some new maps and charts, Hudson's first voyage had been insignificant. Now this second one was a big failure. Only a shipwreck could have made it more of a loss. The arrival in England was grim.

Because trade with Russia on the White Sea was booming, the Muscovy Company stopped sponsoring the kinds of enterprises that Hudson sought to undertake. When the company rejected his request to lead a third venture, his resolve twisted into deep depression. The recent enterprise had already demoralized him with its affronts to his leadership, but pride demanded that he try again. There was just one problem. Hudson's next venture would have to proceed without funding from the Muscovy Company. Like Columbus, Magellan, and the Cabots, Hudson began seeking support outside his homeland. His obsession with finding a passage to the East led him to deal with one of England's rivals: the Netherlands.

The Third Enterprise

The Netherlands wanted to discover a northeast passage for the same reasons as England. The Dutch had also incurred some misadventures, such as the famously bold 1596–1597 enterprise of Willem Barentsz. He and his crew heroically survived extreme winter conditions on a shifting ice pack near Novaya Zemlya in a small wooden shelter. Because of the risk, the union of Dutch provinces had begun discouraging the financing of these enterprises in the later 1590s. However, the state had begun offering a large reward for the discovery of a passage. In Hudson's time, no one had yet succeeded, but many intrepid as well as foolish adventurers had tried.

Hudson was ready to do almost anything to lead an enterprise in search of a route to the East, including bending the rules. In those days, bending the rules was a dicey business that often amounted to treason. Hudson was not dissuaded. He turned first to French and then to Dutch diplomatic officials in England. France and England were enemies at this point.[27] Both admired the riches that Portugal and Spain had acquired with their seafaring ventures, but they were also rivals as they each pursued similar fortunes. Hudson used that rivalry to his advantage, just as he had won a better deal with England for his first enterprise. He was not a great strategist, but he was as tactically adept at managing individuals and institutions as he was at angling around ice bergs and ice floes. Luckily for Hudson, financing in England and Holland usually came from the progenitors of modern business organizations. There were still potentially new kinds of opportunities despite his recent string of failures.

Hudson was familiar with company rule in England, but his reputation was damaged there. Moreover, the Muscovy Company was seeing its sixty-year tradition of spirited exploration weaken. It had settled on trade with Russia and, like Holland, was avoiding risky ventures. The Muscovy model was so profitable that in 1600 and 1602, respectively, the British and the Dutch were compelled to found their own East India companies. These companies were a new sort, aligned with the crown but with commercial activities as prime movers. They were innovative in another way, too: they were the world's first private companies that issued joint stock to a wide array of supporters to procure investment. The formation of joint-stock companies made the competitive markets even more volatile. They rendered more traditional and centralized models, like those in

Portugal and Spain, somewhat inefficient by comparison. The tactical challenges produced by this new commercial turbulence were a
boon for Hudson.

The Iberian Union was still stubbornly hindering Portuguese and
Spanish seafaring ventures with bureaucratic red tape and stalemates.
Indeed, within about a decade, the new English East India Company
was helping England to humiliate and outpace mighty Portugal at
sea. In a dispute in November 1612, for instance, four Portuguese
ships were defeated by four English East India Company ships. The
Portuguese had gone all the way to China in 1516, and now, a century
later, they were defeated on the ocean by ships from a seafaring tradition whose sailors were known for navigating by following European
coastlines. After two centuries of Portuguese seafaring domination,
the balance was shifting.

The early East India companies embodied the spirit of today's
multinational organizations. Indeed, they helped bring great riches
to the English and the Dutch. The French followed suit with an East
India Company in 1664. Hudson planned to take full advantage of
this new sort of financing and shared risk-taking.

Hudson considered the Dutch East India Company to offer
a larger opportunity because it was about four times the size of its
English counterpart. The Dutch were also taking some of the spice
trade from Portugal through aggressive strategies in the Spice Islands.
Hudson went across the North Sea to Amsterdam at the invitation of
the company. He did not speak Dutch but used interpreters and Latin
to communicate with the company directors about his plans. There
were disagreements and doubts, but the company eventually agreed
to sponsor his next venture.

Hudson promised the Dutch a smoother new way to the East. It
was to them a very attractive prospect. The rewards he would receive in
return for success were considerable. He also promised strong trade opportunities for the Dutch East India Company. The company balked,
but having discovered that Hudson had begun additional talks with
the French, a final decision was made on December 28, 1608. Hud-

son had known that the Dutch did not want to risk the French, an enemy, finding a valuable passage or new commercial route first. The contract, dated January 8, 1609, was drafted for "Henry Hudson, Englishman," with assistance from Jodocus Hondius, a cartographer who served as Hudson's interpreter.[28] As for Hudson's failed English enterprise, the stated objective was to seek a northeast passage by going up and over Novaya Zemlya.

After living in Holland for four months preparing for the voyage, Hudson departed from Amsterdam on March 25, 1609, in a Dutch ship called the *Half Moon*. For some inexplicable reason, Juet was on board again. All went as planned at first. In a month, the crew were in the freezing northeastern realms where Hudson had been the previous year. Two months later, the thick fog, ice, wind, and snow generated disaffection. Half the crew were Dutch, and many Dutch sailors preferred the warmer spice-trade routes around the Cape of Good Hope. To them, Hudson was a foreigner, and he did not really understand the Dutch seafaring culture. In fact, the gap between Hudson and his Dutch crew was greater than the gap in the Magellan and Columbus mutinies. In Hudson's case, the language barrier was virtually complete. Indeed, mutinies were most common on enterprises with polyglot crews. Poor communication makes it easy for values to clash in uncertain environments.

Some Dutch historians describe the mutiny on this voyage as due to cultural differences. The gaps in shared values were significant, and they were exacerbated by distrust. A powerful mutiny arose in mid-June, when the *Half Moon*'s mast was damaged in a storm. The ship passed Vardø and was approaching the White Sea before the voyagers realized they were 100 miles (161 km) off course.

Dissension, cultural differences, the language barrier, the missed course, and the damaged mast were synthesized into a mutiny that was as natural as the wind. Juet capitalized on the unrest of the Dutch crew members, over whom he had a certain authority as an Englishman speaking against an English captain. He posed a threat to Hudson but provided an opportunity for the mutineers, who demanded to leave the miserable cold and this dangerous area of the ocean. Hudson maintained authority and quelled the mutiny with a familiar response. He gave the crew two options: they could head southwest for the fortieth parallel, off the American coast, or northwest for the Davis Strait, which lies between Greenland and Canada.[29] The crew chose the former, probably because it was closer to their current location and possibly also because traversing the Davis Strait would have entailed more ice and snow.

Hudson wanted to head west anyway; he wanted to find the long-sought northwest passage. The journals of George Weymouth in his possession influenced him greatly. Weymouth had explored the American coast in 1602 and 1605 and written about a passage to the western sea. Hudson received those journals in Holland from Petrus Plancius, a cartographer and founding member of the Dutch East India Company. Like Hondius, Hudson's Dutch interpreter, Plancius had spent time in England and was now a cartographer in Amsterdam. He had valuable Portuguese charts that he jealously guarded. Plancius had lost faith in the idea of a northeastern passage around Novaya Zemlya, and Hudson respected his opinion. The two options that Hudson gave his crew created a false impression; he intended to keep exploring, and he preferred to explore westward, but he made the crew believe he was proceeding on their terms. A 1613 Amsterdam tract describes the choice as rational: "His course to the east and Nova Zemlya was blocked by ice and snow, [and he sailed west] in order that he might see if there were any hope remaining . . . that he might get some profit for our country and the Directors."[30]

They approached the American coast in early July. Initially, the interactions with natives on the coast of North America, near modern-day Maine, were positive. Things turned grim, however, when members of the *Half Moon* suspected theft, and Juet led a raid of a native settlement on July 25: "Then we manned our boat and scute [a flat-bottomed boat used for transporting heavy loads] with twelve men and muskets, and two stone pieces or murderers, drave the savages from their houses, and took spoyle of them, as they would have done of us."[31] Of all the historical cases presented in this book, this one includes the most shameful actions against natives. Even other ships that the *Half Moon* encountered were not spared aggressive but bumbling advances. Stories of Drake and Hawkins capturing ships in the Spanish Main were certainly familiar to Hudson, but he was no Drake.

In August 1609, the ship followed the shoreline of America seeking inlets and rivers that might cross through to the western ocean. Hudson displayed a navigational style that was thoroughly tactical and involved much shunting about: to the north, then the south; back to the north and then to the southwest; through the shallows and into the deep before coming suddenly upon shoals. The venture retraced its own course several times. The members charted much of Delaware Bay and found Cape Cod, which was promising but ultimately disappointing. Finally, on September 3, Hudson found the mouth of the wide river that Esteban Gómez and Giovanni da Verrazzano had found back in 1524.[32] Hudson called it the River of Mountains, but it was later named for him: the Hudson River. The *Half Moon* ran aground, but the crew explored the river in small boats all the way to where Albany sits today, approximately 140 miles (227 km) from the river's mouth.

Along the way, there were many more interactions with natives. Most were friendly, but according to Juet's journals, Hudson's men feared the natives and took hostages as a form of insurance. They continued to explore the river, fighting and trading along the way. Several skirmishes occurred, and one of Hudson's members was killed by an arrow shot into his neck on September 6. One member shot and killed a native trying to steal the small boat. There were many encounters. Some encounters were positive, but many entailed violent and deadly attacks and constant suspicion on both sides. The interactions became increasingly dangerous.[33] Later Hudson did order members to fire on natives. Indeed, the natives of this region still recalled these events and reported them to explorers many years later. The memory of such episodes complicated future explorations by others.

By October, the decision to either winter over or head back to Europe needed to be made. Hudson wanted to continue to explore. Members disagreed. His capitulations were now a reliable mechanism for dealing with points of contention, and mutiny had essentially become a substitute for leadership. Hudson's Dutch second-in-command favored wintering over, but Hudson feared mutiny if they stayed. This time he had no chance to make a deal. According to Hudson's journal, the members gathered against him naturally in a boldly menacing and mutinous manner.

Hudson's authority was at a new low. Everyone agreed that not enough time had passed for them to go back to Holland. An early return would jeopardize their common financial interests. So they opted to go to Ireland. They crossed the Atlantic, missed Ireland, and landed at Dartmouth, in southwest England, on November 7. Upon arrival, they sent a letter to Amsterdam requesting more money and new members and described a new plan to depart in early March, head northwest to hunt whales, and then go to Holland and make good on the company's investment.

The Dutch East India Company's response arrived two months later. Perfectly clear about what they were dealing with, they ordered the *Half Moon* to return to Holland immediately. Hudson assented. It was January 1610. Unfortunately, by now the English had also ascertained details of the venture, and before the *Half Moon* could leave, Hudson and all the English crew were arrested for working for the Dutch. The Dutch contract meant little to Hudson other than the means to explore, but it meant something different to the English authorities. Hudson already had a poor reputation around England, and the authorities regarded this behavior as treasonous. They believed further that the information gathered about the Hudson River could be useful and perhaps help them find the passage they sought.

Some Dutch writers charitably speculated that Hudson had ascertained the location of a northwest passage but had passed it by to save the discovery for the English. The English were not inclined to a generous interpretation. Hudson was put under house arrest in

London and tried for treason. King James I was angered that Hudson had dared to collaborate with the Dutch, although he would license a Dutch settlement on the Hudson River several years later, a decision that proved to be a mistake. The merchants already felt less strongly. With their open-minded commercial worldview, they could not conceive of a reason why Hudson should not be able to contract with the Dutch East India Company.

Hudson never returned to Holland. In the summer of 1610, the non-English members were allowed to bring the *Half Moon* back to Amsterdam, along with some journals and records that were never recovered. It seems that the English had grounds for taking exception to Hudson's Dutch venture after all. Once James I had allowed for the initial settlement, the Dutch set their sights on the River of Mountains that Hudson had explored and sent many expeditions to the region in the years to come.[34]

The Final Enterprise

Hudson remained as obsessed as ever about making a mark in history. The opportunity came less than half a year later, in March 1610. This time Hudson ventured for England in the *Discovery,* the same ship that Weymouth, his idol, had used a decade earlier. The *Discovery* was larger than the *Hopewell* or the *Half Moon* and had already made at least six transatlantic voyages. The Muscovy Company had sponsored Weymouth in the *Discovery* when he sought a northwest passage in 1602. For Hudson's final enterprise in 1610, he had a refurbished *Discovery,* more of Weymouth's charts, and new charts that he had procured in Holland.

In the early seventeenth century, as England became a richer society, it had become easier for adventurers to raise capital through informal channels when direct ones failed to come through. For his fourth venture, Hudson won funding from several rich merchants in spite of another Muscovy Company rejection. Some of these investors, like Thomas Smythe, were members of the English East India and Virginia companies. A new enterprise called the Company of

Gentlemen, made up of rich merchants and speculators, was a subsidiary of the East India Company. Its members not only coordinated the support for Hudson's new venture but also convinced James I to forget the charges of treason leveled against Hudson, even arranging for Hudson to meet the king's son, the teenage Prince Henry, which helped restore Hudson's damaged reputation.[35] Prince Henry supported Hudson's fourth venture, as did former members of the Muscovy Company.

Hudson boldly claimed during planning meetings that he would reach the East Indies—southeastern Asia—by February 2, 1611. He was provided with resources to upgrade the ship, granted lawful authority to build an organization, and given the freedom to navigate at will, but his strategic leadership proved poorer than ever, and he ended up merely setting the stage for mutiny.

The *Discovery* and its twenty-five members, again including John Hudson, departed from the docks at Saint Katherine's Pool, near the Tower of London, on April 17, 1610. Five days later, Hudson expelled a member named Coleburne and left him at Gravesend, 25 miles (about 40 km) down the Thames River from London. We do not know exactly why Hudson removed him, but we know he was a representative of the Company of Gentlemen and a capable and knowledgeable seafarer. It is probable that Hudson perceived a threat to his own leadership. When he expelled Coleburne at Gravesend, he took on Henry Greene as a replacement.

Hudson was not a keen judge of character. Greene, a venomous man quite the opposite of Coleburne, had acute gambling problems and a criminal record. By most accounts, he was a hothead who liked to fight. Abacuck Pricket, who provided a first-person account of this enterprise, wrote of Greene that through "lewd life and conversation hee lost the good will of all his friends, and spent all that hee had." For some reason, Hudson liked him. Greene was probably brought aboard to serve as Hudson's man, as defense against members like Juet, who was Hudson's mate but not a trusted confidante. After Greene joined, Hudson promised him a future position with Prince

Henry's soldiers. This promise was Greene's payment. The financiers knew nothing about him, and there were no references to Greene in the official documents.

It is unclear why Juet was with Hudson on the third enterprise as a clerk after he orchestrated a mutiny on the second enterprise as its master. But it is truly baffling that Juet was working with Hudson again on the fourth enterprise. We know little about their relationship other than Hudson's remark concerning Juet's mean-spiritedness. Their interpersonal dynamics on Hudson's final enterprise are stranger even than the fact that they were working together yet again.

The *Discovery* exited the Thames and rounded England to the north. On May 11, the crew sighted the east coast of Iceland. They watched a large volcanic eruption from Iceland's Mount Hekla later that month and interpreted the astonishing sight as a bad omen.[36] Frozen seas to the south of Iceland prevented landing, so the *Discovery* sailed up the northwest coast for provisioning. Once that was done, the wind would not permit them to reenter the Atlantic, so they went back to Iceland, landing near modern Reykjavik.

Here in southeastern Iceland at a place they called Lousy Bay, they enjoyed the very best part of the voyage, bathing in hot springs and eating well. Back at sea, Greene got into a fight with the surgeon, Edward Wilson. Hudson intervened, censuring Wilson without knowing the details and offending the crew, who were all suspicious of Greene. If no one trusted Greene, almost everyone doubted Hudson's competence. Worse, Greene made Hudson seem untrustworthy because many believed he was Hudson's spy. Juet had circulated that idea. Hudson caught the rumor and accused Juet of disloyalty. That was a serious word on a seafaring enterprise at this point in history. Hudson threatened to take Juet back to Lousy Bay to go back to England in a fishing boat, even though, at the time of the quarrel, the ship had already traveled 140 miles (220 km) west of Iceland. Hudson was ready to turn around, but he vacillated and changed his mind when members objected.

On June 4, after spending the better part of the day chasing a looming fog bank that they believed was land, they caught sight of Greenland. They intended to land on its east coast, but the ice made that impossible. So they circled south and reached what is today called Kap (Cape) Desolation, at the southern tip of Greenland. A large number of whales were here, three of which came alongside the ship. One bumped the keel and frightened the crew. The *Discovery* crossed the North Atlantic over the next few weeks by way of the Davis Strait, between Greenland and Baffin Island, in the northeastern modern Canada. Owing to currents and winds, Hudson was farther south than he had intended, which was actually fortunate, for the inlets above the southeastern point of Baffin Island (at today's Resolution Island) are dead ends. On June 25, they approached the mouth of what is now known as the Hudson Strait.

Davis, Frobisher, Weymouth, Baffin, and several other English seafarers had all missed the entrance to this particular strait, which Hudson entered between Baffin Island and northern Quebec.[37] The Portuguese had explored and written off the whole region a century earlier. When Hudson entered the strait, he felt the exciting promise of a passage to the East. Members were excited, too. The sea and land, though inhospitable, seemed similar to what they had heard about the Strait of Magellan. The expanse of water into which the strait opened was huge and open. But there were differences. At this time of year the strait, about 400 miles (600 km) south of the Arctic Circle, was filled with large whirling chunks of ice that made the *Discovery* feel disposable and even fragile. Hudson and his members were terrified.

The English had not charted the strait yet. Seafarers like the ones listed above, who may have seen it from a distance, knew the power of ice in this realm. Following Captain John Davis, they all referred to it as the Furious Overfall. Hudson's members had all heard stories about extreme tides, currents, and fog. They knew they had to navigate through mountains of ice that could crush the *Discovery* if it was boxed in. Sure enough, once they cleared Resolution Island, they found themselves in a dangerous whirl of ice floes, not unlike the descriptions in the stories.

Hudson was not always brave, and he was interpersonally ineffective compared to other leaders examined here. But it would be hard to match his bold tactical leadership in the Furious Overfall. He gave orders as the crew pushed around large and slow icebergs, careful not only of dangerous protrusions below the waterline but the thousands of sharp broken chunks that had destroyed other ships. He gave world-class tactical directions. Indeed, seafarers in the same area one hundred years later performed far worse than Hudson did.[38] However, as with Magellan, his deft actions did not build trust in him but merely lowered distrust in his competence.

As the *Discovery* tempted fate in the dangerous ice-filled strait, its overall heading was north by northwest. The crew soon began to make out the northern boundary of the strait. The sighting of land gave a hint of certainty, but the situation grew worse around July 5, when a dark storm appeared in the west. The *Discovery* was soon in the path of a deadly ice floe. Some of the larger pieces spun violently in the current. An entire iceberg flipped over. Hudson made a shrewd decision to take the ship into the middle of a huge field of smaller bits, "into the chiefest of the ice, and there to let her lie," with the idea that the smaller bits would buffer the ship from damage by the larger ones.[39] The maneuver worked. But now they were stuck. As Hudson and his crew watched the ice close in on their wooden ship, they all feared that they might become stranded.

Hudson managed to quell a mutiny that arose on July 6 while they were surrounded by this encroaching ice. Not surprisingly, it was based on a shared concern for safety in light of his decision to continue their journey. Mutiny struck during an open meeting when one crew member famously remarked that if he had one hundred pounds, he would give back ninety just to be in England. Many agreed, but the view was not quite unanimous, for the carpenter, Philip Staffe, countered that he would give nothing back; he would take all his money to England when the venture concluded safely. Thanks to Staffe, and to poor organization (i.e., "many words to no-purpose"), the mutiny fragmented. Hudson took the opportunity to assert himself. He showed the crew members that according to Wey-mouth's chart, they were "entred above an hundred leagues further than ever any English was." Using his tried-and-true tactic, he then "left it to their choice, whether they would proceed any further; yea or nay."[40] Although his motion took advantage of momentary dis-agreements among members, their shared perception of danger and the gap in trust never disappeared.

After a great deal of work the crew freed the *Discovery* by creating a three-mile (4.83 km) channel through the floating ice. They were in what is now named Ungava Bay, a 250-mile (about 400 km) north-to-south shallow body of water south of the entrance to the strait; they had been trapped along this bay's east coast. Now, on the move again, they saw an enormous iceberg, as large as an island, capsize in the distance. It was a fantastic spectacle. Thousands of such bergs had broken up over time and created massive fields of sizable ice chunks covering miles of water as a sharp-edged sheet of uneven ice. When they saw a polar bear exploring the edge of a floe, they pursued it in the small boat and then tried to shoot it with their muskets. As they headed northwest, they sighted modern-day Akpatok Island to the southwest—it is in the center of the bay where the bay bellies down from the strait—and, marveling at its high mist-covered land draped in snow, called it "champaigne land." They continued, veering to the west to avoid more ice before heading north again.

Eleven days later they anchored near some small land forma-tions. Here they witnessed the unbelievable power of the tide, which is among the most extreme tides in the world. Although Ungava Bay is generally shallow, in the west and southwest the tidal change can exceed 59 feet (18 m). On the evening of July 11 they sounded nine fathoms (54 feet, or about 16 m) correctly but noticed large sub-merged rocks. The next morning the same rocks jutted 15 feet (4.6 m) above the surface of the water. They called this place the Isle of

God's Mercy because the tide had not caused the hull to be lanced by those towering rocks.

On July 16, Hudson angled back toward the northwest to double around an ice floe, and by July 19 he and the rest had surmised that they were in a bay. In fact, they were still in Ungava Bay, off the strait. They kept pushing northwest to find a passage through to the East. The *Discovery* traveled between Akpatok Island and Ungava Bay's west coast slowly, believing that the northwestern exit from the bay and then the strait would open to the Pacific Ocean. After another frightening encounter with ice, they cleared the strait at the end of July, passing several large islands as the coast fell away sharply to the south. Then they came upon a large body of water.

For a time, Hudson and his crew experienced the jubilant feeling of success. Believing that they had achieved their objective, they must have felt much the way members of Magellan's enterprise had felt as they exited their strait into the Pacific. Hudson was ecstatic. His energy, like Columbus's, buoyed everyone's spirits for a time. Once the ship entered this "great and whurling sea," he turned the *Discovery* southwest, toward the equator, just as Magellan had turned northwest, toward the equator, and they maintained a slow pace for almost two months, expecting to reach warmer temperatures as they journeyed toward southeastern Asia.[41]

They met with nothing but confusion. Hudson charted islands and inlets and sent crew members ashore to see what they could find. One party found birds that had been killed and stored by natives for food, but Hudson would not agree to fetch them and fired cannon to call the members back to the ship. Hopes fell when they reached shallower waters, which indicated that they were not in an ocean after all. Some members suggested taking a western course, which was the most likely way to the ocean. Hudson, influenced by conversations with Plancius in Holland, was intent on finding a southern passage through the American continent. He made his decision, and the *Discovery* ended up at the bay's southern extremity where it ballooned southward, forming today's smaller but still sizable James Bay.

Hudson had a habit of not justifying his decisions to the crew. Much as he had done when exploring Delaware Bay and Cape Cod for the Dutch, now he began crisscrossing James Bay, making four to five long circuits and taking hundreds of soundings of depth. He gave orders without explanation. Nonetheless, all realized that James Bay was very shallow and small compared to the larger body of water they had discovered.[42] The toilsome activity continued for almost two weeks before its futility was clear.

Juet had been formulating a strategy for mutiny for weeks. Now he saw an opportunity. The aimlessness of their current activities exacerbated the tension aboard ship, which Juet leveraged toward mutiny by deriding Hudson's original claim that he would reach southeastern Asia by February 2, which was still about three months off. Hudson was already anxious about the predicament. He responded with a recollection of Juet's disloyalty after departing Iceland. The retort did not calm the crew, so he went further. He fired Juet, lowered his pay, and accused him of mutiny. That quelled the mutiny for the moment. Hudson then drafted a charge against Juet designed "to punish and cut off farther occasions of the like mutinies." It contained four parts, as documented by member Thomas Widows:

> It was prooved to his [Juet's] face, first with Bennet Mathew our Trumpet upon our first sight of Island [Iceland], and hee confest, that hee supposed that in the action would bee manslaughter, and prove bloodie to some.
>
> Secondly, at our comming from Island, in hearing of the companie, hee did threaten to turne the head of the Ship home from the action, which at that time was by our Master wisely Pacified, hoping of amendment.
>
> Thirdly, it was deposed by Philip Staffe our Carpenter, and Ladlie Arnold, to his face upon the Holy Bible, that hee perswaded them to keepe Muskets charged, and Swords readie in their Cabbins, for they should bee charged with shot, ere the Voyage were over.

Fourthly, wee being pestered in the Ice, hee had used words tending to mutinie, discouragement, and slander of the action, which easily took effect in those that were timorous; and had not the Master in time prevented, it might easily have over-throwne the Voyage: and now lately being imbayed in a deepe Bay, which the Master had desire to see, and some reasons to himselfe knowne, his word tended altogether to put the Com-panie into a fray of extremitie, by wintering in cold: Jesting at our Masters hope to see Bantam by Candlemasse.[43]

Magellan's promise to reach Bantam, an English trading post in today's Indonesia, by the Christian holy day of February 2 was com-ing back to haunt him.[44] As disagreeable as Juet may have been, his was a strong position, and his actions reflected the shared values of the members. By contrast, Hudson's actions countered those values and continued to do so even as he tried to quell the mutiny. For in-stance, Hudson replaced Juet as his mate with his friend Robert Bylot, a competent navigator, but Bylot was seen as an outsider by most members. Hudson fired Clements (Juet's ally) as boatswain for mutinous words spoken in July when they were trapped in the ice in Ungava Bay. A member named William Wilson, not so well regarded by the members, replaced Clements.

Hudson's actions may seem weak in light of the "rope and knife" powers granted to earlier seafaring captains, but by 1610, there were formal codes and institutional regulations regarding mutiny. The direct punishments administered by Magellan and Drake were not feasible for Hudson, which is partly why he used so many pay cuts, demotions, and firings for punitive measures. A portion of Juet's pay was now directed to Bylot and Wilson and a Hudson ally named John King. With matters apparently settled, the *Discovery* continued its traversals and soundings. All might have been well, but then Hudson made a very odd decision. He followed bold action with vacillation, announcing that he would forget all charges and forgive mutineers if they would just conduct themselves honestly. He thus undermined his authority and subverted the rules intended to protect the whole enterprise. Rather than profiting from this kind of error, as Cabot might have done, Hudson compounded it. Another mutiny began to take shape.

Soon the *Discovery* was canvassing James Bay aimlessly again. They headed north yet again, into bad weather, cast anchor in fifty feet (15 m) of water, and stayed for eight days because of a storm. Hudson went against the wishes of everyone by ordering the anchor raised in still-rough seas. Crew members heaved up the anchor as the *Discovery* rocked. When a wave knocked them off balance, the anchor dropped. Staffe, the skillful carpenter who had supported Hudson during the mutiny in early July, was watching and waiting, ax at the ready. He deftly severed the line, saving most of it, but the anchor was lost.

Circumstances worsened as the weather grew colder. Hudson, like Magellan, would need a place to spend the winter. He and his men headed south in James Bay. Noting the dangerous shallows, they turned east for deeper water. Then Hudson took them southwest again. In the shallows again but near land, Hudson sent Abacuck Pricket (who wrote the best primary source accounting of this case) and Staffe to explore. They noted human footprints and brought back firewood for the winter. The tide was extreme here, and rocks they had charted were now invisible as they headed back to the northeast. Like Cabot in Santa Catalina eighty-four years earlier, but with the roles reversed, Staffe told Hudson that they were in danger of running aground. Just as Hudson disagreed, the *Discovery* ran onto the rocks. Fortunately, history was not repeated further. The ship did not sink; the reinforced hull of the *Discovery* held fast. But here they were stuck for twelve hours. Hudson's obsession with finding a passage was turning him into a worse and worse leader.

When the *Discovery* was free, Hudson insisted on heading south, not north, a route that took them back to the extreme southwest region of James Bay by the end of October. Here he sent Pricket and Staffe in the boat to find a place to winter. Upon their return, they directed the *Discovery* to the far southwest, where members hauled the ship onto land on November 1. Ten days later, it was frozen fast in ice that was as solid and hard as rock.

The predicament was disastrous and depressing. As Pricket wrote, "It behooved us to have care of what we had; for, that we were sure of; but what we had not, was uncertaine." They estimated that the current supplies would sustain them for six months. Hudson offered a reward to anyone who brought back edible fowls, fishes, or beasts. However, the land was barren and had little to offer.[45]

In this frozen wasteland, the gunner John Williams died of an illness. According to English seafaring custom, a dead crew member's properties were to be auctioned and sold on deck, with the proceeds going to the family when the enterprise was concluded. This tradition was followed at first, but then Hudson stopped the proceedings and gave Williams's cloak directly to Greene, his pet, distrusted and disliked by everyone else on board. The action violated a tradition upheld by all members, including Hudson's allies, it disrespected Williams's family, and it opened the way for members to violate other traditions, including respect for the captain's authority.

A few days later Hudson offended a longtime ally when he ordered Staffe to build a small cabin on the shore. The carpenter refused on account of inclement weather. It was late November, and winter had closed in. Staffe had suggested to Hudson earlier in the month that a cabin should be built, but Hudson had disagreed. Now Staffe found it impracticable to comply. He cited his own expertise compared to Hudson's regarding when and how to do such work. He told Hudson he was not a house carpenter and asked why his suggestion had been denied weeks earlier. Hudson exploded. He physically "ferreted [Staffe] out of his cabbin to strike him, calling him by many foule names and threatening to hange him." So Staffe created a design, measured and cut wood, and, with a team, constructed a shelter.[46]

Pointless and futile tasks can bring out vile political dynamics that turn small matters into significant problems. As Staffe built the shelter, he became a better friend of Greene's. When the two men

went hunting together, it angered Hudson, who retaliated by ordering that Greene's cloak (from Williams) be given to Bylot, who was
currently his ally. He derided Greene—"If all his friends would not
trust him with 20 shillings, and therefore why should he?"—and
threatened not to help Greene join Prince Henry's soldiers, as he
had promised. That was to be Greene's remuneration for serving on
board. Making enemies with Greene was risky business. Greene soon
began discrediting Hudson with Juet, Staffe, and others.[47]

Crew members were staying alive by eating fish, birds, mosses,
and frogs "as loathsome as a Toade." It was an awful winter. The only
reason the simmering mutiny had not yet come to a boil was because
they were stuck. Deposing Hudson would not remedy their basic
situation. But the desire for mutiny grew in intensity, nurtured by
shared experiences and hopes for a change in circumstances.

The first native they saw approached their camp as the weather
warmed in May. The initial exchange was positive because Hudson
and the crew were in dire need. They traded a knife, a mirror, and
some buttons for whatever food the native had. A day later, the native returned with two large deer and beaver skins. He laid the items
he had already received from Hudson on the skins to indicate potential trades. Hudson offered a hatchet, for which the native offered one
deer skin. But Hudson demanded two skins and ended up threatening with force. The native made the trade and never lost his temper.
Before departing, he indicated he would return, but that was his last
visit.

The *Discovery* was still trapped in ice, but water was now accessible with the small boat, enabling the crew to fish. The members were so miserable that they considered taking the small boat
and deserting. Hudson wanted to use the boat to seek more natives
and trade with them, so he accompanied a group in the boat and
found more natives. But when the Europeans attempted to land, the
natives set fire to the brush along the shore and threatened them.
In the end, they returned to the *Discovery* empty-handed and even
worse off.

In June 1611, after seven months of being iced in, they finally put the *Discovery* back in the water. After dividing the scanty provisions among the thirty crew members, they were free of the ice. The exit to the strait was a daunting 730 miles (1,170 km) up the eastern shore of the bay. Hudson wept as he distributed the scanty inventory. Trust was gone; the atmosphere was tainted. Fights broke out easily. Members argued over minute scraps of food, and Hudson was thought to have been hoarding supplies in his cabin, where he seems to have met with and come to better terms with Staffe. But a week later, before they even exited James Bay, the unthinkable happened: they got stuck in the ice again.

Here in James Bay is where Hudson took the final actions that exacerbated the situation. He ordered everyone's chests and stores searched for provisions. Indeed, some items were found, and Hudson threatened to maroon those members as thieves. It was a way to assert his authority, but it was also the last straw when it came to the basic dignity and values that members shared. The uncertainty of being stuck yet again and not knowing when or how they would depart for home was the last straw.

The mutiny that occurred at this juncture is famous. It has been the subject of books and films. But its linkages with his leadership have only rarely been so clearly delineated as here, where the details come from multiple original sources. Now, having developed a rich perception of his leadership, let us examine this climactic mutiny.

THE FINAL MUTINY

The plan for mutiny against Hudson was finalized as the *Discovery* was stuck in the ice in James Bay. Wilson and Greene approached Pricket as he slept. After waking him, they informed him that a group of men were going to mutiny against Hudson. They would put Hudson and those who were sick into the small boat and set them adrift. Pricket refused, and they dropped it. Juet approached Pricket a bit later to persuade him. Pricket asked that Juet wait a few days while he considered it. He reminded the conspirators that mutiny brought a penalty of death. Moreover, many crew members had families waiting for them in London. Greene responded that it was better to be hanged at home than to be starved abroad. Pricket negotiated. He said he would join them if the *Discovery* was not headed for home within two days. He insisted that they hurt no crew members in their execution of mutiny. Finally, all agreed. Pricket had been successfully recruited. Now they just needed the right moment in which to strike.

That moment came on June 22, 1611. As soon as the *Discovery* was free, Hudson ordered a westerly heading: away from home. He wanted to look for that elusive northwestern passage in James Bay. The mutineers acted. They grabbed King, Hudson's last confidant, and locked him in the hold. They seized Hudson and tied his arms. The men who were sick were roused from their bunks. The captives were quickly organized for transfer to one of the *Discovery*'s two small boats. When King was let out of the hold, he threatened Juet with a sword. Several mutineers assisted Juet in overpowering him. Hudson's son was added to the group to be set adrift.

No reason was given to the captives for what was happening. When Hudson asked, he was told that he would know once he was in the small boat. Once it was hauled near, the captives were all dumped in, Hudson last, with his arms still tied. Pricket reported begging the mutineers not to hurt anyone as they put them in the small boat. Hudson called up that Juet was leading a mutiny. "Nay," Pricket reportedly called back, "it is that villaine Henrie Greene."[48]

Hard decisions were made over who was to go in the small boat. Two sick members were spared because their friends convinced Greene to keep them on the *Discovery*. Nine members were expelled in total—Staffe was among them. He was less of a friend of Hudson's after the way he had been treated during the seven icebound months, but as Pricket recorded, "The chiefest cause was for that the master loved him [Staffe] and made him his mate upon his return out of our wintering place."[49] The action generated significant ramifications; it repaired grievances with Staffe as it chilled relations with Bylot. In

An unknown artist's romanticized depiction of Henry Hudson, his son, and members marooned after the mutiny on the *Discovery*. No image exists that is thought to be a reliable likeness of Hudson. (Courtesy Library of Congress Prints and Photographs Division, Washington, DC.)

deed, Staffe was ready to be expelled from the *Discovery* and be with Hudson rather than be part of a mutiny. In the end, thirteen members remained on board.

The *Discovery* let out its square sails and moved slowly forward. The small boat was in tow, and the line was run out to its end. Finally they cut it, setting Hudson and the others adrift. They had oars, clothes and blankets, a musket with powder and shot, pikes, an iron pot, and some cakes. Greene ordered the mainsails let out and the ship turned to a northeast heading. Those in the small boat rowed after them, so they let fly the topsails and sped along until the small boat disappeared. The writer of one account claimed that muskets were fired at the small boat from the *Discovery* as it departed. Hudson, his son, and those seven members were never seen again.

The mutiny had a treacherous aftermath for most of the mutineers. After they took over the leadership, they searched the *Discovery* and found extra provisions in Hudson's cabin. And after a few days' sailing they landed and hunted, catching several fowl. They continued north, dodging ice and arguing with one another over the best heading.

As Richard Eden's poem of 1553, quoted at the beginning of Part I, suggests, fortune favors the bold but fails those who lack faith. Mutinies can and do become confused once they are put into action, especially if they are successful. An exit strategy and a structure are required to deal with what comes after the leader is deposed.

In this case, such designs were lacking. Greene directed his ire against Pricket, charging him with mutiny against the mutineers. Pricket quieted him by returning the accusation, saying that Greene himself had only informal status as a member. Pricket, the most literate and intelligent among them, may have promised to write an account of the enterprise that would protect all of them if they made it back alive. He was not fully committed to the mutiny anyway. By July 25, a month after the mutiny, the ship had covered the long course to the enormous bay's entrance. As it rounded the point, they drew near shore to land and hunt, accidentally running the *Discovery* aground on a submerged shoal. They managed to free it with lines and stopped to survey the damage. That is when they had visitors.

Forty to fifty natives approached the *Discovery* in canoes. They tied them together into a flotilla, which was a menacing form as it advanced. Yet the interactions were initially friendly. The *Discovery* members were emboldened by the peaceful reception. They were invited to the native settlement, where they marveled at strange large dogs the natives had as pets. The natives taught them how to hunt fowl using a long pole and a snare. Several days later, Greene and five others took the second small boat to the shore one morning and attempted to barter, which inexplicably provoked an attack.[50] Things became deadly very fast. Two of the six barterers were killed outright, two were stabbed in the stomach, and two others were badly wounded. As the four survivors frantically rowed back to the *Discovery*, they were peppered with arrows. Pricket survived a shot in the back. Greene was killed in the attack. A mutineer named Michael Perse fainted and died two days later. For some reason, the natives would not come close to the *Discovery*.

Desperate for provisions, the next day a small group hunted very cautiously on shore. Using the natives' methods, they took many ducks and geese. Then they departed as quickly as possible and headed through the strait to the east. They were only nine members strong, just enough to operate the ship. Bylot, originally Hudson's ally and his former mate, was in command.

Despite fair winds and following seas, the going was tough. There was a lot more fighting. Juet argued for a stop in Newfoundland for provisions, but the wind seemed favorable enough for a smooth journey all the way back to England. Soon they were in the middle of the ocean, eating candle wax fried with seagull bones. Meals were rationed to one pound per week per person. Juet, the last of the mutiny's ringleaders, died of hunger and illness. The eight remaining members reached Bantry Bay, on the southwest coast of Ireland, on September 6, 1611. The food was gone, and they were so lost that they believed they had passed Ireland. Here they sold their line and other supplies for money to buy food. They promised wages to some mariners if they would navigate them to London, where they arrived on October 20. The eight were arrested and soon questioned by members of the Company of Gentlemen.

The deaths of Juet and Greene helped them defend their cause. Juet had been a longtime seafaring partner of Hudson's, known to have caused trouble before, and was the last of the ringleaders to die. Greene was infamously troublesome even before the departure of the enterprise. The company charged them all anyway and recommended hanging. There was a long delay before the trial, however—it occurred sometime in 1618—and a few members did not live long enough to see it. In the interim, a few other members found employment on other ships, even on the *Discovery* for a voyage back to the same bay. England was expanding its empire, and their knowledge was valuable to that larger cause. Perhaps it could even help avoid future mishaps.[51]

As it turned out, the eight mutineers who made it back from Hudson's 1611 enterprise were never formally punished. Mutinies notwithstanding, English seafaring continued to intensify. The belief in a northwest passage was very strong. It persisted as the Age of Discovery came to an end and the Age of Sail began in the first part of the seventeenth century. In 1670 a Hudson's Bay Company was incorporated, and it became hugely successful, one of many other English commercial companies that searched the enormous Hudson Bay in vain for the northwest passage. The lore died hard. It was sought for no less than three more centuries. Even Lewis and Clark's famous 1804 expedition was intended to find a northwest passage over land. Commissioned by President Thomas Jefferson, it carried the same hope as previous attempts: commerce between Asia and the Atlantic states. In this case, it was to support the growth and development of the new United States.

COMMON FEATURES OF MUTINIES

Like Columbus, Magellan, and Cabot before him, Hudson was a passionate and experienced leader of a bold venture. But his obsession with finding a northwest passage not only strained multiple relationships but created a large gap between him and his crew. The gap widened when his leadership decisions offended the shared values of members. When an uncertain environment includes passion and conflicting values, mutiny comes and goes naturally. For Columbus, the trigger for mutiny was a false sighting of land after many promises. For Magellan, it was the replacement of a captain trusted by members with one who was not trusted by members (but was trusted by him). Cabot, a master at avoiding and preempting mutiny, finally had his authority deposed when he hanged Lepe. For Hudson, the incitement to mutiny came with his decision to continue canvassing James Bay after being trapped in the ice for many months. In each instance, such an action would not have sparked mutiny under normal circumstances. But because of the status of trust, the violation of shared values, the uncertainty in the environment, and the presence of a ringleader to incite and coordinate action, mutiny occurred.

When shared values are threatened or violated, members of a group naturally begin to invent preferable substitutes for the offensive and distrusted leadership. An uncertain environment, a ringleader, and a decision that violates members' shared values are a volatile mix. The potential for mutiny can gather for a very long time despite the existence of these elements because mutiny stems from values, which are deep elements of human nature. To shift such values in organization members is a task beyond most leaders, even if a quite competent one, as we saw in Magellan's case. If shared values are violated, then the blowback can be sudden, intense, and overwhelming. In an organization, mutiny is the channel for the blowback.

Trust is an aspect of mutiny that was germane to all of the mutinies examined in Part I. As we briefly mentioned in the introduction, it is possible to trust and distrust a leader simultaneously. That is not the simpler way that people usually think about trust. Instead, trust and distrust are seen as a forced tradeoff. That conceptualization is specious in organizational settings, however. This deeper aspect of human nature is important to mutiny. We will examine it more formally in Part II and reflect on the historic cases along the way.

Another aspect of mutiny that we will examine in Part II is the functional role of values. After all, values constitute what is shared and violated in a mutiny. To be sure, values in the Age of Discovery differ from the values shared by members in modern organizations. But this difference is in content, not function. The mechanisms by which values are shared by members and violated by leaders are still the same.

In addition to trust and values, we will examine the important role of a ringleader. In the historic cases, some mutinies had identifiable ringleaders (e.g., Magellan's, Hudson's); in others, that aspect of the case was not clear (e.g., Columbus's, Cabot's). Because a mutiny is rather similar to a small and adaptable entrepreneurial venture in a hostile environment, the ringleader serves a vital function that can dramatically increase the power of a mutiny and its chances of achieving its objective, not least by coordinating the plan to depose the leader. We will draw from the historic cases to make a rich and rigorous examination of these elements of mutiny in Part II.

Part Two

SWORDS BECAME WORDS

When mutiny feels strong it is wild and cruel. But this same mutiny, when power is not on its side, is infinitely base and cowardly. And no one can so easily change from arrogant pose to humble slavishness as mutiny.

—Ilya Tolstoy

Throughout history, the sea has captured the imagination of many entrepreneurial minds. As Nicholas Breton suggested in 1616, in the quotation at the beginning of chapter 4, adventurers and merchants have often been linked to the ocean. For adventurers in the Age of Discovery, the sea was an infinite and intimidating realm: the embodiment of uncertainty.

Excellent leadership in an environment of opportunity and risk is not so different today from what it was then, just as organization members' reactions are similar in such environments. Human nature remains human nature. Today's entrepreneurs and leaders face many of the same kinds of problems as ship captains and fleet commanders used to. Members of modern firms can and do naturally move to depose a leader for the same basic reasons, and the leader's response is just as vital to how the action unfolds. Some leaders rise to the challenge; others sink.

In the historic cases examined here, mutiny occurred upon the convergence of key elements: environmental uncertainty, problems of trust and distrust, violations of members' shared values by leadership actions, and structural enablers such as ringleaders and coordination. Those elements moved toward convergence as they evolved. Rigorous examination of how those elements reinforced and interacted with one another offers valuable insights into the function of coordinated upward defiance in organizations in general and the function of mutiny in firms. The historic cases and primary source data in Part 1 provide certain insights that are almost impossible to grasp otherwise.

Modern organizations differ from one another categorically. Generalizable insights are impossible when business models, structures, populations, cultures, and other aspects are not reliably comparable. The result is bound to be a superficial understanding or one that applies only to a particular case. This makes it hard to know which elements matter and which ones do not in a mutiny situation. Moreover, today's firms are so much a standard part of our environment that we cannot view them without an immutable and subtle sort of subjectivity. To get around these problems, we examined historic mutinies in detail. Here we will apply some of the lessons to today's settings with specific references to the historic cases. We will also briefly describe some more contemporary cases that reflect the experiences of Columbus, Magellan, Cabot, and Hudson.

By definition, a mutiny involves deep opposition expressed by two sides who are sharply divided based on distinct perspectives and realities. There is a gap between the sides; their views are black and white without much gray area in between. The difference between the sides is largely determined by the structures that distinguish leaders from members in organizations. In other words, the difference is not determined by the deeper values that the two sides have in common. This observation explains why mutiny, for centuries, was seen as expressing the dominant will of the members of an enterprise. Cabot's 1553 memo to Willoughby and Chancellor and Drake's 1578 execution of Doughty signaled a basic change in how mutiny was viewed. Both also reflected a change in the times as seafaring ventures became formalized operations, driven by company rule and more closely engineered to minimize risk. The problem with minimizing risk, as entrepreneurs understand, is that the reward is also minimized. Leaders in the Age of Discovery learned to deal with mutiny based on this logic.

Leaders today are usually assumed to be the good guys, mutineers the bad guys, because of the organizational context, *not* because the purpose of every mutiny is inherently bad. Trying to make sense of these perceptions leads into dizzying spirals of human nature, but the endeavor sheds light on why mutiny and leadership are so poorly understood.

In this part of the book, we will show that mutinies have a great deal to do with trust and distrust. In organizational settings, trust is a matter of shared values. It resides in the members, not the structures. Leaders' actions that violate shared values can generate mutinous reactions. Distrust, by contrast, has to do with the more immediate organizational context. Other triggers of mutiny pertain to uncertainty in the environment and the presence of a ringleader. Mutiny brings all of these items together, not unlike a highly adaptive entrepreneurial venture. This conceptualization clarifies linkages between these elements that are usually invisible, especially for actors who are in the middle of an uncertain situation. Applying the conceptualization provides a practical perspective on how both leaders and mutineers can best take action in a mutiny.

5

The Power of Shared Values

A witness heard Francisco de Lepe say as he was taken to be
hanged, that he had been blamed and would pay for all so
that God would give them a good voyage as he knew he was
about to die.

—Statement by a member of Sebastian Cabot's enterprise
after its return to Seville in July 1530

S hared values, trust, and distrust each come up many times in
the historic cases in Part I. Service for a foreign power, which
was common in the Age of Discovery, often entailed working
with enemies of one's homeland. Service aboard a ship often entailed
working with people speaking different languages and adhering to
different cultural norms and customs. Since exploring oceans was a
dangerous business, and a seafarer's life was to a large extent in the
leader's hands, issues of trust and distrust could become matters of
life or death. Moreover, they almost always mattered to the success
or failure of an enterprise. In this chapter we shall examine trust and
distrust in organizations, with a focus on the vital importance of the
values that organizational members share.

Magellan dealt with grave matters related to these issues. In his
case, members did not trust him because of his background. As a
Portuguese working for the Castilian crown and leading an enterprise with many Spanish members, Magellan was a foreigner aboard
his own ship. The tensions between Portugal and Spain were exter-

nal, but such tensions can often emerge *inside* an organization, especially if the environment is uncertain, because values transcend people. Magellan aimed to protect his authority by selecting leaders who shared his values, building trust among the leadership team, and achieving a specifically defined objective. As he did so, he generated trust via shared experiences that spread the trust down into the fabric of the enterprise itself. In the end, success and the validation of his public predictions and espoused objective resolved most of those issues.

Hudson's final voyage provides another example. From his point of view, he was leading a bold expedition, just as Magellan had done ninety years earlier. That was how he perceived his obsessive search for a northwest passage. Promising signs of a passage as the ship entered the enormous James Bay encouraged his belief that ceasing to search would equal failure. Members, by contrast, perceived his obsession as misguided. A gap emerged between him and them. They did not trust his decisions and wanted mainly to survive. Although a heroic feat of leadership or fortune might have bridged the gap, the absence of something to unite success with Hudson's decisions made even his confidants turn on him. Hudson saw as destructive the actions that members undertook to protect themselves and save the expedition (e.g., Staffe's request to build a shelter). When trust is low, such differences in perception are almost impossible to resolve through rational means.

Tapping into shared values and capitalizing on them is thus part of transformational leadership. The same actions can also lead to mutiny, however. We need a framework that shows how different results come about.

The Good and the Bad

In an organization, two sides of certain issues can be functionally opposed, even to the extent that risks and rewards are wholly reversed. Threats to the business of an organization can become opportunities for a mutiny inside that same organization. Indeed, the two sides speak different languages because they have different shared values. The result, functionally, is two organizations: one large and one small. The larger one subsumes the smaller one although they are oriented against each other. Leaders oppose the mutiny, the mutineers oppose the leadership, and their nested arrangement may preclude an easy solution.

Both sides can appeal to the same larger purpose. But the real difference is not in objectives, however much that may seem to be the case. In the historic cases, leaders and members emphasized differences in objectives even though both truly wanted the same thing: a successful enterprise. When a mutiny emerged, the differences were radicalized and became extreme. Larger contexts and unfalsifiable explanations that seemed natural were usually spun and concocted to explain the sharp differences.[1] Yet such differences between leaders and members were in *perceptions* of the actions that would lead to the common objective; they did not reflect the practical reality of the situation, in which both sides had a great deal of control that could be used to address the grievances.

The problems associated with this kind of impasse become knotty because organizational actions are cooperative and coordinated in a formal sense. Leadership decisions and authority can easily violate shared values even when a violation is unintended. Once values are violated, or even perceived to be violated, other elements can exacerbate the situation. Limited options for exiting the enterprise, for instance, can drive organization members to desperate measures to protect what they value. Uncertainty in the environment amplifies the perceived threat further. Mutiny thus becomes a method to restore certainty, a mechanism to promote and protect shared values. That is, it becomes a substitute for leadership.

Do such differences in perspective mean differences in objectives, or do they concern differences in strategies leading to objectives? Mistaking strategies for objectives makes it tempting to frame a mutiny situation in terms of good versus bad. However, such an approach is misguided. It generates uncertainty for both sides, effectively obscuring the fact that objectives are shared but values are not. For exactly that reason, leadership and mutiny can seem antithetic even though they release the exact same bottom-up force in an organization.

Thinking of mutiny as a force of human nature reframes some traditional industrial organizational leadership paradigms. It casts leadership and mutiny as something of the yin and yang of organizational life and less as a matter of good and bad. Such a reframing requires more than can be expressed in absolutes. There is a logic to it: if flawed leadership can hurt an organization, then an effective mutiny can help an organization. It is hard to reconcile such statements in general, and it is almost impossible for most leaders to do so, especially if a leader forgets that the logic of organizational performance applies equally to members and leaders.

Uncertainty is not a matter of good and bad either, because it can drive a mutiny just as it can be used to reinforce leadership. In the case of Columbus's first mutiny, for instance, when it was still very uncertain that land would be discovered, Columbus used the uncertainty to his advantage. Uncertainty is often bad for an organization. But it gave Columbus an opportunity to introduce organizational certainty through an agreement with members. Mutiny came when he made the last in a string of flawed navigational decisions that raised distrust by degrees. Columbus's quelling tactic would have lacked force had the enterprise not been brought to the brink of mutiny. Because the mutiny constituted a clean break from normal operations, he quelled it even though the objective had not yet been achieved. The event renewed the crew's spirit. In Columbus's second mutiny, a poorly executed one, when Pinzón and the *Pinta* deserted, the ships had already made landfall, so there was certainty based on having achieved the objective. The second mutiny, then, occurred because of low trust (not high distrust) in Columbus's leadership.

The practical methods by which to undertake a mutiny can vary widely. But mutiny itself always starts with a critical incident that provides an opportunity to act, and it always requires coordination. A soundly executed mutiny can transform an organization and even result in retaining the leader with reformed and reduced authority. Hudson's actions on his second voyage incurred such a mutiny. That mutiny even included its own term sheet, like the bulleted lists of policies and conditions that entrepreneurs and investors use to protect themselves. Hudson was depressed by the mutiny, but he did not regard it as bad. How do we know? The evidence is that he hired Juet, its ringleader, on multiple subsequent occasions. Hudson's last mutiny shows how poor coordination can turn mutiny into a stalemate, a blackmail situation, or something worse. Staying coordinated is hard because a mutiny is a volatile action. In Magellan's case, once the mutiny in the Bay of Saint Julian lost its coordination, Magellan was able to quell it by imposing extreme certainty with assassinations, arrests, and beheadings.

Mutiny transcends notions of good and bad because it is a force that can be leveraged in the service of performance. It generates opportunities to change or intensify the activities of members. Columbus used the first mutiny on his venture in this way; his response yielded three additional days of performance from members. He also benefited from serendipity, but fortune is not divorced from good leadership. Luck matters. His agreement to turn back if land was not sighted within three days supplied certainty in place of the trust in him that crew members lacked, and it mitigated the uncertainty of the environment. Mutiny gave him the opportunity to lead a smoother operation with motivated members for a few more days. It restored cohesion among the members. By using its force to a positive end, Columbus managed to travel farther than they otherwise would have and achieve a momentous objective.

Still, like other social phenomena, a mutiny occurs in a context. It should not be encouraged for its own sake. A mutiny that grows out of a set of circumstances emerges naturally, and a bold enterprise is more likely to engender passionate actions than less risky ones. Leaders who expect their organizations to achieve revolutionary outcomes should also expect to deal with mutinies. Moreover, they, like Columbus, should think about ways to leverage mutiny to make better organizational decisions and pursue better actions. Like transformational leadership, mutiny taps into a value-laden context that subsumes the organization. It can emerge even if a leader does almost everything right.

THE VALUE OF UNCERTAINTY

The opposite of good organization is not necessarily chaos. To assume so promotes a mindset that is not helpful to bold enterprise. High levels of structure work only when the environment in which an organization operates is also highly structured. Such an environment is rare in almost any entrepreneurial or business setting, just as it was rare for ventures in the Age of Discovery. When an environment is uncertain, an organization must also admit some uncertainty. If it does not, then mutinous activity is liable to establish uncertainty naturally.

Leadership and mutiny interface with uncertainty in similar ways. Sebastian Cabot's venture into the Río de La Plata region is an example. That region is more complicated than the regions navigated by any other venture chronicled in this book. Its nebulous channels and hundreds of islands made for a complex exercise in problem-solving that kept Cabot's members busy for almost three years. Such uncertainty was matched by the contingencies of Cabot's actions. Had he led with rigidity, a mutiny might have inserted the necessary contingencies. Cabot held the enterprise together by providing opportunities for members to exit, but he could lead very boldly when necessary. He quelled the mutiny at Santa Catalina by marooning Méndez, Rodas, and Rojas. But he also offered exit options to disaffected members at the Canary Islands, São Vicente, and other places. As Cabot crossed the ocean to and from Seville, his leadership style became aloof, unlike in the Río de La Plata. He even relied on delegation during the return crossing. In the Río de La Plata, by contrast, he was omnipresent.

Such events amid uncertainty show that trust does not operate along a single dimension. After all, a changing leadership style can make the leader seem unreliable and not trustworthy. In fact, the notion of changing one's leadership style is an oversimplification. How does a leader know when to go with the flow? When to buck the system? We all know leaders who are well liked but not experts at their jobs. Those leaders go with the flow. We also all know leaders who are experts but are hard to relate to. Those leaders buck the system. Both types can succeed, fail, or incur mutinies. The existence of radically different types of successful leaders shows that trust in organizations is a multidimensional construct.

TRUST AND DISTRUST

Trust shared among leaders and members amplifies the motivation to perform and excel. However, trust is also vital to a mutiny. Most leaders of bold enterprises know that trust is important, but they do not normally think about it until things start to go poorly. That is usually too late for trust to be recovered.

Sometimes a leader is trusted because of a special connection with organization members. For example, the Pinzón brothers led the *Niña* and the *Pinta* of Columbus's enterprise, and they enjoyed strong trust with members by virtue of the fact that, like the members, they were Castilians and from Palos. Most members had known of them for years. Trust was established and practically unbreakable. Most of the time, trust must be earned through shared experiences. That is why earning trust as a professional manager can come at a cost in time and activities. However, the relationship between leader and members is enduring once that trust is earned.

Trust is quite separate from competence or expertise. It is a deeper aspect of human nature. Magellan's high levels of competence did not build trust. He shared a connection with members, but that had more to do with his competence. Full trust was established only after his small armada exited the strait that now bears his name. Earning trust required an incredible shared experience in which his specific and falsifiable prediction became real and verified. The hardships faced on the Pacific Ocean during the following three months were the worst of the entire voyage. Almost everyone died. Nonetheless, no more mutinies against Magellan occurred.[2] Before that magic moment, the potential for mutiny was constant. Such trust-winning moments are rare. So, if Magellan's members did not trust him before they exited the strait, how did he maintain influence up to that point?

Before winning trust, Magellan led effectively because of a low level of distrust. Low distrust is different from high trust. Trust and distrust are not functionally equivalent in organizational settings. In most settings, even a leader who is not highly trusted can usually wield influence if distrust is kept low. Similarly, a leader who is distrusted because of low expertise can be influential if trust in his or her values is kept high. This framing of the issue offers insight into how and where mutiny fits into an organization. Distrust pertains to actions, correct management decisions, and expertise. It is easier to keep distrust low than it is to earn trust. Low distrust is also easier to lose: it entails actions that are superficial and observable compared to shared values. It involves personal characteristics that are behavioral. Trust, by contrast, pertains to shared values. It is more complex.

This important difference explains how members can respect a leader's competence while privately questioning what is driving the leader's actions. Much exists under the surface, and sub-surface explosion is possible if success becomes dubious and the environment becomes uncertain. The explosion can and will come in a powerful flash. Several of the mutinies in the historic cases illustrate this effect, which comes when the right constellation of elements converge. For instance, once success becomes unlikely (for example, because of low supplies) and uncertainty increases (for example, because of approaching winter weather), a leader's action can set off the explosion. Then, the mutiny.

The wait for the moment to arrive may be lengthy even though low trust and high distrust are a volatile combination. Certainly, mutiny will emerge suddenly when events, personalities, or circumstances force it to, but it tends to develop over long periods, growing endogenously because the social reality of organizational structures compels leaders and members to behave on multiple levels and even in contradictory ways. Management theory thus acknowledges that members can simultaneously trust and distrust their leaders.[3] Members may act one way toward each other but another way toward their leader. Even if members are not critical of a leader's motives because he or she performs well, it does not mean that they *trust* that leader. It merely indicates that their distrust is low. This notion of operating on multiple levels is familiar to experienced businesspeople. Doing so can produce tension, or it can reduce or prevent tension between leaders and members. Still, understanding how this permutation of trust and distrust relates to mutiny potential is not easy, because trust is usually confused with the absence of distrust. In organizations these two dimensions are best regarded as distinct.

Trust is a connection between people. It is rooted in values, beliefs, or other basic shared assumptions. Organization members have faith in leaders whom they trust. Distrust, by contrast, applies to behavior. A lack of expertise, little experience, and poor management decisions give rise to distrust. Because behavior is more superficial than values, distrust is more easily won and lost. In an organization, it is better for the distrust dimension to be low. The trust-distrust diagram shown here gives some insight into mutiny by illustrating the two-dimensional context in which it can emerge.

Quadrant I describes circumstances in which trust is high and distrust is low. In such a setting, members will continue embracing the leader's vision, even if circumstances become very unpleasant. This explains much about how Cabot was able to avoid mutiny for

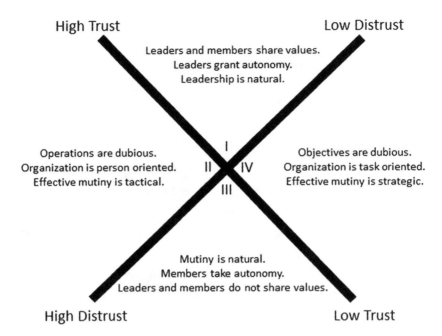

High Trust   Low Distrust

Leaders and members share values.
Leaders grant autonomy.
Leadership is natural.

Operations are dubious.   I   Objectives are dubious.
Organization is person oriented.   II   IV   Organization is task oriented.
Effective mutiny is tactical.   III   Effective mutiny is strategic.

Mutiny is natural.
Members take autonomy.
Leaders and members do not share values.

High Distrust   Low Trust

Organizational circumstances with respect to leadership and mutiny based on
varying levels of trust and distrust

the three years spent exploring the Río de La Plata. He had an amazing ability to establish trust with others and capitalized on their willingness to give him the benefit of the doubt. His seafaring competence was another story: many noted his lack of genuine skill. How did Cabot handle distrust from members? One's actual skill level is visible only in the context of the tasks one undertakes. Cabot managed impressions; he strategically determined not to seek Magellan's strait because that was an undertaking beyond his ability. Exploring the Río de La Plata was a far less daunting task and a better match with his skill level. Or so he thought. Choosing the right level of challenge helps minimize distrust. Cabot masterfully kept himself within the circumstances defined by quadrant I, despite a constant trend toward higher distrust (quadrant II).

Cabot could manipulate trust masterfully, but he raised distrust at Santa Catalina when he clumsily sank the *Capitana*. He then lowered distrust when he strategically revised the enterprise's objective. His enterprise was among the least successful of the historic cases, and Cabot engaged in activities that were unethical and treasonous. Yet his ability to strategically manage mutiny and use it to his advantage was legendary. Several strategic mutinies were formulated against him, but his strategic responses were too cunning for the mutineers. A simpler, more tactical mutiny, requiring an immediate short-term response, might have been more effective. After all, we saw how Cabot reacted to sudden situations. He relented to members only after they had wandered a labyrinth of rivers for months, apparently to no purpose and amid frightening encounters with natives—that is, after the tactical circumstances had become extremely uncertain. Cabot used the potential for mutiny as a force over long stretches of time, and when mutiny was leveled against him strategically, he would foil it. Those instances occurred when distrust became high. He did not face a tactical mutiny that required a tactical response, as Magellan did. Cabot regularly granted autonomy, in the form of frequent exit options to members, for example, and was able to make many believe that he shared their values. Indeed, today's leaders may not admire his ethics, but one can learn a great deal about strategically channeling the force of mutiny and turning failure into success by studying Sebastian Cabot and his 1526 enterprise.

What about when distrust and trust between leaders and members remain high, as in quadrant II? Sometimes leader incompetence forces distrust to stay high even though members feel a connection with the leader. Although Hudson had tactical competence, for instance, as shown by his maneuvering through treacherous ice floes, he was a bad strategic navigator. He was born into a tradition of only modestly challenging navigation and received his leadership position in part because of his family name. His level of strategic navigational skill was not evident until the enormous expanse of the Hudson Bay tested him. The Portuguese had already explored that region a century earlier. If they had concluded that it was bereft of valuable resources or a practical passage, as it certainly was, then why was

Hudson not able to draw the same conclusion? Despite this incompetence, Hudson was still trusted enough to be given the leadership of four distinct enterprises. For all but one of them, trust in Hudson derived from his name and the fact that he hailed from the same culture as most of his crew. On his third enterprise, for the Dutch, even having a diverse crew that could not always communicate with one another did not seem to cause trust problems; and even after he came back to his home country, he was once again trusted with the leadership of a fourth English venture. Trust is hard to lose. Yet, it says little about expertise.

High distrust was Hudson's bane. Shifts in the external environment were mutiny triggers because they put his venture in circumstances he could not understand or deal with. In such contexts, any leader's deeper connection with members is the only element left to hold the organization together. That kind of high trust is evidenced by granting autonomy (like Cabot) or leading naturally (like Columbus). As Hudson's case showed, he did not have high trust.

A likable but incompetent leader, then, fits with the conditions that quadrant II describes. Hudson had become less well-liked before the mutiny on his fourth enterprise occurred. He was not as adaptable as Cabot and had lost his closest allies, including Greene and Staffe (though the trust shared with Staffe was ultimately restored). The mutiny simmered for a long time until he made his critical decision to take another western heading across the bay immediately after the ship was finally free from the ice. The mutiny occurred suddenly, as a hellish tactical nightmare. The Hudson case also shows just how long mutiny can remain under the surface. The action can appear powerfully and suddenly even though the key elements have been present for months or years.

Quadrant III describes conditions under which members do not relate well to a leader who is also low in competence. Mutiny emerges most naturally in such a case, as it almost did during a brief interval in the first part of Cabot's voyage, when he was crossing the Atlantic. In fact, that mutiny was forming naturally even before the ships departed from Seville. As we know, Cabot used aloofness and exit options to deal with it strategically as he cunningly built trust. Hudson did the opposite, effectively putting himself in quadrant III.

When leaders have trusted individuals close to them who also connect with other organization members, they can help prevent a mutiny from occurring. Part of Cabot's strategy was the use of allies to maintain order and keep connected, as when he quelled the mutiny coordinated strategically by Lepe and Orosco. When Hudson managed to lose the trust of key individuals and the environment became uncertain, then it became natural for the members to depose him. All the key elements for a mutiny converged. Even so, Staffe chose to go in the small boat with Hudson instead of staying on the *Discovery,* showing again that trust dies hard. Hudson's intemperate order to build a shelter damaged but did not completely destroy the values the two men shared.

Finally, a leader who is competent but does not share values with members of an enterprise fits in quadrant IV. Members may not trust that leader, but since distrust is also low, things run smoothly so long as the environment does not generate uncertainty. When it does, technical expertise is still important, but it takes more than that to hold an organization together. A sense of belonging and a feeling of familiarity both matter, and both derive from shared values. Members feel comfortable amid uncertainty only when they feel a strong connection to a leader.

Mutinies associated with quadrant IV are most effective if they are strategic. The mutinies that Magellan faced illustrate the quadrant IV circumstances. However, those mutinies were highly tactical. Magellan was a bold expert who struggled with earning trust. A man of few words, he led with actions. An excellent navigator, he managed an enterprise that changed human history and gave his life in the process of doing so. Before exiting the strait, members constantly questioned his motives and felt a degree of dislike despite his competence. Back when the armada wintered in the Bay of Saint Julian, uncertainty became high, and that is when the lack of connection between him and the crew members enabled a couple of ringleaders to coordinate a mutiny in a shorter amount of time than it took to organize the ones against Cabot. As we saw, the mutiny in the Bay of Saint Julian was as tactical as a game of chess. That mutiny, as well as the earlier one on the Atlantic, were pulled together tactically, and some of the mutineers wavered in their commitment to it. Magellan's tactical responses were bold and devastating. Had Cartagena, Mendoza, and Quesada been more strategic, the outcome may have been different.

In summary, if a leader does not have a deep connection with the shared values of members, then trust needs to be earned. If a leader is incompetent, then distrust needs to be avoided. One way to earn trust is by cultivating relationships, and one way to avoid distrust is by demonstrating expertise. Trust and distrust can be earned and lost. The notion that the levels can shift is straightforward enough, but it is not easy to conceptualize in practical terms. The historic cases illustrate nicely some of the ways these shifts can occur.

EARNING AND LOSING TRUST AND DISTRUST

Aside from managing relationships, a leader can earn trust through external environmental changes that unite strategic objectives with shared member values. That is what happened with Magellan and Columbus. Business managers and economists have long known that success raises the level of cohesion in organizations. If success is defined specifically and clearly before it is achieved, then its realization becomes a powerful shared experience pursuant to the realization of value.

In Magellan's case, once the ships exited the strait and entered the Pacific Ocean, members had that moment of realization. The objective that Magellan had pursued so doggedly was key to the shared experience. There were no more mutinies after that, at least while Magellan was still alive. Success had a somewhat similar effect for Columbus, even though his objective was more general and one of his commanders defied his authority a few months later. Why did success earn trust? The vital aspect was that the two leaders made clear public declarations about their objectives.

Publicly declaring a specific objective and then achieving it is a way to ensure that success brings members and leaders together. Such shared experiences can promote shared values in an organization. However, the tactic introduces a kind of risk. What if the objective is not achieved? Hudson predicted that his enterprise would reach Java by Candlemass and failed to do so, and the members set him adrift in a small boat. The tactic of declaring an objective can help a leader engage the minds and hearts of members by focusing on circumstances that all share. Achieving success entails some luck, to be sure, but most landmark organizational outcomes do entail some luck, especially in entrepreneurial settings. After all, leaders have some freedom to select the objective. If the risks are managed carefully, the tactic is a way to promote better performance. Publicly declaring a specific objective and then achieving it amounts to more than words. It makes words real. It enhances and reframes leadership into a force that can quell a mutiny.

Ways to earn trust may be familiar, but ways to lower distrust probably are not. A leader lowers distrust through changes in the *internal* organizational environment, where the knowledge, skills, abilities, and competencies of leadership are evident to members. It may involve the management of impressions. As Cabot demonstrated, the internal organizational environment can be controlled profoundly. Lowering distrust is the opposite of earning trust in a practical sense because it is tactical and less strategic. Lowering distrust takes less time to achieve, for internal organizational elements can change quickly. Procedures, activities, and policies all bear directly on distrust when members perceive the leader dealing with them.

On Hudson's fourth voyage, for example, the crew's attitude toward Hudson vacillated between low and high levels of distrust. He expertly conducted the *Discovery* through ice but clumsily canvassed the enormous bay. Distrust varied accordingly. In contrast to Hudson, Cabot approached the maintenance of low distrust by arranging circumstances so the navigational requirements did not exceed his abilities. Consequently, crew members perceived him as more technically competent than he actually was, and that impression enabled him to maintain cohesion.

Levels of trust and distrust can help forecast mutiny. The trust-distrust diagram is a useful tool. The first step is to determine which quadrant fits the organizational circumstances. Since a leader has control over some circumstances, the next step is to change those circumstances as appropriate. Since organizations are social settings and leaders are self-aware, a leader has some control over which quadrant is most salient. Therefore, a leader has a degree of influence over whether a mutiny is natural or must be forced. As noted, trust is harder to earn or lose than distrust. It is deeply interpersonal, but it can stem from elements largely external to the organization. Distrust rises and falls more easily; it is managed internally. For healthy operations, quadrant I is the best, and quadrant III is the worst. In circumstances described by quadrant III, a ringleader and a bit of planning are all it can take to give rise to an effective mutiny. We will discuss such effective mutinies in a later chapter. Here, let us close this chapter by considering three implications of our mutiny research, which yielded three actions that can help prevent mutiny.[4]

Gaps between Echelons

The first implication of our mutiny research is that there are stark divisions between members and leader: a gap between echelons. The nature of that space is what we are talking about. In some instances—as when Cabot crossed the Atlantic—the space can fill a function. But over the long run it can create a barrier to upward communication, communication that a leader can use to stay sharp. Because a leader makes decisions whose effects members must live with daily, the connection with members and the ability to manage it are vital. The connection is not wholly ad hoc; it derives partially from the structure of the organization. If this gap between echelons is not easy to bridge, then it can put middle managers in a difficult position. They must navigate the discontinuity between upper and lower echelons. If they feel a closer connection to the lower levels of the structure, then it can lead to mutiny, as with Magellan's Castilian captains and as with Martín Alonso Pinzón on Columbus's voyage. Two indicators of a gap are aloof leadership and unclear communication channels with members.

Failure to manage the gap between echelons involves more than just being out of touch. By being out of touch, leaders can very easily make decisions that violate shared values among members. The gap hinders understanding about what is best for the organization. Magellan managed that gap by methodically and strategically replacing his captains with new ones who shared his values. Columbus managed it by being a constant presence as his small armada crossed the Atlantic. Leaders who understand and manage the echelon gap can do much to diffuse or avoid mutinous action when uncertainty increases. This tactic goes beyond managing members directly. It concerns the structural link between members and leader. If the gap between the echelons is significant and uncertain, then one condition for mutiny is sure to be intact.

Sources of Disgruntlement

The second key implication of our mutiny research builds on the former implication. It concerns which critical areas a leader should address across the echelon gap. The critical areas are reflected in working conditions, reactions to leadership decisions, compensation, opportunities, and more. Members share positive or negative perceptions of these items. High distrust can cause a leader to know that members are concerned about something but to be oblivious to the details. Low trust can cause a leader to try to respond to every complaint that members make but still fail to understand the underlying problem.

A leader successfully addresses sources of disgruntlement by making consistent management decisions that explicitly or implicitly relate to the shared values of members. Doing so brings a leader closer to members and, even more important, to what is most important to them. Then, even if a leader's actions contradict or violate those shared values, he or she can acknowledge the contradiction and effectively ameliorate the clash. Cabot was a master of this tactic. He used it dozens of times to keep trust high and distrust low. He addressed disgruntlement effectively. If sources of disgruntlement remain unaddressed, then the potential for mutiny is only natural.

Continuous Competence

The notions of bridging the gap between echelons and addressing sources of disgruntlement demystify some of the linkages between mutiny and leadership. The demarcation between what is the leader's fault and what is a property of the situation begins to be clear. The third implication of our mutiny research concerns this demarcation. It is the notion of developing competence continuously. Continuing to develop competence helps a leader avoid mutinous action. Why? Because competence comes in technical *and* interpersonal forms. Leaders should develop competence continuously because the criteria of performance change over time. Without constant updates to competence, a gap between echelons will develop over time, as will the concomitant sources of disgruntlement.

Each of the enterprises in Part I went through stages that required the leaders to draw on different kinds of competencies. Columbus used intense optimism as a form of social competence to lead his armada across the Atlantic. Once the enterprise achieved its goal, his style became less transformational and more technically strategic. The Hudson case is a negative example. It was almost as if he developed incompetence. He seemed least competent on his fourth and final enterprise. Once he displayed low technical skill, made poor strategic decisions, and damaged trust after exiting the ice trap, the mutiny that had been simmering under the surface for so many months erupted like a force of nature.

These three notions map onto trust and distrust in many ways.

They also relate to each other. If the gap between echelons and the disgruntlement issues are critical, then trust is bound to be damaged. If an uncertain situation epitomizes distrust in a leader's competence, the potential for mutiny will rise, forming an opportunity for a ring leader to coordinate and begin to take action. The next consideration for leaders and mutineers is how to handle a mutiny once it has begun. By that point, trust and distrust are less important and action is what matters.

As the epigraph to this chapter indicates, an organizational member can be utterly fearless when acting on behalf of values shared with fellow members. That is when speaking truth to power in an organization becomes most natural. Therefore, since a mutiny can occur naturally in an organization, the shared values of mutineers tend to reflect the actual culture of that organization. That is where mutiny begins. It ends with a clash between those values and an existing authority structure. The trust-distrust framework in this chapter offers some additional insights into the actions that leaders can take when such a clash happens. We shall examine those insights and actions next.

6

Architectures of Inversion

The mutiny was the turning point of Magellan's career.

—Francis H. H. Guillemard

T he previous chapter focused on trust and distrust to illustrate circumstances that precede mutiny. In this chapter, we shift our focus to external elements of mutiny to provide a broader conceptual architecture. Considering the nature of external environments and the fitness of organizations within them not only sheds light on what a leader can do if a mutiny occurs, but also gives insight into the strategic actions that can make a mutiny succeed or fail. Since we do have some firsthand experiences with mutiny, we will begin this chapter with Ray Coye's reflections on his own experiences and observations of different leaders.

EXPERIENCE WITH MUTINY

The mutiny in Coye's experience was not nearly as violent or dramatic as the ones in Part I. Nonetheless, he did experience mutinous activity in 1972, during his time as an officer in the U.S. Coast Guard (USCG). After battling a severe North Atlantic gale for days, the aging cutter on which he was an officer developed a hull leak. Almost everyone knew about the leak, but no one talked about it publicly. At first, some crew members threatened to refuse to work because of the situation. They demanded an assurance from the leadership that repairs were in progress or that the cutter would return to a safe harbor instead of staying on the ocean in a violent storm. Indeed, the storm was a big part of the problem because of the uncertainty it added.

But another part of the problem was internal. It stemmed from the captain's known reluctance to abandon a mission unless circumstances were extreme. All of the members knew it. That was his leadership style, and it connoted certain values like order, control, and perseverance. Since the storm threatened and even precluded attainment of many of their objectives on this particular venture, most crew members believed it simply made no sense to take the risk of staying at sea.

Some anxious off-duty members eventually gathered on the mess deck. That was the setting in which the leader's decisions and actions began to clash with the values they shared about safety and practicality. No ringleader had yet emerged, but as crew members organized, they clearly attracted the attention of the leadership.

Mutinies do not usually happen just because organization members perceive danger. The potential becomes real only when the perceived danger occurs at a time when there is a gap between leaders and members, when the leader makes decisions that violate shared values, and when an uncertain environment prevails. In Coye's case, the captain came to the area where the members had gathered and communicated directly with them. Despite his usual aloofness and low interpersonal skills, he acknowledged that he understood their concerns and said that he shared their value of safety. Then he provided information on what was being done about the hull leak. He commented on the nature of the leak and its risk to the ship and the mission.

Even though the larger situation did not change, this interaction raised trust because it highlighted the values they all shared. Although he was a disciplinarian and somewhat disliked, he was highly technically competent. His credibility as an expert made the level of distrust very low. That is why the unexpected direct interpersonal engagement defused the situation. In fact, the captain's speech was very similar to the two communications that Magellan, also a disciplinarian, delivered to his members. Magellan's first one was in the Bay of Saint Julian when he gave a summary rationale for why members should not be concerned. His second occurred in the strait not long before entering the Pacific Ocean. In both instances, the tension was mitigated, but mutinies occurred shortly afterward. In Coye's case, the mutinous assembly dissipated, although grumblings persisted. Here, the difference was that Magellan's mutiny had ringleaders. Had there been a ringleader on the cutter in 1972, the situation might have evolved differently. We will have more to say about ringleaders later.

Experience with Leaders

Our interest in mutiny during the Age of Discovery derives in part from our own experiences in the maritime services and our experiences with leaders in the business world and in academia. Leadership is part of this story anyway, so we would like to also share some of Coye's experiences with radically different leaders during his time as a USCG officer. Each experience provided illustrative lessons about the relationship between leaders and members.

Leadership is multidimensional and dynamic. We all have shorthand personal rules that help us evaluate good and bad leaders and that can guide the actions of leaders and group members during critical incidents. During Coye's time as a USCG officer, his own shorthand rules came in the form of two questions to himself. These questions map onto the difference between trust and distrust that we examined in the previous chapter. The first question was, "If we were sinking and in a violent storm, would I willingly get into a small boat with this leader?" That is a question of technical competence. Its answer derives from the level of distrust in the leader. The second question was, "How willing am I to do extra work given the way this leader treats me and others?" That is a question about interpersonal competence or emotional intelligence. Its answer derives from the level of trust in the leader.

In a practical sense, the answer to the second question can influence the answer to the first one because of the power of shared values, as explained in chapter 5. After all, the answer to the second question is likely to be tacitly assumed. There is no need to think very much about one's willingness; the answer is self-evident because the question concerns shared experiences that are implicitly human. By contrast, the answer to the first question cannot influence the answer to the second one very much because distrust and trust are independent dimensions, and it is easier to affect the level of distrust that others have in one's competence than it is to build trust with others on the basis of shared values.

The first leader in Coye's experience was a veteran of North Atlantic convoys in World War II. He exuded technical competence. He was an expert. His navigational skill was complemented by a sense of humor, genuine understanding, and a concern for members. He knew what was going on in the organization without being intrusive. He had legitimate authority from the organizational structure, but he never abused it. In fact, he rarely needed to call on it to get tasks accomplished. He gave direct orders, but members responded less to the authority and more to their trust in him.

Technical competence is critical to the success of most enterprises. It lowers distrust in a leader. In fact, if a leader shares values with members and there is a level of trust, then members tend to have greater autonomy to develop their own technical competence. This combination of technical competence and emotional intelligence minimizes the importance of traditional structural authority. This first leader with whom Coye worked was very effective. He seemingly combined the technical expertise of Magellan with the emotional intelligence of Cabot. Would Coye get in this leader's small boat in an emergency? Definitely. This leader had a way of convincing others that even if he were absent, they would still be able to handle the situation, and everyone was part of the mission.

Coye's next leader was an administrator whose expertise was in mission logistics. He excelled at knowing details. Rarely did a chat or an item of minutiae escape his attention. His knowledge of navigation and the international rules of the road was low, however. He was also unable to connect with members. In fact, Coye's experiences with him were the genesis of his doctoral dissertation research on substitutes for leadership.

Substitutes for leadership are aspects of individuals, tasks, or organizations (e.g., experience, ambiguity, formalization) that can substitute for or neutralize the influence of individuals in leadership positions. What Coye learned from this leader was that it is possible, though not easy or pleasant, to achieve objectives when the leader is technically incompetent. In these circumstances, members create their own ways to get jobs done. But they can also waste energy protecting their work from dysfunctional intervention. That inefficiency is related to distrust. It can create gaps between echelons, especially if trust is low. Staffe's vacillating relationship with Hudson through the experience of being Hudson's mate, being ordered to build a fort, and finally joining Hudson in the small boat were similarly complex. In such cases, members may even undertake actions contrary to policy to accomplish tasks that are actually good for the enterprise. Would Coye have readily boarded his leader's small boat in an emergency? Unlike Staffe, not a chance.

The third leader with whom Coye worked transformed his personal concept of leadership. A principal leadership challenge is that the best way to perform is usually unique. It derives from the idiosyncratic relations between leader and context. Coye admired this leader for his ship-handling skills and his management talents. What was less admirable and made no sense, however, was that a leader with such competence commanded with fear. Coye and his fellow officers dreaded meeting with him because they knew they would face his condemnation. In this case, low distrust was balanced by the low trust they had in him as a person. Members of his group recognized his wisdom but had nothing else in common with him. His objectives were dubious. They did not share the values driving his actions. The lesson from this experience was that expertise cannot compensate for interpersonal skills. Again, the answer to the first question does not influence the answer to the second; distrust and trust operate on separate dimensions. Would Coye get in this leader's small boat during an emergency? Yes, but only for survival, and only if there were no other options.

Coye's experience with this leader tells some more about what Magellan's members felt during the winter in the Bay of Saint Julian and raises important issues. The fact that members follow a leader for different reasons in different situations complicates generalizations about leadership effectiveness. When it comes to how and why a mutiny occurs, emphasizing the importance of individual style can fill in some gaps in the understanding of leadership. That is why it is important to think about leadership and mutiny with an explicit formal reference to distrust and trust. The framework adds a degree of freedom in that it allows a leader to be effective on more than one level even as it clarifies and defines the most natural setting in which mutiny can occur (i.e., quadrant III, in the previous chapter).

The fourth leader in Coye's experience was in charge of a very large base and oversaw many search and rescue teams. Officers like Coye, who were essentially middle managers with line authority, were important to a variety of administrative functions. However, in this leader's view, experienced first-line supervisors were the most important people in the operation. Those members were valuable and accomplished their goals. But this leader went around certain aspects of the standard organizational structure to become involved in situations more appropriately handled by other officers.

Subverting the structure resulted in junior officers having a lack of trust in him. When Hudson gave undue authority to Greene on his fourth voyage, he subverted the structure in a very similar way. Greene was experienced and capable but had no formal authority. Giving him such an important role in formal operations violated member-shared assumptions about the organization and thus undermined Hudson's authority, especially with those members who did have formal authority and valued the organization's structure. The lesson here is to lead an enterprise in a manner that does not violate norms or traditions that may be important to structure and stability. Subverting norms can generate inefficiencies just as affronted values can fester into mutinous intentions, as happened in the case of Hudson.

In Coye's case, the managers at his level shared certain values about the organization, but the actions of the leader, by transgressing against those values, damaged trust, and members became oriented against the leader. Had the organization faced extreme uncertainty or if a ringleader had appeared, mutiny might have naturally emerged. This leader also, like Cabot, had an uncanny ability to build interpersonal relations with all members at informal and individual levels. Would Coye get in this commanding officer's boat? Yes, but only if other experienced members were in it, too.

The fifth leader in Coye's experience assumed command of the same base and made many changes. Quiet competence, attention to detail, regular feedback, and concern for others characterized his leadership style. An unobtrusive presence during critical activities was comforting. Lines of authority were reaffirmed, resulting in increased morale because members were more certain about where they fit in the structure. The lesson here is that transformational leadership is not always about force of personality. It is often about building and harnessing trust by enabling members to take personal responsibility for success. It is the loosing of members' drives and volition via leadership that creates a context in which that force can be set free. Shared values already exist, and in these contexts they become aligned with organizational purpose via their expression.

Would Coye get in this leader's boat in an emergency at sea? Without a doubt. The circumstances he created were marked by trust. Mutiny was unthinkable because there was no channel or reason for it.

The sixth and final leader in Coye's experience was in charge of a marine safety office that handled traffic control, pollution responses, law enforcement, and safety inspections. This leader had a very relaxed style. He also knew the details of the regulations that the organization was charged with enforcing. He could relay many anecdotes about each one. The level of distrust in him was low. His hands-off style was appreciated but could be problematic. For example, members valued control over their own activities but sometimes needed a leadership presence, particularly when a situation was uncertain. This leader rarely provided such guidance. Similarly, we saw that Cabot's members rarely dealt with him as they headed west across the Atlantic in 1526. When they did, the exchange was usually individual, and it was rich and meaningful. But they were all generally unsure what to make of him. Because of his strategic lack of engagement, they could not even sense whether he shared their values.

Coye's lesson from this experience was that a leader can fail to promote the accomplishment of objectives in times of uncertainty if the leader not only lacks trust but has failed to take opportunities to build trust. Just like Columbus, and a bit like Cabot, this leader critiqued poor performance and, in the next breath, offered praise. Coye would probably not get in this leader's boat in an emergency. Even after working with him for a year, nobody knew who he was, what he really stood for, or what he was ready to contribute. There was too much of a gap between him and the group members.

No leader is perfect. Coye's experiences reflect that truth and also illustrate several ideas and themes from the historic cases. The cases in your experience probably revealed similar insights to you. It is a good idea for organizational professionals to undertake an audit of their own experiences similar to the one we just undertook in the case of Coye. An audit begins to illustrate that certain leadership styles are more likely to promote mutiny because they instigate formal causes by violating shared values. In our experience and research, we have observed four such formal causes.

MUTINY'S FORMAL CAUSES

Mutinies push boundaries. They were natural during the Age of Discovery because the ventures during which they occurred also pushed boundaries. As seafaring nations expanded to protect their territories and lines of commerce, mutiny grew in tandem. However, a far stricter code on mutiny developed based on Cabot's document and Drake's circumnavigation, as we have noted, making it less likely to occur naturally and more likely to be immediately punished without question. Increasingly, the assumption was that authority and organization should be preserved against the constant threat of mutiny: that mutiny was an omnipresent and negative force. Enterprises still push boundaries and create settings where mutiny emerges naturally, and mutiny still tends to be suppressed unnaturally. Fortunately, a mutiny today is not such a violent or physical act as it was during the days of rope and knife, but it can still be very intense indeed. It can also be frightening. The formal causes of mutiny fall into four categories, each one having trust and distrust as a foundation.

Shared Grievances

Shared grievances invoke the purely social component of an organization. Although many cases of mutiny across history were based on shared grievances, a great many come from the British navy in the eighteenth century. By that point, the burgeoning British Empire had evolved out of the tradition that began with Cabot, Drake, and others. Two famous examples of mutinies are the Spithead and Nore anchorage mutinies of 1797. The "Great Rebellion," or Indian Mutiny, of 1857 is even more famous, if not technically a mutiny. The literature on these cases is voluminous, and the mutinies unfolded in cultures and periods that were different from the Age of Discovery. Suffice it to say that their formal causes involved coercive power, injustices, and resource shortages—all the subject of grievances.[1]

Coercive power, which forces or unduly compels others to act, creates grievances among group members. It was common in the Age of Discovery. We saw it explicitly in the case of Magellan, when he was a Portuguese foreigner punishing Castilians. It was particularly relevant in the Cabot case, too, when he abused Méndez and tried to prevent him from joining the enterprise in Seville and later executed Lepe.

The modern equivalents of these acts are such management decisions as employment terminations and reclassifications. Members tend to discuss such events until consensus emerges. The events can eventually become part of the lore of an organization as the consensus generates shared values that align or clash with a leader's actions or decisions. These *socialized* grievances are significant. Indeed, if all the members share values, then poor treatment of members often aggrieves even members who are not poorly treated. A mutiny is, in this case, a means to protect shared values. Organizational life has highly organic aspects. Leaders must understand that they lead a single organization, not just a plurality of members, no matter how diverse those members may be. The connection among members is a more vital element of an organization.

Members of today's firms are not usually starving or risking their lives because of limited resources or navigational hazards. But modern grievances come in other forms that still entail shared values that go far beyond staying alive and safe. For instance, members of an organization may not have the tools to do their jobs. That lack may not be sufficient to drive a mutiny against a leader. But what if members share a certain value about those tools and then a leader violates that shared value? For example, software engineers, investment bankers, construction workers, accountants, police officers, and most specialists require tools and technologies to undertake their work and, in each case, share a certain perspective about the value of those tools and technologies. When an organizational decision affronts the shared value that defines that perspective, there is often an expressed grievance in response.

If there is a gap between leaders and members, the shared grievance may be invisible to the leader but acutely obvious to members. Moreover, members may not be able to communicate that concern because of the echelon gap, and the inability to communicate may reinforce the shared grievance. The only thing required for a mutiny at that point is a ringleader and an opportunity. Because a gap between leaders and members can cause members to associate shared grievances with bad leadership decisions, even erroneously, a mutiny can form based on an imagined affront. Near the end of Cabot's explorations in the Río de La Plata, for example, members were seeking almost any possible excuse to mutiny.

Detached leadership generates decisions that violate shared values very easily. In Hudson's case, he even seemed to be emphasizing the gap between echelons in the weeks leading up to the final mutiny. Not intentionally, of course. Ordering Staffe to build a shelter and awarding Williams's cloak directly to Greene (and later taking it back with impunity) merely exacerbated existing shared grievances and widened the gap between Hudson and the members. Like an exceedingly passionate nascent entrepreneur, he was obsessed with seizing the potential opportunities of his enterprise. But he had become gravely oblivious to the threats that can accompany opportunities. Juet and Greene undertook the mutiny by seizing their own opportunity, which emerged squarely in the context of the threats to which Hudson was oblivious.

Danger and Uncertainty

The potential for mutiny increases when perceptions of danger combine with uncertainty. That combination constitutes the second category of the formal causes of mutiny. A leader's actions can create a critical juncture where members are at risk and a situation is uncertain. Mutinies based on perceived danger were rare, however, even in the Age of Discovery. Broadly speaking, members usually know if the work is dangerous before they join an enterprise. Even if they do not know about possible danger and discover it later, in the middle of the operation, the problems are seldom insurmountable. Columbus and Magellan both described their ventures to potential members conservatively to manage members' impressions of danger. Being misleading at the outset did not itself generate problems, because perceived danger alone is not a full cause of mutiny in an organization. It is half a cause.

When uncertainty enters the equation, it multiplies the prospects of danger. To deal with the uncertain situation, members start to take it upon themselves to add certainty. Leaders mitigate this process by explaining the external environment so that members gain certainty that way rather than turning to their own devices. The first mutiny on Columbus's voyage, which he quelled, had this same cause. Members associated the distance from Spain with danger and uncertainty. The mutiny potential grew over time, although Columbus tried to manage it with the considerable power of his personality. Once a critical juncture was reached, sheer personality was not enough. That is when he supplied a rational argument to add certainty, which bought him the valuable time that afforded his landmark achievement. Cabot was also quite masterful at maintaining a cohesive enterprise despite uncertainty. Not until the expedition reached Santa Ana and the objective seemed utterly hopeless was he compelled to move out of the Río de La Plata.

Levels of the Environment

The third formal cause of mutinies pertains to opportunities and threats across the external environment. Mutinies connect with the environment in complex ways, just as organizations do. However, because the strategy of a mutiny runs counter to the strategy of the organization, the nature of that connection with the environment is different. Elements affecting the organization in one way will relate to the mutiny in a different way.

To explain this category, we must delineate two perspectives. The first one concerns the relation between the mutiny and the organization. Since the mutiny is opposed to the subsuming organization by definition, it is not so different from a risky entrepreneurial venture. And just as an entrepreneurial venture faces tough challenges when it enters a hostile market environment, so, too, do mutineers when they undertake their action. For them, the organizational environment is hostile. There are threats, opportunities, and barriers. Their venture can be very threatening to the established players. These elements are precisely why a mutiny must be strategic. Private information and novel means of performance are important to planning and coordination. A more tactical mutiny can get away with less secretiveness because operations are usually dubious when distrust in a leader is high. In both settings, whether a mutiny is strategic or tactical, some level of planning and coordination is required. Enter the importance of ringleaders.

The ringleader of a mutiny is as vital to its effectiveness as the leader is to the organization. In fact, the importance of a ringleader to a mutiny is comparatively greater because a mutiny's environment (i.e., the organization) is comparatively more acutely hostile to that mutiny than an organization's environment (i.e., a market) is to that organization. One of the most important elements of a mutiny, therefore, is a very effective leader who performs a role similar to that of the leader of an entrepreneurial venture.

For the leader of an organization, the best strategy for quelling a mutiny is to first depose its ringleader. In fact, one of the reasons Columbus so easily quelled the first mutiny on his 1492 voyage is because there was no ringleader. That was a vital missing element. It was much harder for him to deal with Pinzón's coordinated defiance of his authority later. In fact, Columbus chose not to deal with that mutiny: the goals had already been met anyway. The importance of a ringleader also explains why Magellan took such bold action against Quesada and Cartagena and not the other mutineers. Similarly, Cabot dealt aggressively with ringleaders on multiple occasions, marooning Méndez, Rodas, Rojas, and at least six other crew members at Santa Catalina and later executing Lepe and Martín.

The second perspective concerns the nature of the broader environment. An organization's internal environment (functions, divisions, departments) is the first layer of a mutiny's *external* environment. The first layer of the organization's environment (competitors, customers, suppliers, distributors) is the *second* layer of the mutiny's environment. Finally, the second layer of the organization's environment (technologies, demographics, economic forces, sociocultural values, etc.) is actually the *third* layer of the mutiny's environment. Opportunities and threats are flipped; across these environmental layers, they relate to a mutiny in almost the opposite way from how they relate to the organization subsuming that mutiny. Moreover, with an additional environmental layer, the mutiny's situation is more complex.

It follows that the best strategies or tactics for a mutiny are often the opposite of the organization's strategies and tactics in very certain ways. A threat to the organization can be an opportunity for the mutineers. The ringleader of a mutiny looks at the environmental layers with a reversed lens in search of opportunities to depose the leadership or authority structure. This logic is quite reliable. That is, the opportunities a ringleader recognizes are usually known threats to the organization. For instance, if there is a broader social movement based on certain values hostile to the organization, the mutineers can leverage that movement to depose authority. Or the mutineers could gain power and influence by taking advantage of a new technology that is a bona fide threat to the organization's business operations.

Understanding the environment is the first step in the traditional course of strategic planning. Thus, when dealing with a mutiny, if the leader is aware of it, careful stock should be taken of threats in the environment that could help that mutiny. The first attempted mutiny that Magellan faced occurred after leaving the Canary Islands and before crossing the Atlantic offers an example. Although Cartagena derided Magellan for sailing so close to the African coast and used that fact to question Magellan's authority, we know that Magellan chose the course to avoid the threat of the Portuguese caravels that had been tracking his armada. Thus, what Magellan saw as a threat to the enterprise was identical to the opportunity for Cartagena to attempt mutiny. Magellan's response was to remove Cartagena, the ringleader, from his position and replace him with Coca, with whom he shared values.

Ringleaders of mutinies and leaders of organizations must both act strategically and tactically in accordance with the reversal of threats and opportunities. The historic cases provided many examples. Consider the case of Cabot. When Méndez wrote a letter to the Spanish king reporting Cabot's incompetence, he was implementing the mutiny strategy he had formulated with Rodas and Rojas. The king's authority could easily become a threat to Cabot if confidence in the mission was lost. That threat to Cabot was Méndez's opportunity. There are multiple ways to respond to such acts. Magellan, for instance, might have removed Méndez at that moment. Instead, Cabot neutralized the threat with clever guile by intercepting Méndez's letter and quietly disposing of it.

Personal Intentions

The worst of human nature can be put on display in a mutiny situation. Drama and tragedy, which often accompany mutiny, shape popular perceptions of it. Human nature is in fact the fourth and final formal cause of mutiny, although the historical record indicates that it is not the chief cause. Even so, it is still the most complex. Mutiny caused by human nature happens in departments, divisions, and whole organizations. Personal intentions often drive subtle affairs that defy formal understanding. In Part I, at least two mutinies were undertaken for reasons that had to do with the leader as a person. Magellan faced peculiar challenges based on personal jealousies and his foreigner status. One mutineer, Gómez, was against Magellan because Charles V rejected his venture plan.

Cabot's expedition offers another example of the dark personal element of mutiny. Like Columbus and Magellan, he was a foreigner to his members, but he had a personal aura of mystery. The gap between Cabot and his members would have damaged trust for most leaders, but Cabot was able to turn threats into opportunities for himself. His case is a prime example of reversal, seemingly related to his general ability to become powerful during dire moments and not otherwise. Cabot faced the most determined mutiny of all those discussed in this book. Méndez, Rodas, and Rojas were not only jealous of him but often saw through his clever posturing. They had begun plotting in a church before leaving Seville, and their intentions simmered even as they initially progressed down the Guadalquivir River to enter the ocean at San Lucar some weeks later.

We close this chapter with some reflections on these architectures of inversion and offer some rules of thumb for leaders and members. Perhaps the most basic lesson that we draw from the examples presented here is that shared grievances can turn into a rationale for mutiny if they are not perceived or understood by a leader. Another lesson is that if members share perceptions of danger and uncertainty, those perceptions can prompt the fabrication of grievances that then orient mutinous action. Human nature comes into play here. As Richard Biddle wrote in 1831, "But pretexts will never be wanting where a mutinous temper exists."[2]

Like entrepreneurs, mutineers search constantly for opportunities to act. An unceasing search for ways to rebel can twist perceptions of reality and induce the seekers to go to great lengths to reach that personal objective. Brilliant tacticians like Magellan and Hudson thus have good reason to think carefully about internal and external environments and any possible opportunities for a strategically designed mutiny. Magellan did so, for example, by contemplating the composition of shared values on the *Victoria* before quelling the mutiny tactically. Hudson did not think about his enterprise at this level. It is vital that a leader understand that shared values underpin mutinous action. A meaningful response to a mutiny is possible if, and only if, an understanding of those shared values exists.

Different levels of the environment, the third formal cause of mutiny, are what make mutiny strategic. The internal organizational environment brings particular opportunities and threats, which make planning and coordination essential. These activities call for a mutiny to have an appropriate structure. Effective organizational leaders routinely examine opportunities and threats in order to structure the organization according to what they find. Ringleaders of a mutiny ought to do the same thing. Those who would quell a mutiny should use the same approach in turn.

We should note that organizational life has a darker side. A leader is sometimes just not likable, and some leaders excite jealousies. When personal animus leads to mutiny, the fomenters are usually a small number of individuals, perhaps just one, with specific and often misguided perceptions. Founded or unfounded, such perceptions can and do become realities in the social context of organizational life. Great leaders know that their decisions and actions convey values to members of the organizations they lead, and members' perceptions of any single leader decision will vary. It is thus important for a leader to convey values to members so that such decisions can be more easily interpreted. Irrespective of agreement with member shared values, a leader's values must be made clear. Otherwise, a gap can form and mutiny can emerge based on perceived or invented affronts.

The act of mutiny is usually less malicious and purposeful than it seems to leaders. Much of the affair has to with ignorance on both sides. Members and leaders that see their own causes as righteous carry distinct biases, which generate different social realities and can be volatile if they intersect. That is why mutiny has aspects of a clash in values and also why the tension can build for a long time.

All business schools deliver courses that intensely examine organizational strategies and competitive environments. There should probably be seminars on mutiny and its importance to highly adaptive innovation activities. Mutinous groups can develop into small, sui generis organizations, after all. The effects on a market system or environment can be profound. Indeed, mutiny can have its bounty. California's Silicon Valley provides an undeniable example. The original population of ventures that developed into the Silicon Valley, currently the most important high-technology region in the world, can be traced back to a mutiny at Shockley Semiconductor Laboratory in 1957. By the 1970s, more than forty firms had been founded in the lineage that sprang from that mutiny. By the early 1990s, the number was well over a hundred. As in the Age of Discovery, mutiny is relevant to entrepreneurship and innovation in organizational settings.[3]

Why is mutiny so relevant? Because it is as germane as leadership in any cultural setting in which entrepreneurship and innovation are defining elements. Firm structures or operations that prevent coordinated upward defiance, one consequence of the industrial organizational paradigm, also hinder innovative and adaptive activity. That is why, at first blush, the concept of mutiny does not fit with the popular conception of how innovation actually works. That popular conception is provincial, even jaundiced. Mutiny can be regarded as dangerous, to be sure. It is powerful. But viewing it as inherently bad can be a costly mistake, however easy it is to do so. Mutiny almost always happens for reasons that are worth considering. In entrepreneurial environments, the potential for mutiny can help a firm make better decisions amidst uncertainty and enhance discovery and innovation. It can bring a venture toward options that were previously unreachable, just as it can steer a venture around threats that were previously invisible. The same force that drives mutiny can propel a firm beyond its own boundaries as it revolutionizes an industry or market space in the name of a strong mission.

As the epigraph to this chapter suggests, the event can have a profound effect on a leader's effectiveness. Indeed, Magellan's authority structure was not established until after the mutiny in the Bay of Saint Julian. The architectures of inversion we examined in this chapter can thus enable leaders to connect better with the shared values of members as they undertake ventures over time. Mutiny is implicitly human but it is also an organizational phenomenon that capitalizes on the raw force of human nature germane to a firm's members. As we have said, it is functionally equivalent to transformational leadership, which is why it can transform internal human nature into external organizational outcomes that are revolutionary.

7

C H A P T E R

Double-Edged Blades

Mendez and Rojas were the recognized leaders in this movement of insubordination and mutiny, and it may be that becoming bold from the number and zeal of their followers,
they did not go so cautiously to work as the dangerousness of
the affair required.

—Francesco Tarducci

On a practical and operational level, mutiny seems like the
antithesis of transformational leadership. Yet the forces
driving both are functionally equivalent at a deep level. In
this chapter, we shed light on these forces by examining some more
current mutinies. Along the way, we will present a few insights that
will be especially useful not just for leaders but also for those wishing
to execute a mutiny.

The 1952 Pulitzer Prize–winning novel *The Caine Mutiny,* which
brought the connection between leadership and mutiny to twentieth-
century attention, had an impact on public perception on par with
Cabot's 1553 document or Drake's actions during his 1577 voyage
around the world. Conflicting rationales for mutiny, mixed with
knotty questions about justification for disciplinary, military, and
personal actions, show how maddeningly complex these situations
can be. Even the ending of the film captures the complexity, for it
effectively shows the potential misguidedness of ascribing right and
wrong to the members and leaders participating in a mutiny.[1]

Anyone who has seen the 1954 film based on the novel will remember the moment when Lieutenant Commander Queeg's officers
depose him. It is a highlight of the film. Humphrey Bogart immortalized the eccentric leadership style of Queeg. Queeg's predecessor
had not emphasized basic task discipline, but he did share a connection with the men. Most of the crew were competent at their
jobs and had trusted their previous leader. As a leader, Queeg was
his predecessor's opposite. He was technically able but abhorred the
crew's slovenly habits. Members perceived him as foreign. They were
unwelcoming and did not share many of his values. Over time, his
relationship with those reporting directly to him soured. Disgruntlement simmered for weeks until a typhoon created a dangerous and
uncertain environment at sea. Mutiny emerged very quickly when
the executive officer moved the ship to a safer heading and Queeg
ordered him to reverse that action, an order that clashed with the
members' shared value of safety. Because the situation was uncertain
and trust between Queeg and the members was low, the mutiny
flashed. The executive officer forcibly deposed Queeg, calling him "a
sick man." Queeg, shocked, retorted, "You'll all hang for collusion in
mutiny. I kid you not about that."

The industrial organizational paradigm evolved in response to
uncertain environments. Lawful authority is designed to rest with
the leader. But the leader still has responsibility for what members
do in coordination. Framing a mutiny situation in terms of two sides
thus turns out to be arbitrary because leadership and mutiny are both
defined by coordinated participation, which begins and ends with
the organization of which leaders and members are part.

TRANSFORMATIONAL LEADERSHIP AND MUTINY

The characteristics and the actions of a leader convey certain values
that can interact with values shared by members. Transformational
leaders create a context in which the best talents and competencies
of members are set free. The leader enables, fosters, and coordinates

the organization with a future goal in mind, which can align or clash with member shared values. It is important to understand that the shared values of members have a future-oriented character: they clarify what should be done in new situations. That is why successful leaders play less of a direct role in organizational performance than many people think they do. In fact, such leaders usually do not explain their performance in terms of what they do, but in terms of the members who made success possible. Many go so far as to say that they would not be successful without members' actions. The truth is that transformational leaders are far more facilitative than directive.

Mutiny and leadership are similar for the same reasons that leadership and management are different. Legitimate power and authority are the underpinnings of influence merely in a management (not leadership) sense, and those two elements of control derive from the policies and structure of the organization. By contrast, leadership (not management) sets loose a bottom-up force that emerges from what is shared among members. The basic phenomenon of mutiny and transformational leadership is thus largely the same. It is a force of human nature. When the force serves a ritualistic or sociological function as a natural release of tensions, the effect is cathartic. But as a coordinated breakout of human feelings channeled into action, the force can nonetheless clash with the structure of the organization and test existing limits. If a coordinated breakout by members aligns with the leader and the leader's goals, then it looks like leadership. If it is in opposition to the leader and the leader's goals, then it looks like mutiny.

Because shared values drive a force that can clash with existing structures, mutineers must manage perceptions. Of course, leaders do, too. Even though both mutineers and leaders are managing perceptions, the perceptions appear very different because of the nature of organizational settings. The values-circumstances diagram shown here depicts possible contexts.

One dimension shows the degree to which values are shared between leaders and members. The other dimension shows the level of

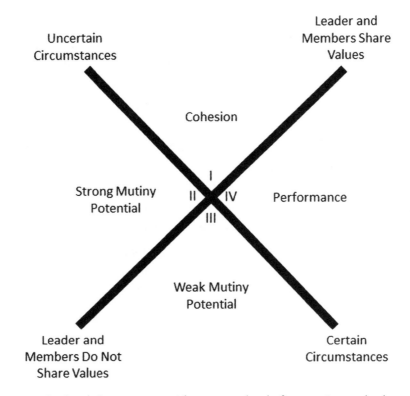

Organizational circumstances with respect to level of uncertainty and values
shared by members and leaders

uncertainty surrounding the organization. Quadrants II and III integrate what is illustrated in earlier chapters regarding shared values and uncertainty. When environments become adverse or uncertain and when members and leaders do not share values (quadrant II), the potential for mutiny goes up. Some leadership action or decision usually calls attention to the gap in shared values by violating those values. That is a mutiny trigger. This framework is straightforward and useful, but it also opens the way to establishing certain boundary conditions. Trust and shared values have certain limits in organizations. It is important to understand those limits in order to appreciate not only the similarities between transformational leadership and mutiny but also the differences.

THE LIMITS OF TRUST

As with most aspects of human nature, the effects of trust are not absolute. Quadrants I and IV help us to think about the limits of its effects. We know that shared values (quadrants I and IV) can work against the development of mutiny. Values shared between members and a *competent* leader help keep an enterprise on course. As we saw, Magellan's achievement of a specific performance outcome put him in quadrant IV and enabled him to avoid the mutiny quadrants, II and III, once and for all. Values shared between members and a *trusted* leader can bring cohesion to an enterprise. Columbus's intense optimism encouraged members even as he led the enterprise into uncertainty. He constantly tried to build trust and highlight shared values as underlying tension gathered. In this way, he stayed in quadrant I and actively avoided the mutiny quadrants.

Quadrants I and IV still miss one aspect of mutiny outside the boundaries of the trust-distrust paradigm: what happens when leaders and members become *too familiar* and trust is *too high*. Cohesion and performance can actually enable the deposition of authority if an organization lacks a clear objective and structure. Although the second mutiny against Columbus by Pinzón is related to this principle, we know of one example during the Age of Sail (not the Age of Discovery). It is a perfect illustration and an interesting case of how familiarity can breed contempt and how performance and cohesion can run amok. Let us examine it briefly.

On October 23, 1813, the USS *Essex* stopped to refit and refresh at Nooaheeva Island in the Marquesas, in the South Pacific between South America and Austrialia.[2] Its captain was an American, David Porter. With approximately three hundred members, it was a much larger sailing ship than the caravels and carracks of the Age of Discovery. Seafaring had become very routinized, and sailing ships were highly developed by this point in history. When the *Essex* stopped at the Marquesas, it had just completed a phenomenally successful fifteen-month operation against British shipping lines and whaling vessels during the War of 1812. Before reaching Nooaheeva, the disciplined and tightly knit captain and crew had captured or destroyed at least twelve British ships. Once in the port, however, discipline all but vanished. Porter, for instance, undertook a flagrant relationship with a young native woman named Piteenee, the granddaughter of a powerful island leader named Gattanewa. Before long, several members of the leadership group became enamored of her. Porter encouraged crew members to pursue liaisons of amusement and repose. It became clear that Gattanewa also had his own designs, for his granddaughter became instrumental in enmeshing Porter and his crew in tribal wars.

The actions of the *Essex*'s crew members were clashing with the shared values that had heretofore defined the culture of the enterprise. The decision to enjoy the liberties of the island paradise and to help Gattanewa against his enemies seemed to make sense in context, but in retrospect, we can see how it undermined Porter's authority. Porter, who enjoyed the trust of his crew and was enormously competent, tried to do the right thing by encouraging recreation. For example, when friendly women on shore sought to visit the *Essex* and the captured British ships in the harbor, Porter set up shuttle runs. The result was "a scene of merriment such as is very uncommon in a man-of-war."[3]

These kinds of actions had a powerful transformational effect on *how* Porter's crew members trusted him. The culture of the enterprise had been forged in intense shared experiences under his leadership. Now the external situation was straining those shared values. The bedrock of trust was bound to fracture.

The subtle but powerful pressures were invisible to Porter until plans were being made for departure. They became starkly clear when he left the *Essex* for a few days, members mutinied, and a lieutenant barely quelled the uprising. Porter quelled additional mutinies after his return. But now he displayed a new tendency for vacillation in punishment, not unlike Hudson two hundred years earlier. His wake-up call came when several members swam to shore the night before the *Essex* was to depart. Such breaches of discipline were unthinkable. Now he knew unavoidably that the culture of the ship had shifted. Members no longer valued the mission and might even mutiny rather than depart. The potential for mutiny had been simmering for weeks, changing the shared values and shifting them away from Porter's and those of the mission. Although Porter's values had not changed, his actions in the new environment had shifted the values of the members. Before departure, he had to restore commonality and discipline.

According to historical accounts and Porter's journals, the familiarity between leader and members was high because of the success of the mission. After months of less-serious actions had effectively trivialized the original mission, the easy and certain environment of Nooaheeva became a substitute for Porter's leadership. His familiarity with members now became a detriment to his authority.

The critical juncture came with Porter's order to depart. According to the member's new shared values, there was simply no reason to leave Nooaheeva, especially since, in their perception, the ocean was full of belligerent enemy ships and the United States was winning the war. Why enter that uncertain environment? Time was on their side. They had been there for months, so what was the harm in staying a while longer? A ringleader named Robert White coordinated the mutinous action along such purpose.

Porter made an amazingly risky move. As we know from the discussion in chapter 5, it was a perfect tactical response to White's strategic angling. It was probably the only thing Porter could have done to quell the mutiny besides staying at Nooaheeva. After all were on board and the *Essex* was ready to sail, but before the grumbling intensified, he called the entire crew together and swore in a rage that if there was a mutiny, he would "put a match to the magazine, and blow all hands into eternity."[4] His threat restored his authority temporarily. To prevent a resurgence of the mutiny, now he needed to destroy its coordination.

Porter called White to the fore and banished him from the *Essex*, putting him in a canoe with male natives. In a tradition dating back to the Age of Discovery, members who had deserted or been marooned were scattered about on islands; it was not uncommon to find them. In fact, Porter and his crew had encountered several such individuals living in the Marquesas. Deserters and those punished by being marooned were rarely trustworthy and were often dangerous. They often became pirates, taking over ships and using them to their own ends. White's mutiny strategy fit that mold. An opportunity for the mutineers amounted to a threat to the mission. But with White gone, the mutinous members lost their ringleader. Porter had extinguished the mutiny by destroying its coordination.

Porter reportedly had the band play a moving tune as they departed. Hundreds of natives gathered for the sendoff, singing goodbyes, dancing, dripping seawater down their faces to look like tears, playfully cutting themselves with white stones that they pretended were sharks' teeth, hitting themselves on the head with soft blades of grass, and laughingly threatening to drown themselves if their departing friends would not stay.[5] And as they departed, Porter assured the members again, but in a far gentler tone, that any hint of mutiny would result in his blowing the *Essex* up.

A few months later, the *Essex* was caught in a storm off the coast of Valparaiso, Chile. Two British vessels, the *Cherub* and the *Phoebe,* spotted it, strategized, and attacked. The *Essex* caught fire, and more than half of its members were killed before Porter surrendered and the ship was captured. The survivors were taken prisoner. Under a wartime agreement they were given passage to New York on April 27, 1814, and there they were given a parade and a hero's welcome for their actions before Nooaheeva. Porter was given command of a new ship, also named the *Essex.* The original USS *Essex* was now the HMS *Essex,* flying a British flag.

SOCIAL AND INTELLECTUAL MUTINIES

Indeed, swords have become words over the centuries. As we have emphasized in this book, mutinies in modern organizations entail many of the same dynamics as historic ones, but the dynamics are harder to delineate and the cases are not as well documented. They are nuanced and subtle affairs, and case data are highly subjective. Many experienced managers have shared their stories with us after hearing about our research. One of them shared the following account, which illustrates trust and distrust in a modern setting while drawing clear parallels with the historic mutinies examined here. In this case, the leader has an eerie resemblance to Cabot, except for her inability to sense and avoid mutiny. The importance of a ringleader is evident here also, as are the linkages between mutiny and transformational leadership.

The manager who related this account is a financial analyst, here called Kevin.[6] In the 1990s, having completed an MBA in the United States and worked in finance in Hong Kong for two years, Kevin returned to the States and joined the new online trading division of a large, well-known brokerage firm as finance manager. The firm was in the midst of change. The Internet had become popular while he was out of the country, and the financial business that he previously knew so well was now high-tech and filled with unfamiliar jargon. Given that his foreign experience had taken him a bit out of the loop, he was surprised that he had been hired at all, especially in the electronics division of a prominent company.

Kevin's specific responsibilities as a manager involved overseeing budgeting and planning for the new division. His team included three analysts as direct reports. At his same level were a manager who handled competitive intelligence and a manager who handled information systems. His boss, Franz, reported to the senior vice president who was responsible for the whole online trading division.

The existing team members had been at the firm for several years, and all of them seemed highly competent. Kevin was excited to work with them. In his first week, he was invited to a meeting to discuss the wrap-up of the latest budget iteration. Franz ran that meeting because he and the analysts had most of the background knowledge. Kevin met another new person at this meeting. Her name was Anne, and it was her first day, too. Kevin was not told exactly what her role was.

During that first meeting, Anne interrupted frequently and kept asking strange questions peppered with buzzwords and jargon. After the meeting, Kevin asked Franz what Anne's job was. "She's the new division controller, my new boss," Franz responded.

Anne introduced much uncertainty into the division. From Kevin's perspective, over the next two years Anne's decisions caused what amounted to a shipwreck in slow motion. Anne's capacity to speak facile jargon initially led Kevin to believe that the uncertainty was his problem, not hers. He and his peers frequently bore Anne's tongue-lashings, although why she was angry was unclear. As they began to share their perceptions with one another, they commiserated over their common inability to understand what she wanted or how it related to their work or the firm's objectives. Above all, they failed to grasp why she was hostile toward them. Franz's advice was to go along with Anne's directives and adjust to her style.

But Kevin and his colleagues found the climate very tense with Anne in charge. Once she ordered Kevin to fire an analyst for a minor mistake. When he objected, Franz stepped in and directly told Kevin to do it. A few months later, Anne directed Franz to demote Kevin from his management position. Franz did so but never explained the situation to Kevin. The decision was cast in the context of a department restructuring. In fact, Kevin did not even know that he had been demoted until he happened to notice that his pay grade had changed in the directory listing. His salary stayed the same.

Within eight months, Anne had transformed the division into a fiefdom. She had hired new directors and another vice president, all of whom reported to her. Kevin and the other members did not understand the reasons for the new positions. In less than a year, the division no longer comprised a small seven-member team. Now there were more than twenty division members who failed to understand what their colleagues were doing. They shared similar values and grievances but did not have the coordination to do anything about them.

James, one of the directors whom Anne had hired, did not suffer fools gladly. Sometime after joining the firm, he began to openly regard Anne as incompetent. He had tuned into the tension that had been building over the past year. Heretofore, Anne had benefited from her uncanny ability to manage others' impressions of her intelligence and wit. She had used that ability to gain influence with her superiors and external individuals. Nonetheless, several months after joining the firm, James pulled the other directors together to discuss what might be done to ease tension and resolve their grievances. Kevin learned later that Franz had resisted going to the meeting, but James finally pressured him into attending.

After the disgruntled division members organized, James suggested that they send a summary memo of their grievances to the human resources department and a copy to Anne. The memo stated formally that they would resign and seek jobs elsewhere if Anne remained in her position as leader. It included a list of examples of her performance, with linkages to firm performance. Within a matter of days, she was fired.

The reputations of James and the mutineers were damaged initially. But it became clear to all that their shared values were aligned with good company performance. Anne's leadership, by contrast, had not been. A new controller named Mary was promoted from within to rehabilitate the team. She reorganized the department and cut positions. James became Kevin's new boss and restored Kevin's title of manager. A good mentor, he helped improve Kevin's self-confidence and helped him earn a promotion to director. In that new position, Kevin was assigned many of the tasks for which Anne had been responsible.

Anne's strategy of hiring too many people admitted the very element that led to her deposition: one of the individuals she brought into the organization as a buffer was the one who took the strategic actions to depose her. The same thing had happened with Henry Hudson, who hired Henry Greene near the outset of his fourth voyage only to regret it later. Like Greene, James was a "foreigner"; he came from outside. Foreigner status can aid the ringleader of a mutiny for the same reason that it can hamper the leader of an organization, especially if the leader is aligned somehow with an external threat.

The shared values that guide a mutiny usually stand directly against the leader's values. However, individuals in the group are sometimes too close to both sets of values to see the overlap between them. Both leaders and members easily become overly subjective because they are both integral parts of the dynamic. It is clear that Anne was behaving based on a set of values that were different from the ones that Kevin and his colleagues shared. Kevin's case illustrates this important lesson. Indeed, he reported to us that the experience showed him in retrospect that organization members do not have to put up with an incompetent leader, even if grievances are subjective. With the benefit of hindsight, he said that the mutiny not only helped the firm in objective ways but also improved his own life. He would not hesitate to act as James had if he were in a similar situation in the future.

Let us close this chapter by examining how a mutiny is executed. Since mutinies are almost always different from one another at the practical and the empirical levels, the principles enumerated in the following section are not definitive or exhaustive, but potential mutineers—especially people in organizations with bad leaders—should find them useful. These general principles can be adapted liberally to suit specific purposes.[7]

Mutiny's Entrepreneurial Aspects

Coordinated upward force in an organization is a weapon. It can be used to reform an organization, or, like any weapon, it can be seized by the enemy if wielded poorly. How it is used depends on who is wielding it. Indeed, like a sword, it can cut in different ways. The concepts of aiming and accuracy are thus very important. Mutiny is directionally opposed to leadership, but not to all leadership. Rather, the focus of a mutiny is a particular organization's leadership. A mutiny as we have defined it is never the result of anarchist or anti-establishment values. Those values belong to revolutions, not mutinies, and can actually disserve a mutiny because they are not suitably strategic or tactical. Effective mutinies benefit enormously from some level of design and planning, even with their own leadership and structure.

One or more members of a mutiny can fulfill the all-important ringleader role. Sometimes these members determine whether or not a mutiny will succeed just by participating in it. The role contributes coordination and strategic decision making to the mutiny. Although the mutiny may arise from lower echelons of the larger organization, the key players are often middle-level members. Let us consider how these elements make a difference in mutiny settings by using what is known about small, bold, and risky enterprises.

A mutiny is an entrepreneurial act in many basic ways. Just as a successful entrepreneurial enterprise evolves via internal and external drivers, a successful mutiny is also subject to such drivers. A mutiny's internal aspects involve members and ringleaders determining to organize and act strategically to depose a larger organization's leadership. The external aspects come into play when the larger organization's leadership accepts that things must change one way or the other and takes the mutiny seriously. Ringleaders, structures, and strategies are vital to clearing the internal and the external stages effectively, and they largely determine whether a mutiny can be successful.

Finding similarities between mutinies and entrepreneurial ventures is a powerful way to think about mutiny. Mutinies and entrepreneurial ventures are both relatively small and agile compared with more established organizations. Size and agility are important because being successful requires an innovative strategy that may need to change quickly. Both kinds of undertakings are typically disruptive to some existing order because they threaten the elements that currently occupy the organizational environment. Another similarity is that entrepreneurial ventures and mutinies do not often follow existing policies or regulations. Because they are concerned with a new way of doing things, the old rules may not apply. Both begin on a small scale but gain momentum and size over time. Thus, both are oriented toward growth. When they do emerge in an observable way, their appearance may seem sudden even though the planning that went into them took a lot of time. Finally, some kind of exit strategy is important in entrepreneurship as well as in mutiny. Given all these similarities, the underpinnings of entrepreneurial success can be instructive in understanding mutiny success.

When a group recognizes an opportunity for action in an entrepreneurial context, that opportunity already exists. The group's principal tasks are to understand that opportunity and then to formulate an idea that creates a new way to take advantage of it. This becomes a matter of strategic formulation, implementation, and even operations management. For example, customers in a given market segment may have a definite need for a service. And there may be some innovative notion that has not yet been developed into an actual service that can fulfill that need. Notion begins to equal opportunity. The task of an entrepreneurial team is formulating a response to that opportunity, a response that includes executing the plan while avoiding threats. Because immature ventures do not have ample resources to handle errors, execution is vital; one mistake can be fatal. This logic is natural in entrepreneurial settings. It is almost identical to the logic of mutiny.

In a mutiny, as the opportunity becomes defined more clearly, members can think strategically about objectives and smart courses of action. It is much harder to develop strategic ideas if the opportunity is unclear. In the case of the mutiny that Kevin experienced, for instance, he originally had the idea that Anne was bad for the company as division controller. His colleagues came to agree with him about that idea. Her decisions and actions routinely violated their shared values, thus generating a need for something to be done about it. Indeed, they all had a common perspective and even had examples to illustrate their view. However, practically speaking, having a common idea does not by itself lead to mutiny. For Kevin and his colleagues, an opportunity did not emerge until James joined the company as a director. That is when the sense of what was needed began to form; before that point it had been invisible because deposing Anne's authority seemed impossible. James's position was higher than Kevin's and his colleagues. He was also newer, giving him an outsider's point of view that was more objective. But most important, he shared their values from the outset. He saw the elements that constituted an opportunity for mutiny more fully and provided the final element needed. He championed sending a memo to company leaders and to Anne. Had Anne been more like Cabot, she might have sensed and neutralized that memo, as Cabot had done when he burned Méndez's letter of complaint to the king. She was not as sensitive to internal disaffection as Cabot was, and Kevin and his colleagues executed their mutiny.

The individual who first formulates the idea (here, Kevin) might not lead the mutiny. Different members of a group will have different strengths. Moreover, the one who formulates the idea may not be the one to recognize the opportunity or execute the action. Multiple members must coordinate to achieve success; that is, team and structure are important. But ideas, opportunities, and execution also have important differences. Let us consider some aspects of those differences before addressing ringleaders and teams.

The first stage of a successful mutiny occurs when a small group of members in a larger organization recognizes an opportunity to undertake one. Just as an entrepreneurial venture aims to control a larger share of a market and gain influence, so, too, do mutineers aim to control a larger share of the organization as they gain influence. In both instances, one or more individuals usually recognize the opportunity by scanning the environment. The opportunity may be unclear and ill-defined at first. Indeed, the opportunity may be nothing more than the notion that "something is not right here." Some examples include an organizational inefficiency, a suboptimal time lag, counterproductive behavior on the part of a leader, or an uncoordinated department. These organizational flaws indicate potential opportunities to act. But again, an opportunity is not nearly enough. It is just one part of a successful mutiny's foundation. Another part of that foundation is the idea.

In a mutiny context, an idea can be an alternative way to carry out existing organizational processes, an instrument of practical value, or a new method for eliminating undesirable organizational elements. Such ideas usually come from the unique perspective of one or two members and emerge in personal and subjective ways. What makes an idea for mutiny good or bad is how well it offers a viable solution with respect to an opportunity for mutiny and the problem the mutiny intends to address. Ideas become actions, and those actions are more effective if the opportunity and the idea are distinct and complement one another.

Those who understand how an idea can be made real, as James did in Kevin's case, often end up as the ringleaders. However, they can yield that position to others. Ringleaders are often middle managers whose position and knowledge enable a deeper understanding of circumstances and often make them ideal coordinators or planners. Still, it is very important for all mutineers to share information, with guile if necessary, and reach a strong common perspective. The idea and the opportunity must not only be clear and distinct, they must reflect the shared values driving the mutiny.

If those two elements are not developed properly, then the execution will be difficult. Indeed, lack of clarity around the execution may be a sign that mutiny is a bad option. After all, as with risky ventures for Age of Discovery seafarers down to today's entrepreneurs, failure can be costly. Eventually the idea *and* the opportunity for mutiny should be embraced by all even if initially resisted. Only then should execution become the focus.

Mutiny's Execution

The set of members who recognize an opportunity and formulate an idea for mutiny is sometimes not large enough to undertake an effective one. The right team of members is necessary. It is important for this team to be cohesive even if the larger organization is not. The level of trust among mutineers must be absolute because discretion is a strategic weapon.

There is a potential internal threat here. If disagreements occur among mutineers, they can be of a particularly thorny nature. Disagreement in purpose is almost always a bad sign and can bring worse trouble than in other group settings; every possible effort to detect and address it must be made at the outset. The presence of shared values implies a cohesive team, but the diversity of tasks that a mutiny will require means that each member needs to make unique contributions. The mix of required tasks has team-building aspects, even though the team should remain lean. Not just anyone should be able to join the mutiny; a mutiny entails selection decisions. Having more members does not necessarily mean better chances of success, because larger teams tend to be less adaptable and cohesive than smaller ones. What begins as a private matter will eventually require public actions by several people if a mutiny is going to change an organization's reality. With a team of appropriate size and thoughtfully selected members, planning for those outcomes becomes far easier.

A ringleader not only supplies coordination but performs an important selection function. The position carries a level of authority. As in almost every case examined in this book, someone has to approach potential members. This activity is an art. It is risky too, as Lepe and Martín found out when Cabot seized them based on leaked information. But once the team and its leader are established, a mutiny needs a very rudimentary model for operations over time. The model should make sense in the context of the larger organizational environment.

Assigning the right tasks to the right individuals aids the effectiveness of the operational model. For instance, in the Hudson case, Juet communicated and coordinated the mutineers before and during the mutiny whereas Greene handled the rougher aspects of execution as they deposed Hudson and took control of the *Discovery*. Again, if the idea and the opportunity are not clear, the model will face threats from internal sources (e.g., member disagreements) and external sources (e.g., being discovered by the organization) because important actions will be less certain. Some level of formality is vital for a mutiny, as Kevin and his colleagues exemplified by gathering information for an official memo whose delivery to the firm's leaders James orchestrated. Finally, secrecy must be strictly maintained. As with many early-stage entrepreneurial projects, implementation and action are not advisable until the idea, the opportunity, the team, the strategy, and the operational model are all very sharp and clear. Before that juncture, mutiny is not worth the risk.

Indeed, as the epigraph to this chapter shows, the two ringleaders in one of the mutinies in the Cabot case made this serious mistake. They seem to have proceeded prematurely, swept away in the zeal of their purpose.

The earlier actions of forming a mutiny are the most difficult. The remaining actions, those that come after its execution, are also very important, however, and we will discuss them in the final chapter. We will also consider why those who undertake a mutiny must also take special care to remember one step that is vital but often forgotten: a smart exit strategy.

8

CHAPTER

A Force of Human Nature

In such a case, the mutiny would have been justified.

—Lawrence J. Burpee, on Hudson's situation in June 1611

In a landmark treatise on social science methodology, *The Poverty of Historicism,* Karl Popper asks, "If it is possible for astronomy to predict eclipses, why should it not be possible for sociology to predict revolutions?"[1] The question broaches issues of organizational dynamism that are too often ignored. Human nature does not lend itself to reliability (or predictability) over time in performance contexts, even though the purpose of organization is to create such reliability. This makes perfect sense. One of human nature's most reliable aspects is that people find new ways to do old things. What works in one setting is not likely to work in another setting. That does not mean that books like this one lack practical value. These pages contain practical insights concerning the constellation of elements that promote a mutiny. Knowing what people did in a mutiny is important, but what is far more important is to understand the logic driving the action. Mutiny is complex. For those who undertake to delineate its logic and make sense of it, defining it explicitly and examining it rigorously are necessary.

A mutiny is a more clearly defined event than, say, a revolution. As we have seen, a mutiny is comparable to a small and nimble entrepreneurial venture, which makes it a simpler construct than other sociological constructs describing transformational change. But it is still a dynamic construct that compounds human purposes. In fact, it is too dynamic to allow for prediction or reliable control. Copying the actions of others who have undertaken successful mutiny may not lead likewise to success. Like any purposeful individual, a would-be mutineer must determine the actions that suit a particular situation. What is most useful for people in business settings is to share concepts that can be tied to purposes and employ them as aids for making decisions and taking action. That is why the theories and frameworks in Part II offer practical value.

Every mutiny is unique. Like most organizational phenomena, each mutiny has an idiosyncratic set of empirical factors and causes. To copy the behavior of subjects in case studies—those in this book or elsewhere—would be a mistake. However similar the situations, they are still necessarily different, in particular ways, from other particular situations. However, what is important and very useful is to grasp the essence of the action and underlying principles of mutiny and then to adapt them to application in the context.

The leaders we know who have experienced a mutiny attest to how unnerving it can be and how difficult it is to respond appropriately. They see value in a conceptual approach that makes sense out of a novel and intense situation. For organization members, the trials of working under bad leadership in uncertain environments can become insufferable. We have met many individuals working under such conditions, some who have worked for years under a leader who deserves to be removed. Most of those individuals do not understand that they can depose bad leadership. Effective mutiny becomes possible using concepts in this book.

Some remaining questions are addressed in this chapter: what underpins mutiny in an organization, when to take action, and how to plan an exit strategy.

MUTINY'S ESSENTIAL STRUCTURES

Membership means that something is shared. Essentially what is shared are certain values related to membership, including cultural values, strategic objectives or purposes, perceptions of a common destiny, or aspects of identity. Shared values have been mentioned again and again in this book. In an organization they acquire a definite status and become a valuable, generally recognized element of organizational life. That is why affronts to shared values can and do turn into mutinies.

Maslow's hierarchy of needs is a well-known conceptual framework. It holds that we are motivated to satisfy needs in a certain order, from the basic needs of human existence to higher-level needs: needs related to physiology, safety, belonging, esteem, and self-actualization. It is hierarchical: once a person is satisfied in terms of one need, then the need immediately above it in the hierarchy becomes the key motivator.[2] This arrangement can shed light on the mutiny mechanism. In Part I, we saw how mutinies could be violent and deadly. They involved fights, arrests, murder, and executions. Each of those instances entailed a leadership decision or action that violated basic shared values of the membership in an uncertain environment. The result was a fleeting moment during which members, if coordinated and prepared, had an opportunity to depose authority.

Columbus's members wanted to return home for safety, but he kept urging them forward. Magellan's members also wanted to return home but had misgivings about his Portuguese background and were concerned about dwindling supplies. Cabot's members, concerned about his competence as a navigator, tried to mutiny when safety was threatened by his poor navigation on the Atlantic and among the dangers of the Río de La Plata. On Hudson's last enterprise, members finally mutinied with ferocity after his decision to continue a futile search with insufficient stores after a harrowing winter in the ice.

In each historical case, the shared values that the leader violated involved the basic needs of human existence; these physiological and safety needs are at the lower levels of Maslow's hierarchy. Leaders' decisions or actions that threatened survival created an affront. The mutinous action that came in response was basic because survival is a basic value. To quell such a basic reaction, leaders often reacted on the same basic level.

Mutiny in today's enterprises follows the same pattern. Leaders can and do make decisions that violate the shared values of members, but the shared values generally pertain to higher-level needs. Even though needs related to physiology and safety are still shared by members, those needs are not normally jeopardized in a direct way. But the values higher in Maslow's hierarchy, such as belonging and esteem, are certainly violated directly.

Members of organizations share a sense of community that comes from membership itself; they mutually value opportunities for achievement and growth, and they all want to be treated with dignity. Leaders are very often in positions to make decisions that violate these shared values. Usually the violation is unintentional. A decision that breaks up an affinity group, for instance, can arouse discontent and grumbling. Failing to offer individual respect and opportunities for personal growth in an uncertain environment can evoke a coordinated response that is designed to preserve and promote them.

Modern mutinies are not as violent as the historical ones because the shared values in question are represented at the upper levels of Maslow's hierarchy. Actions based on those values are more social and intellectual than physical. In today's enterprises, physical violence is no longer necessary to fight, depose a leader, or punish or remove a member. Words can do the job. Even so, parallels between past and present persist. Stress and anxiety, for example, are still quite intense in most mutinies because shared values reside as deeply within the human psyche as ever.

Maslow's model addresses individual human needs. Those do not represent the only shared values that are relevant here. Shared values are also associated with nations and homelands, as well as many other kinds of groups. We saw in all four historical cases that Columbus, Magellan, Cabot, and Hudson faced backlashes in part because they and their members hailed from a range of cultures. It is easy to violate a cultural value when one is a foreigner, and the violation opens the way for doubt about competence, a matter of distrust. Trust, which is different from distrust, can be very hard to earn when different cultural values are in play, and especially so when the environment is uncertain.

Organizational cultures function much like national cultures. Although they are not as deeply engrained, strong organizational cultures entail a clearly defined set of values that members share. People often enter organizations and take a leadership position when they are not yet acculturated. Their decisions may well violate those values or be seen as violating those values. The effect is enhanced in uncertain environments. In fact, as we have seen in the historical cases, sometimes malcontents even seek their own real or imagined reasons to mutiny.

Whatever the values being challenged, a mutiny requires an idea and an opportunity. Moreover, as we saw, a mutiny requires a clear sense of each. The opportunity is part of the external context in which the mutiny occurs, and the idea comes from those individuals who are undertaking the mutiny. This paradigm facilitates a strategic and tactical approach to the execution of the mutiny. One more element that is just as important as all these elements is timing.

TIMING

In a dynamic situation, one of the biggest questions is the best time to act. If a firm launches a revolutionary new product before a market is ready for it, then that firm will likely incur related costs until the market becomes receptive. Of course, the firm may even fail during that interim if the mistake is large enough. Premature action calls for internal adjustments that inflate costs. Similarly, if a firm launches a new project after the core idea has become irrelevant, low revenue or failure is a probable result. Timing is important. It is no different for mutinies.

Being able to identify the right moment to act is important in a mutiny. Undertaking a mutiny too early or too late is liable to lead to failure. In Kevin's case, for example, sending the mutiny memo too soon and in an undeveloped form would have been like launching a product before it was fully developed. Sending the memo before James could serve as a channel would have been like entering a market or serving customers incorrectly. In both cases, the memo would have had less of an effect. Had the mutineers waited too long, the leader they sought to depose might have detected their strategic posture and taken action to suppress the mutiny.

The historical cases provide several illustrations of the importance of timing. In Cabot's case, for instance, Méndez moved too soon when he sent his letter. In Hudson's final mutiny, Juet, Wilson, and Greene acted only when their shared values were apparent and the opportunity emerged. Yet their timing still was not perfect. There was friction among them as they executed their plan, and even more friction after Hudson was deposed. Where did that friction come from?

Shared values have a special relation to the concept of timing and can ensure smoother activities after a mutiny occurs. A mutiny develops as a natural process because shared values have the character of expectations. They imply a definite orientation and purpose with regard to action in future situations, including after a mutiny is executed. The mutiny that occurred on Hudson's second voyage, in 1608, provides an excellent illustration of a clear idea and a clear opportunity. The shared values were obvious, which clarified the idea and the opportunity. The mutineers knew the organization well thanks to Juet. Clarity around the idea and the opportunity facilitated the execution of mutiny at the right time because the mutineers had such a strong sense of the values they shared. Hudson, by contrast, was out of touch with the shared values driving the mutineers' action. Because he was out of touch with those shared values, a gap had emerged. Therefore, the mutiny was invisible to him until it was too late for him to do anything about it.

Amid confusion, the right timing for action in a mutiny becomes a guessing game. And that is when a mutiny is dangerous to everyone. Magellan understood this, which is why he first targeted Mendoza on the *Victoria* when quelling the mutiny in the Bay of Saint Julian. The *Victoria* had a lower level of shared values among the membership, which meant that the idea for mutiny was weakest on that ship. Not only do unclear ideas result in a guess about timing, but a mutiny based on unclear ideas will disintegrate fast if the prospect of success becomes uncertain. The Magellan mutiny disintegrated quickly when mutineers immediately switched allegiances back to Magellan.

No matter how strong the mutineers' sense of purpose, if the opportunity for mutiny is unclear, then the timing will be uncertain, and the mutiny is not liable to be effective. Leaders are usually able to quell badly timed and badly targeted mutinies. Understanding the internal organizational environment is important here, and the ringleader must have that understanding. As in most of the cases illustrated, the ringleader often has a higher position in the overall organization than the other members undertaking the mutiny. He or she understands aspects of the organization that other members do not. This understanding not only helps the mutineers recognize the right opportunity to act, but enables them to act effectively.

Ringleaders, then, are vital. Disgruntled organization members have good reason to find and recruit members with information about the organization, beyond just the ability to coordinate action or communicate well. Similarly, leaders of the larger organization have good reason to look to the same organization members when seeking to quell a mutiny. A mutiny without strong, informed leadership is liable to fail for the same reasons as any other risky enterprise.

Because events that occur in the aftermath of a mutiny can be damaging to the mutineers even if the mutiny is successful at deposing the leadership, it is important to anticipate the ramifications of the mutiny and plan carefully for them. A good exit strategy can bring a happy ending to the mutineers and to the larger organization. It describes a way for the mutineers and the organization both to realize a benefit. An exit strategy is not easy to formulate, however, and it hinges almost fully on smart execution of the mutiny itself. Mutineers, like entrepreneurs, often struggle with this particular aspect more than with any other aspect.

EXIT STRATEGY

The best way to begin formulating an exit strategy for a mutiny involves defining clearly which specific and formal parts of an organization the mutiny is intended to change and which parts it does not. Relying on existing rules as a basis of authority is a poor way for a leader to quell a mutiny. Why? Because those existing rules and circumstances are often liable to be a key part of what the mutiny intends to change. Using them as a quelling tactic can exacerbate the situation by reinforcing the shared values of the mutineers. From the perspective of the mutineers, the success of an exit strategy depends on changing existing rules or getting around them. For both sides to admit that the mutiny is outside the boundaries of existing regulations is a very important first step in terms of effectiveness and exit strategy. It also helps ensure that those rules will not be used to punish mutineers or harm the ringleader after the mutiny is over.

Backlash is likely if the mutiny does not invert the targeted authority structures. Today's cases provide almost no examples of good exit strategies; mutineers, even in successful mutinies, are usually penalized. Kevin's peers, for example, saw some damage to their careers in the aftermath of their mutiny. There is also often a cover-up.

The historic cases offer insights. The first mutiny on Columbus's voyage entailed an ad hoc deal between Columbus and crew: his promise to turn back if land was not sighted within three days. The arrangement was formal but not part of the formal authority structure. It assured an exit strategy that protected Columbus as well as the members. The mutiny on Hudson's second enterprise was similar. In today's firms, such a formal arrangement can turn into something unethical or illegal. But we are not dealing with formal organizational aspects when we deal with effective mutiny. Organizations do not make unprogrammed decisions: people make unprogrammed decisions, and a mutiny has everything to do with people and the informal aspects of organizations that they populate. Today's leaders can easily make ad hoc management decisions, unprogrammed but lawful, if members approach them as a cohesive entity the way Columbus's and Hudson's members approached them. In both of those cases, the idea was so well designed that it protected the leaders and the mutineers.

The initial exit strategy for the mutiny on Cabot's enterprise was the leadership succession plan supplied by the Spanish crown in case Cabot was lost. It was a formal organizational instrument that was never enacted. Rather, the mutineers coopted it. No change in this part of the formal rules was needed for the mutiny because the succession plan could actually serve the mutiny's purpose. Though designed to sustain the enterprise, it could be leveraged as a threat to Cabot. Rarely does a formal rule or process play such a role. Mutineers would do well to recognize such possibilities, as they did in that case.

An exit strategy is a kind of plan, after all. It requires beginning with the end in mind; it is formulated at the outset, during a mutiny's planning stages. Thinking about a successful exit will make other aspects of the plan more feasible and illuminate which ones are misguided. An exit strategy is a sort of insurance for mutineers with regard to repercussions. Failed mutinies are risky affairs, but even a successful one can also be risky for other reasons. The intent is to benefit the whole organization, but a mutiny, like leadership, can inadvertently champion what it would destroy. A mutiny should protect the leader being deposed. A truly great exit strategy extends formal operations in such a way that it protects all members from the rules that govern those formal operations.

CONCLUSION

Throughout history, controlled power may have generated some of humankind's darkest horrors, but it has also generated many of its best achievements. Organizations are the social tools that enable these feats. As organizational scholars, we are incurable optimists when it comes to the goodness of people, the promise of enterprise, and the discipline of management. Still, the industrial organizational paradigm has profound flaws that deserve critical attention in a constructive spirit. One of these flaws is the lack of voice given to organization members when bad leadership outruns its own purpose. Another flaw concerns its deficient capacity to function well internally in dynamic and uncertain environments. For organizational leadership to be openly and vigorously challenged is important not only to innovation and adaptivity but also to the well-being of all people.

As this chapter's epigraph indicates, even the best leadership has limits. Hudson, as we read in chapter 4, was driven by an obsessive desire to discover a northwest passage. Members did not share the values that justified pursuing such a desire, and, moreover, the uncertain environment made it impossible. When such gaps emerge between leaders and members in an organization along these lines, grievances cannot be adequately addressed. At that point, when there are such gaps between leaders and members, mutiny and leadership begin to overlap. If the force of mutiny is crushed, then the vital spirit of continuous improvement can be lost. At such times, as history shows us, organizations can easily take a grave turn. In today's enterprises the outcomes include member unhappiness, loss of jobs, loss of savings, and worse.[3] The ability of all members in any organization to act in coordinated ways to depose leadership is vital to the spirit of improvement. That is why mutiny is fundamentally entrepreneurial. Critical and vigorous attention to broadening our understanding of how it can be embedded in the logic of adaptive organizations will be valuable to future generations.

Those generations will read about our enterprises in their works of history. They will be shocked and fascinated, as we have been by the enterprises that came before us. And they will be able to improve their own future by studying the past, just as we can. What we have learned from the Age of Discovery is that mutiny can serve a functional role if it is executed well. This provocative notion deserves attention and examination. Mutiny today occurs in many innovative firms that take entrepreneurial risks. Asking new questions about mutiny can help the business world redefine (and refine) what values and structures to cultivate in organizational life and what qualities make a great leader. Turning loose the force of human nature even in forms that look a lot like mutinies can generate unimagined positive effects in the enterprises of the future.

NOTES

1. An exception to our definition is found in the United States Uniform Code of Military Justice (Article 94) as it pertains to "mutiny or sedition." The definition repeatedly specifies action "in concert with any other person" but admits the possibility of charging an individual person with mutiny.

2. Measurement and recording were common activities on ships during the Age of Discovery. The term "logbook" itself emerged directly from the strong tradition of physical measurement. In the Age of Discovery sailors used a log tied to a knotted line to measure rate of speed. An earlier method involved throwing an object overboard and using a sandglass to measure the time the object took to travel between two fixed points on the ship itself. The later method involved dropping the log overboard while a ship was under way, paying out the line for a set time interval, and counting the equidistant knots. The knots were spaced approximately 42–48 feet (13–15 m) apart. The space between them (or between the fixed points on the ship itself) was in proportion to a league, a unit of distance that varied from culture to culture. As charts and maps improved over time, the spacing between the knots was integrated with the nautical mile, which is a distance of one minute of latitude at the equator (6,076 feet; 1,852 m). The collected data were recorded in the ship's "logbook"; and "knots" became the unit for measuring speed on the water. These seafaring inventions, like most other significant ones in general use, derive originally from Portugal.

3. Hudson's Dutch East India Company contract is reprinted verbatim in Murphy (pp. 34–36).

4. The Tropic of Capricorn is the earth's southernmost point at which the sun is directly overhead at its zenith.

5. See Gardner and Rowan.

6. The most authoritative reference for research on substitutes for leadership that defines leadership in terms of important contextual factors is Kerr and Jermier.

PART I. ROPE AND KNIFE

1. Eden's 1553 poem is translated here into modern English. The original can be found in Eden (p. 42). Its first, untranslated verse appears here in the epigraph.

CHAPTER 1. COLUMBUS

1. Castilian historical development during this period, along with its evolution into the country of Spain, is chronicled expertly in Chapman (pp. 111–124), the primary source for this summary background. Castile's de jure union with Aragon unfolded over the course of two hundred years. It was not de facto until much later, with the Nueva Planta decrees of 1707 under King Philip V, Spain's first Bourbon ruler. As many of the events discussed in this book occurred during the years that Castile and Aragon developed into Spain, we sometimes use Castile and Spain interchangeably.

2. Here a minor qualification is in order. Philip II united Castile and Portugal in 1580 after the death of Portugal's Sebastien I and then controlled the union. However, Portugal remained essentially unchanged under an agreement preventing it from becoming Castilian property. This personal union lasted sixty years, until the Portuguese Revolution and Restoration War in 1640, which led to the Treaty of Lisbon in 1668 (ratified with England's influence) and Portugal's return to sovereignty.

3. The alliance that Portugal's King Ferdinand and Queen Eleanor formed with England's King Edward III in 1373 is the longest-running international alliance and is preserved in the world's oldest active treaty. Originally intended to promote mutual support, it was reinforced with the Treaty of Windsor in 1386, when Portugal's new King John I married England's Philippa of Lancaster. It was rendered largely meaningless during the sixty-year Iberian Union (1580–1640) but had been reaffirmed several times before the union and was reaffirmed after the union once Portugal reclaimed its sovereignty.

4. Many regarded the Mediterranean Sea as the center of the world in the fourteenth and fifteenth centuries, as its name suggests. The Romans had called it Mare Nostrum ("our sea"), a term that resurfaced several times in Italian history. In the early Age of Discovery, the much rougher "ocean sea"—the Atlantic—was being explored by Europeans but was still mostly uncharted.

5. In 1415 in the Battle of Ceuta, a Portuguese army conquered the Muslim stronghold just across the Strait of Gibraltar. Spain ended the Portuguese occupation in 1580 with the Iberian Union. Ceuta thus became increasingly cul-

turally Spanish despite its Portuguese foundations, which are still recognizable today.

6. It stands to reason that Magellan and Columbus both took Portuguese maps and information with them to Spain as they sought to win financing for ventures, although there is no direct evidence that they had such material in hand. The Planisphere is named for Alberto Cantino (see chapter 3, note 8).

7. Oviedo, a contemporary historian of the period, wrote that the achievement of Magellan's enterprise "is the most wonderful thing and greatest novelty that has ever been seen from the time God created the first man and ordered the world unto our own day. Neither has anything more notable in navigation ever been heard or described since the voyage of the patriarch Noah." That passage is quoted in Guillemard (p. 310). Oviedo's praise echoes that of Maximilianus Transylvanus, secretary for Charles V, who similarly began his famous 1523 account based on interviews with Magellan's crew. A translation of the latter in its entirety appears in Stanley (pp. 179–210).

8. Each of the four cities still exists today, although Palos is no longer an active port. We measured estimates of distance in this book directly using Global Positioning System (GPS) data accessed via Google Earth. In fact, many of the specific places we describe, even small islands and rock formations that the seafarers charted or mentioned, can be found and viewed using Google Earth.

9. Certain optical phenomena at sea had effects on early seafarers that are hard to appreciate today. Seafarers would swear that they had witnessed the supernatural. The illusions take many forms, such as "towering and stooping" and "looming and sinking." Other phenomena were known as fata morgana and fata bromosa. Their effects are powerful. A fata morgana, for instance, occurs when temperature differences refract and actually bend visible light. The effect is transient and causes viewers to see distant objects actually below the horizon appear and disappear suddenly. Depending on the thermal composition of the air over a long distance, such physical objects as land, clouds, mountains, and ships can be replicated on top of one another vertically, appear inverted, or be distorted horizontally to the extent that they are unrecognizable. These illusions are understood by meteorologists today, but they were not well understood during the Age of Discovery, and could be frightening and mysterious to seafarers.

Another phenomenon was the glowing electricity of Saint Elmo's fire at the tops of masts. Saint Elmo's fire is a discharge of static electricity that tends to appear near the end of storms, which led seafarers to interpret it as a sign that divine providence was delivering them to safety. Anthony Pigafetta reports that Magellan's members called the effect "the body of Saint Anselme"; see Stanley (p. 42). However, Pigafetta wrote in Italian, and "Elmo" was probably mistranslated as Anselme. Saint Anselme was archbishop of Canterbury in the late eleventh century. "Elmo" is actually an Italian version of "Erasmus." In fact, Saint Elmo's fire was not named for Saint Anselme of Canterbury but for Saint Erasmus of Formiae, who came from the Balkan Peninsula and was persecuted by the Roman emperors Diocletian and Maximilian in the late second century.

Strange optical phenomena were more common for English and Dutch seafarers to see because the phenomena occur more frequently near the earth's poles. They account for the belief in such phantom lands as Hy-Brasil (which Columbus and John Cabot saw marked on charts) and Willoughby's Island. The legend of the ghost ship the *Flying Dutchman* was based on seeing distant (refracted) ships appear and disappear, loom up in the air, and sail and even fly upside down. If a sighting occurred at night, with the sighted ship in the distance below the horizon where it was daylight, the ship would have glowed. Such phenomena and their lore inspired Samuel Taylor Coleridge's *Rime of the Ancient Mariner* (1797).

10. See Adams (pp. 34–73) for a lively and rich accounting, based on original correspondences and records, of Columbus's persistent attempts to procure support for his enterprise from Portugal, England, France, and Spain.

11. Dias's discovery was a significant culmination of two centuries of Portuguese exploration of the African coast. After rounding the southern point of Africa, a mutiny compelled him to return home. Dias had called the region where he turned back the Cape of Storms (Cabo dos Tormentas) because of its violent local seas. But his return generated such high spirits in Portugal that King John II changed its name to Cape of Good Hope (Cabo da Boa Esperança). The cape is technically not the southernmost point of Africa, but it is a distinctive headland on the southern coast.

12. The bureaucratic delays were largely attributable to Juan Rodriguez de Fonseca (1451–1524), chaplain to Queen Isabella. We shall learn more about Fonseca in subsequent chapters.

13. Columbus's original copy of Marco Polo's writings is housed in the Columbian Museum in Seville, Spain.

14. The two quotations are reproduced in Adams (p. 78).

15. The mariner's astrolabe was Portugal's synthesis of the slide rule and the quadrant, both of which had long been used by seafarers to chart the heavens

and navigate ships. The astrolabe was developed in the early to mid 1400s as the Portuguese charted the coast of Africa. This innovation was one of the distinct advantages from the time of Henry the Navigator that put Portugal far ahead of the rest of the world in seafaring. Like other valuable Portuguese knowledge and innovations, the astrolabe was jealously guarded but was eventually adopted elsewhere.

16. *Volta do mar* means "turn of the sea" or "circle of the sea" and refers to enormous wind patterns on the open ocean, clockwise in the northern hemisphere and counterclockwise in the southern hemisphere. For seafarers in the Age of Discovery, these wind patterns necessitated navigational headings that could be highly counterintuitive depending on one's position and intended destination.

17. The first enterprise of Columbus was marked by at least two mutinies. Various historic sources report that Magellan's entire circumnavigation involved four or five mutinies. Mutinies were so normal in the Age of Discovery that they did not always result in punishments, especially on successful enterprises. The Portuguese explorer Vasco de Gama, for instance, suppressed a fierce mutiny in 1497 as he extended Dias's 1488 voyage and passed the violent seas off the Cape of Good Hope to reach the Indian Ocean, making him the first to sail directly there from Europe. Many other seafarers in the Age of Discovery (e.g., Balboa, Cabral, Côrte-Real, Drake, Frobisher, Hawkins, Loaysa, Méndez, Pinzón, Solís) faced multiple documented mutinies.

18. These data and other quotations attributed here to Columbus are based on the original record and appear in many places. We drew mostly from C. Markham's 1893 publication of Columbus's original journal and other documents.

19. In the Age of Discovery, caravels usually had triangular lateen (Latin-rig) sails because they enhanced maneuverability. The older-style square sails on the *Pinta* were less useful for tacking into the wind. However, at this point in history, ships sailing from Spain often changed from lateen to square sails in the Canary Islands before entering the wide open ocean to enable faster running with the wind.

20. Although the Pinzóns commanded these two ships, each also had a couple of members aboard who were either partial owners or members of the families that owned the ships. The *Niña* was named after its owners, the Niño family.

21. That is, they covered 21.5 leagues. The league represented the distance a person generally covered on foot in one hour. It varied by region owing to

differences in terrain, just as there are different distances for a mile depending on context (geographical, nautical, maritime) or technology (data, telegraph, radar). A league usually corresponded to about 3.2 nautical miles (3.68 standard miles; 6 km). In Portugal, there were several different versions of the league (*légua*). The 21.5 leagues that Columbus recorded here equaled about 68.8 of the miles (111 km) used by the Portuguese and the Spanish. Different versions of the mile existed, too, and Columbus almost always used the Italian mile, which was a third shorter than a Spanish mile. With advances in navigation, Spain abolished the league in 1568, but a version of the league corresponding to approximately 4 miles (6.44 km) is sometimes still used in Brazil.

22. This date has been reported as October 11 because of the early hour. The moon had crossed its zenith on October 5 and was in its third quarter on October 12. This date and time puts the moon behind the three ships about 39 degrees above the western horizon at the time of the sighting. According to the logs, the sky was clear and the moon shone on the sandy coast brightly as they approached it. A reward (a silken jacket and ten thousand *maravedis*) had been promised to the first person to sight land. In spite of Triana's well-documented claim, perhaps unsurprisingly, Columbus's own record shows him as having already sighted land from the *Santa Maria* at ten the previous evening, which indeed would have been October 11. Columbus writes that Pero Gutierrez of the king's court and Rodrigo Sanchez of Segovia witnessed his initial sighting of "a light" at that time, securing the sovereign's reward for himself. Columbus was lucky indeed, for as Beazley (p. 47) notes, had the course not been interrupted by islands (they did not reach the continent on this first enterprise), it would have taken longer than three days to sight land, and the mutiny would have deposed his leadership.

23. Some accounts hold this number to be thirty-nine, but the official list of those left behind with the wreck of the *Santa Maria* contains forty-four names, part of the required notice for next of kin to apply for wages due. See C. Markham (*Journal*, pp. 144–145).

24. On January 8, 1493, Columbus recorded that he "saw three mermaids, which rose well out of the sea; but they are not so beautiful as they are painted, though to some extent they have the form of a human face." It is almost certain that Columbus saw manatees, which still exist in the region. Manatees can and do orient themselves vertically and rise out of the water with outstretched pectoral fins, which look somewhat more like limbs than typical fins, and they can turn their heads to look side to side. These unusual mammals were rarely seen,

and given the extant stories about mermaids, made a powerful impression. Columbus also wrote that he saw "mermaids" near Guinea earlier when he was sailing for Portugal; they would not have been manatees but a very similar marine mammal called the dugong. See C. Markham (*Journal*, p. 154 n. 1).

25. This new dividing line was a factor in Magellan's decision to sail for Spain as he sought his own passage to the eastern world. The treaty led to problems, such as when Pedro Álvares Cabral claimed Brazil for Portugal in 1500. Cabral had superior charts, which showed the true extent of the eastern bulge of the South American continent across the meridian. Brazil remained disputed territory until Spain and Portugal's first Treaty of San Ildefonso in 1777. By then, Portugal's influence had expanded west across the dividing line and into the South American continent. Portugal probably knew more about the true location and dimensions of this territory than they revealed as they negotiated with Spain and the pope over the location of the meridian. The issue came up again at the Council of Badajos in April 1524, attended by Columbus's son Fernando, Juan Sebastián Elcano (sometimes written as "del Cano," whom we shall read about in chapter 2), and by Sebastian Cabot (whom we shall read about in chapter 3).

CHAPTER 2. MAGELLAN

1. The Portuguese court featured many long-running and complex intrigues. They were highly fashionable, to be sure, but they were also a natural response to the need to keep priceless secrets safe from outsiders while dealing with the many cunning seafarers seeking financing and distinction. For example, support for Vasco da Gama's voyage to India in 1498 and Pedro Álvares Cabral's voyage to Brazil in 1500 was accompanied by intense intrigues. These two Portuguese seafarers even had their own coalitions of clever lobbyists. The king hated their jealous feuding and expelled anyone who discussed it. Like Magellan (but unlike Gama), Cabral earned King Manuel's disfavor, but for reasons that are unclear. To express his displeasure, the king replaced Cabral as leader of a locally famed voyage to India just three days before its departure in 1502, putting Gama in charge instead. The purpose of the monstrous twenty-ship "revenge fleet" was to assault Calicut in response to the uprising of Indians and Arabs two years earlier that resulted in the deaths of about fifty Portuguese in a spice warehouse. This historic Portuguese event foreshadowed but pales in comparison to the "Indian Mutiny" (which was actually not a mutiny) and the retaliation by a British "army of retribution" about 360 years later.

2. Magellan's move to Spain earned him Portugal's lasting ill will. *The Lusiads* (*Os Lusíadas*), a celebrated 1572 epic poem by Luís Vaz de Camões that glorifies the achievements of Portuguese seafaring, hardly even mentions him. Magellan is mentioned in the second canto merely as "an injured Lusian," a reference to his knee injury incurred in Morocco, and is cited briefly in its tenth (and final) canto, where he is described as "in all but loyalty, of Lusian soul." The term "Lusian" derives from the popular belief that the Portuguese were children of the Roman god Lusus (a partner or son of the Roman god Bacchus) and occupants of the ancient Roman province Lusitania (established circa 25 BCE). Studies of the early history, such as Stephens's *Story of Nations,* show that the Lusitanians in fact had Celtic origins and resisted Roman expansion. The Portuguese were never Lusitanians, but the Roman provincial area of Lusitania did include most of the region that Portugal eventually occupied.

3. Columbus and Magellan both benefited from well-placed marriages.

4. Magellan's estimates were surprisingly accurate. Ober (*Cabot,* pp. 141–142) draws from Pigafetta's account of Magellan in the Bay of Saint Julian, in which he describes that position as "twelve or thirteen degrees nearer the Antarctic pole than lies the Cape of Good Hope." We checked such estimates by Magellan by converting the distances to miles and cross-referencing them with GPS data. In this case, we used the formula rad = $x^*(\pi/180)$ to express "twelve or thirteen degrees" as 0.218 radians. An oblate spheroid like the earth has 2π (i.e., 6.283) radians. The formula shows that the distance Magellan estimated at the Bay of Saint Julian is 3.47 percent of the earth's north-south circumference of 24,860 miles (40,008 km), which is about 862.7 miles (1,388 km). Magellan did not know the circumference of the earth, of course, and radians were not understood until the eighteenth century, but this method proves that his estimates were not far off. Our calculations also show that the strait he discovered just over 200 miles (321.9 km) south of the Bay of Saint Julian is indeed about 1,000 miles (1,609 km) farther south than the Cape of Good Hope, which is amazingly consistent with estimates he made at this point, before his enterprise departed Seville. As described in note 8 of chapter 1, we checked estimates by observing distances directly using current GPS data in Google Earth.

5. Though familiar to Portuguese cartographers, the portable globe must have made a very strong impression on Charles V and his Spanish ministers. Unlike a two-dimensional map, a three-dimensional model of the earth reinforced the idea of a strait offering a western passage to the East with a continuous tracing of the course and no doubling back.

6. The document reads: "para buscar el estrecho de aquellas mares." Historians have noted that the rare use of the definite article "el" (the) in such an authorization implies a strong expectation concerning the existence of the strait.

7. King Charles V was born on February 24, 1500, making him eighteen at the time.

8. One problem in his dealings with Portugal was personal. A Portuguese friend of Magellan's named Ruy Faleiro, who came to Spain with him and facilitated his presentation to the court, began to create an unfavorable impression in Seville. Faleiro was brilliant and probably a genius, but many thought he had bizarre manners and was of unsound mind. Fellow Portuguese like Costa described him as "half-crazy" in letters to Manuel I. Once in Spain, Magellan and Faleiro acquired lasting and tarnished reputations in Portugal. Guillemard (p. 83) quotes Damião António de Lemos Faria e Castro, an eighteenth-century Portuguese historian, who wrote, "The two monsters Magellan and Faleiro, traitors to the King whom it was their duty to serve, barbarians towards the country for which it was their duty to die, conspired to bring about a fatal war between the two neighbouring and friendly powers." Faleiro was supposed to join Magellan's enterprise, but he did not. Some historians reason that he faked madness because his astrological chart predicted disastrous outcomes. Others describe him as jealous. What actually happened is that a letter from Charles V on July 26, 1519, removed Faleiro from Magellan's enterprise by royal order even after the original mandate had been dispatched and even though Faleiro had long been active in the preparations at Seville. The record suggests that Faleiro had gone insane or become afflicted in some way. He returned to Portugal, only to be imprisoned, but then seems to have returned to Seville, where he died in 1523.

9. The Portuguese attempt to thwart Magellan did not stop at the funding decision. The maneuverings were quite sophisticated. Costa connected with another Portuguese navigator in Castile, Esteban Gómez, as an agent of the Portuguese king. Gómez was against Magellan because he himself had applied to Charles V's court with a plan for a similar but less ambitious enterprise. His project was considered, but his strategy was less developed, and Magellan won the award. An experienced sailor, as we shall see, Gómez became a pivotal member of Magellan's fleet less than one year later. Portuguese spies also interfered with provisioning before the fleet departed from Seville. And on one occasion, Portuguese flags were surreptitiously placed on Magellan's flagship to excite and offend the local Castilian populace.

10. During the Age of Discovery, "rope and knife" meant that a captain had

the authority to hang or cut the throat of any member who stood against him. The risk of death for an individual challenging the captain is why coordination among multiple members was necessary for an effective mutiny.

11. Guillemard (p. 136) quotes the letter that Charles V wrote from Barcelona on June 17, 1519, ordering repeatedly that no more than five Portuguese members be allowed to join the crew. Earlier, in a July 5 letter to Ruy Faleiro, who asked to bring his brother along, Charles V had agreed but had made the stipulation that Faleiro's brother be counted in the quota of five Portuguese. The king emphasized the condition again in the letter of July 26 (cited in note 8, above), which removed Faleiro from the enterprise. Despite all such orders, the records suggest that at least thirty-seven Portuguese joined Magellan, along with men of many different nationalities.

12. Dias, who rounded Africa in 1488, sailed with Cabral on this 1500 voyage but died when his ship was wrecked off the Cape of Good Hope. Vicente Yañez Pinzón (of Columbus's voyage) claimed to have discovered Brazil on January 26, 1500. Yet the Treaty of Tordesillas gave the territory to Portugal. As we suggest in chapter 1, note 25, the Portuguese knew just how far the South American continent extended to the east and how close it came to Africa. They pushed for the meridian to be moved west so they would have space to explore the African coastline. A westward move would also balance how far the meridian shifted on the other side of the world, where the Spice Islands were located. Portuguese seafarers had almost certainly sighted and charted Brazil before Pinzón and kept this information secret until after the treaty was signed, when it was safe for Cabral to make a more lawful Portuguese discovery of the territory.

13. The *San Antonio* was the only caravel in Magellan's fleet. The other four ships were carracks. This form of carrack, which the Portuguese called a *não*, was sturdier and more maneuverable than Columbus's carrack, the *Santa Maria*, which he sailed almost thirty years earlier.

14. Besides Columbus and Magellan, many foreign explorers sailed for Castile, including Amerigo Vespucci (1454–1512). He once experienced a peculiar mutiny in which Portuguese crew members removed their Portuguese captain and put him, an Italian, in command. Sebastian Cabot, another Italian, is the subject of the next chapter.

15. See Stanley (p. 37).

16. Many seafarers before and after Magellan had turned around and headed for home or found an excuse not to go any farther south by the time they reached the region where Argentina now exists. The large river at that juncture, which

Juan Díaz de Solís entered in 1515 and we shall see Sebastian Cabot enter in the next chapter, was not yet known as the Río de La Plata. At this point in the case, Magellan's enterprise is already about 900 miles (1,448 km) south of that river.

17. See Navarrette (pp. 56–57).

18. During the Age of Discovery, the value of Asian spices to Western empires was comparable to that of gold or oil to industrialized nations in the nineteenth and twentieth centuries. Spices not only served as a culinary luxury that enjoyed enormous markets where the food could be rather bland but also cloaked the foul taste and stench of meats that had spoiled in the heat or during long transits.

19. Cartagena was the illegitimate son of Juan Rodriguez de Fonseca. Coca was the illegitimate son of Fonseca's brother. In those days, such relations were usually open secrets referred to in terms of "uncle" and "nephew." Cartagena and Coca were thus "cousins" who had powerful "uncles." As well-placed Castilians, the two men were strong antagonists of Magellan. In such oblique ways, Fonseca was a pernicious presence in the careers of Columbus, Magellan, and even Sebastian Cabot. Whether or not Magellan made management decisions based on the subtext is speculative, but the notion aligns with Coca's replacement by Mesquita, who was Magellan's actual cousin.

20. Even extreme violence was not uncommon in the sixteenth century. Roman law still had a strong influence on European society, and the European legal system, including trials, was rather barbaric by today's standards. Moreover, not unlike today, risky maritime enterprises often had greater need for strong leadership and discipline than ordinary terrestrial society did.

21. See Guillemard (p. 172).

22. Several of these primary sources also diverge on certain facts. For instance, a couple of them incorrectly cite the *Concepción* (not the *San Antonio*) as being under Quesada's command and making a desperate break for the ocean. Quesada had *formerly* commanded the *Concepción*, but he had moved to the *San Antonio* during the mutiny on April 1–2, 1520. Some accounts also incorrectly report Cartagena, not Quesada, as being executed in the bay. The best primary sources are in the General Archives of the Indies in Seville. They include records of examinations of witnesses and accounts of survivors of the circumnavigation recorded on October 18, 1522. A letter from the Contador Recalde to the bishop of Burgos reporting evidence from the *San Antonio* also offers some valid information but is probably unreliable given the circumstances of its desertion from the armada, as we shall see.

23. See Stanley (p. 249).

24. It took Magellan almost two days to quell the mutiny. The day before, when he watched the skiff with the watering party return from the *San Antonio*, he had told members of the *Trinidad* that he would crush any hint of mutiny before sundown of that day.

25. Lorriaga did not die immediately. He succumbed to his injuries on July 15, after the mutiny but before the armada departed from the Bay of Saint Julian.

26. As we shall see, Sir Francis Drake found the two gibbets and the skeletons of Mendoza and Quesada fifty-eight years later (on June 20, 1578).

27. By this point in the Age of Discovery, marooning was gaining in popularity as a lenient sentence, but it did not always work out well. When Sebastian Cabot marooned several mutinous Spaniards on Santa Catalina Island, two of them were picked up by Portuguese ships and made it back to Spain before Cabot. As we shall see in the next chapter, when Cabot returned, those members' families had built a coalition and convinced the court to charge him. Marooning created other problems, too. By the late seventeenth century, many marooned sailors had become pirates. This trend was pronounced with the rise of English seafaring in the Caribbean.

28. Coca, former commander of the *San Antonio*, was linked by blood to Cartagena and a participant in the mutiny. However, there is no record of his being punished. There are no detailed records of what happened during the three days of trials (April 3–6, 1520), but if a decision was made not to punish Coca, it would have been made at that juncture.

29. Translated from Barros and reprinted in Stanley (pp. 177–178).

30. Andrés de San Martín's original journals from Magellan's enterprise were Barros's primary source for his publication of Magellan's order in 1777, which was in turn translated into English and published by the Hakluyt Society in 1874; see Stanley.

31. In the Age of Discovery, cartographers synthesized information not only from seafarers' reports but also from astronomy, folklore, and mysticism, among other disparate sources. The globes that Magellan described were highly prized by Manuel I and constituted a step toward objectivity. The specific one he referred to was created in Nuremberg by either Martin Behaim (Martin of Bohemia) around 1490–1492 or by his countryman Joseph Schöner in 1515 or 1520.

Behaim, who received patronage for his craftsmanship from Portugal's King John II, created at least two famous globes. Globes had a powerful effect on thinkers of the age. Behaim's first globe was called *Erdapfel* (German for "earth apple"). It is regarded as the first three-dimensional scale model of the world. It is possible that this kind of model was known quite early in Portugal, in the mid-1400s. The travels of Henry the Navigator's eldest son to Rome and Venice in the 1420s were rumored to have yielded a map that deepened Behaim's thinking years later. The map depicted a very long, curved "dragon's tail" with a passage through it at the tip. The dragon's tail was what would come to be known as the South American continent. Combining that smooth arcing projection with assumptions of a spherical earth would have required only a small intellectual leap for a talented cartographer to infer a passage through it. Much was still unknown, however. North and South America are absent from Behaim's models, which were based on Marco Polo's accounts, Ptolemaic geography, and mysticism. Behaim's globes reflect Columbus's concurrent understanding of the earth, although there is no evidence that Columbus saw them. The two globes influenced Schöner, whose subsequent and improved globe-making even influenced Nicolaus Copernicus, who published his revolutionary heliocentric theory in 1543.

Magellan may have seen one of Behaim's globes in Portugal when he was still a young page in Queen Eleanor's court under John II. He certainly would have known of the *Erdapfel*. The genius of Schöner's globes, by contrast, was what influenced the mature Magellan. These globes benefited from inferences based on an astronomical tracing of the course of the planet Mercury, Columbus's discoveries in 1492, and the cartography of another German, named Martin Waldseemüller (an acquaintance of Copernicus's and also Schöner's teacher). Schöner owned a map by Waldseemüller that did show the South American continent. This famous map, the *Universalis Cosmographia*, completed in 1507, was the first map to show the name "America." Amerigo Vespucci's ventures to this region for Portugal's Manuel I in 1499–1502 influenced the choice of name. An improved Ptolemaic map with latitude and even longitude lines, the mapmaker obviously drew inspiration from the Cantino Planisphere, which had been smuggled to Italy from Portugal and predated it by only five to seven years. Waldseemüller was the first to cut these two-dimensional maps into gores, which enabled them to be pasted onto three-dimensional globes by protégés like Schöner. Magellan, along with his astronomer friend Faleiro, likely appreciated the globes deeply. Both Behaim and Schöner, despite their radical ingeniousness in creating the globes, drastically underestimated the world's size, just as Columbus and Magellan underestimated the distances across the Atlantic and Pacific oceans, respectively.

Contrary to several historical accounts, Westerners generally regarded the earth as round (not flat) even before Henry the Navigator sailed in the early to mid 1400s. The original notion stemmed from classical Greece during a pre-Socratic period of enlightenment in the sixth–fifth centuries BCE. Thales thought of the earth as a ship floating on the sea, a model formulated in part to explain earthquakes. Anaximander built on Thales' view with a model of the earth as a disconnected floating drum held stationary by being equally distant from all things. These first bold models, both posited by men from the Ionian colony of Miletus, were basic to Western thought. Parmenides, who was from a Greek colonial city-state in the south of Italy called Elea, eventually refuted Anaximander's model. He conceptualized the earth as a sphere in the fifth century BCE in his only written work that still exists, *On Nature*. In verse he describes the intense love of the moon (Selene) for the sun (Helios) as reflected in Selene's gaze, which faithfully turns toward Helios as they spin around each other and around the earth. His model influenced Xenophanes, Plato, and even Isaac Newton many centuries later. So, by the Age of Discovery, this idea of a spherical earth was well established.

It was one thing to discuss and embrace the idea of a spherical earth. It was another thing altogether to act on the idea. Behaim's and Schöner's globes were truly revolutionary. No one had put the idea of a spherical earth into a practical model in coordination with existing knowledge of navigation and astronomy. No one had ever before depicted the world on a physical scale with practical implications for circumnavigating the earth. The implications were profound.

32. Had Coca been on the *San Antonio* at this juncture, conspiring with Gómez would have been even more natural. It is not recorded when Coca was moved off the *San Antonio*, but it is known that he crossed the Pacific with the *Trinidad,* the *Victoria,* and the *Concepción* and died in the Ladrone Islands (today's Mariana Islands).

33. See Stanley (p. 61).

34. The historical record does not specify exactly when the *San Antonio* deserted Magellan's armada in the strait. Several accounts note a council in which Gómez spoke against Magellan but offer conflicting dates. Magellan's order of the day in which he called the council is dated November 21, but it does not mention the *San Antonio.* If Gómez led a mutiny and deserted shortly after Magellan's communiqué, then it would explain why Magellan did not mention the incident.

35. A second native prisoner was on the *Trinidad,* and he died one month

later, just as the fleet entered the Pacific Ocean. For a brief account of the *San Antonio* after it deserted and after its arrival in Seville, see Guillemard (pp. 214–217).

36. Gómez may have discovered what became known as the Falkland Islands after entering the Atlantic. Before the *San Antonio* exited the strait, it probably had some close calls and was almost spotted by the other ships in the complex channels as the *Trinidad, Victoria,* and *Concepción* retraced their courses and waited for four–six days. Once it had arrived back in Seville, sixteen months before the *Victoria* completed the circumnavigation, Gómez and Guerra had crafted a strong statement of justification that tarnished Magellan's reputation, which was filed on May 22, 1521. Magellan's father-in-law, Diogo Barbosa, worked in his defense, but the statement landed Mesquita in prison as Magellan's accomplice. Spain also put Gómez and Guerra and Magellan's wife (Beatriz) under observation. Beatriz died in March 1522, before the *Victoria* returned. Magellan and Beatriz's son died in September 1521, during Magellan's circumnavigation. Moreover, Beatriz was pregnant when Magellan departed, and that child was eventually stillborn. Beatriz's brother Duarte, with Magellan on the enterprise, died after Magellan during the circumnavigation. Diogo Barbosa died in 1525. The facts slowly came to light after the *Victoria* returned, but Magellan's reputation was never fully restored.

37. As of 2012, there was only one native speaker of the Yaghan language still living, named Cristina Calderón.

38. For more on the "dragon's tail," see note 31.

39. Two years earlier, Elcano had been one of the mutineers in the Bay of Saint Julian. By a twist of fate, he ended up on the *Victoria* and commanded it on its journey back to Seville. Although he was very generously treated for completing the first circumnavigation, over time his fame diminished as the facts emerged and the record of the case circulated. Four years later, in 1526, Elcano led another venture for Spain with Garcia de Loaysa. It began with 450 crew members on seven ships and finished with only nine members and no ships. Loaysa died of scurvy on July 30, 1526, while crossing the Pacific Ocean. Elcano died of the same affliction six days later, on August 4. The enterprise essentially disintegrated, with a scattered handful of its original members arriving in Spain on Portuguese ships as late as 1536. However, this enterprise did technically amount to the second circumnavigation of the earth.

40. Only eighteen men were on the *Victoria* when it reached Spain. Thirteen of the members had been arrested when it was seized by the Portuguese

in the Cape Verde Islands several days earlier. Once the thirty-one men were vouched for by the Castilian court, the thirteen who had been captured were released by the Portuguese and sent to Spain. One of those thirteen, Martin Méndez, joined Sebastian Cabot's crew and participated in a mutiny against him, which we shall explore in the next chapter.

CHAPTER 3. CABOT

1. The advent of the caravel and the rich discoveries it brought to Portugal and Spain slowly shifted wealth and trade dominance away from Italy, and enterprising seafarers like Columbus and Cabot followed it to the Iberian Peninsula. England adopted the caravel from Portugal. Both countries needed a ship for traveling on the rougher Atlantic.

2. Like Columbus, John Cabot had also gone to Portugal and Spain seeking support. He must have known that his countryman Columbus requested support from the English king, Henry VII (via his brother Bartholomew). After Columbus's achievement for Spain, this knowledge was a factor in his decision to go to England. Beazley (pp. 39–40) draws on the words of the Spanish diplomat Pedro de Ayala (who, like Cabot, hailed from Italy) regarding John Cabot's clandestine visit to Mecca.

3. Such myths stem from a story about Brendan, a fifth-century Irish monk. Irish sea tales concerning a journey into the unknown, or *Immrams,* usually with religious overtones, can come in several forms. One of the later ones describes Brendan and sixty of his fellows sailing to the Isle of the Blessed, an earthly paradise. Once they finally land, the isle turns out to be a large whale, which explains its elusiveness. Works of Lucian and Dante Alighieri and the story of Sinbad in the Arabian *One Thousand and One Nights* all reflect this basic plot. Less prominent in Portuguese and Spanish seafaring, the legend is still important because many seafarers in the late fifteenth century, including Columbus and the elder Cabot, studied it and wrote about it. Phantom islands marked on their charts or believed to exist in the middle of the ocean were sometimes part of their original objectives.

4. Columbus had encountered members of the same Portuguese communities when he landed at Santa Maria in the Azores on February 18, 1493, on his return from his first voyage.

5. Perhaps the richest historic treatments of the fate of John Cabot are Biddle, chap. 10, and Tarducci, chap. 6. However, the two accounts are vague and often conflict with each other. Biddle suggests confusion (p. 7) and deception

(p. 89) by the Hakluyt Society, and Tarducci (p. 76) confounds John Cabot's achievements with Sebastian Cabot's.

6. See Harrisse (pp. 166–167).

7. Their presence aboard is indicated by sponsorship documents. Sebastian Cabot sailed for England in 1508, but little is known of his two brothers other than that letters patent were granted to John Cabot on March 5, 1496.

8. Rodrigues and Devezas (p. 176) cite two letters dated October 17 and 18, 1501, from Alberto Cantino from Portugal to his benefactor Hercule d'Este, Duke of Ferrara. Cantino was in Portugal as a wealthy "horse trader" but in fact he was a spy for Italy. The two letters report being in the presence of Portugal's King Manuel I and hearing Gaspar Côrte-Real (see chapter 1, note 17) describe his most recent venture with his brother Miguel to Newfoundland. We described the Cantino Planisphere in chapter 1 and again in chapter 2, note 31, for its influence on Waldseemüller, Behaim, and Schöner.

9. Biddle (chap. 17). It is unknown whether Sebastian Cabot resorted to the tactic used by Columbus, his father's contemporary, to manage mutiny during the 1508–1509 voyage. Coming to a final agreement was a standard tactic. Cabot might have done so, given his closeness to his father and his father's connection to Columbus.

10. Sebastian Cabot claimed to have been born in England as well as in Italy. In 1553, Richard Eden wrote, "Sebastian Cabote tould me that he was borne in Bristowe, and that at iiii yeare owld he was caried with his father to Venice and so returned ageyne into England with his father after certayne years wherby he was thought to haue bin born in Venice." Beazley (p. 75) quotes Peter Martyr, by contrast, who in 1515–1516 described Cabot as "a Venetian-born" and shows (p. 42) that Cabot told Venetian ambassador Contarini that he had been born in Venice.

11. Juan Rodriguez de Fonseca (b. 1451), one of these enemies, played an important role in three of the cases in this book. A master of intrigue, he was chaplain to Ferdinand and Isabella and a bishop of several minor Castilian kingdoms. He was a famous enemy of Columbus's and was largely responsible for the bureaucratic delays in the Castilian court before Columbus's venture was approved. He also promoted the removal of Columbus from a governorship in 1499. As noted in chapter 2, note 19, Cartagena was thought to be the illegitimate son of Fonseca; Coca, the illegitimate son of Fonseca's brother. Evidence of Fonseca's designs against Sebastian Cabot, another foreigner in Spain, again shows his jealousy of foreigners. Fonseca was a factor in Cabot's decision to return to England after Ferdinand's death. Cabot had little chance of support

in Spain until Fonseca was gone. Fonseca died in 1524, and it was not until 1525 that Cabot received authorization to lead an enterprise.

12. Some contemporary sources use "Pert" for his name, but most primary sources use "Spert." The ending of his given name, Thomas, may have been a phonetic factor in the use of the "s."

13. The conflicting descriptions of events are apparent in Biddle's and Tarducci's treatments of the record. A poem penned around 1517 practically lampooned cowardice in early English seafarers like Cabot and Spert, attributing loss of nerve to a "faint heart" or the vile "sweating sickness," an English epidemic at the time. Historians of the age cruelly used lack of seafaring prowess as the reason why Seville's treasures outmatched those in the Tower of London. Cabot and Spert were lucky to escape the Spanish and even luckier not to have confronted the Portuguese, whose caravels were infamous for being fast and ruthless. Portuguese ships with their sleek hulls covered with jet-black pitch were a formidable sight in formation.

14. See Herbert (pp. 410–412).

15. Contarini's detailed report of this surreptitious interaction with the council appears in "Venice: December 1522," and the council's reply appears in "Venice: April 1523." The account gives some insight into Cabot's interpersonal power to persuade. Contarini expounded to the Ten that Cabot discussed "a variety of geographical topics with me," mentioning, "among other things, a very clever method observed by him, which had never been previously discovered by any one, for ascertaining by the needle the distance between two places from east to west, as your Serenity will hear from himself if he comes." Indeed, the search for a way to measure longitude lasted for centuries and led to many navigational errors during the Age of Discovery. Latitude was measured based on the sun's position. The problem of measuring longitude, by contrast, baffled some of history's greatest minds, among them Galileo Galilei and Edmund Halley. The problem was so important that there was even a national contest in England to encourage its solution. The first practical solution to the long-standing problem utilized measures of lunar distance and did not emerge until 250 years later, in the 1760s, with the work of John Harrison and Nevil Maskelyne. The latter became England's royal astronomer in 1765. In 1767 he published the first *Nautical Almanac and Astronomical Ephemeris*, which was instrumental in the standardization of the prime meridian and Greenwich mean time (GMT). Yet, in 1522, Cabot was somehow able to convince others, such as Ambassador Gaspar Contarini, a wise and knowledgeable man, that he had discovered a solution.

16. Before the armada departed in September 20, 1519, Magellan and his pilots must have met Cabot. His authority as pilot major in Spain (held from February 5, 1518) would have required a meeting. As Ober (*Cabot,* p. 191) notes, "It is quite impossible that Magellan and Cabot should not have met, and, having met, of course they held long and earnest conversations on the topic in which both were intensely interested." The record of such a meeting would be fascinating but unfortunately, there is no evidence of one. Given Cabot's usual expressly negative regard for other seafarers, as we see in this case, we can infer that Cabot might have had sour views. The historical record suggests, by contrast, that Magellan never said much, positively or negatively, about other seafarers (see note 35, below).

17. Cabot's contract from the Council of the Indies is cited in Peter Martyr's *De Orbe Novo* (The New World), decade VII, book VI, which appeared posthumously in 1530. Much of this work was written before and during Cabot's 1526 voyage and gives insight into how this enterprise was seen at the time. Martyr uses present tense, and he wrote the decade before any news of the enterprise arrived in Seville. MacNutt provides a translation of the Latin; Cabot's authorization is described in vol. 2, p. 288. Martyr praises Cabot as a seafarer—another instance of Cabot's ability to manage impressions—effusively lauding him as superior to Magellan. Unfortunately, he also acclaims Cabot as the "discoverer of the country of Baccalaos," a mythical island (probably in the Azores), much like the islands of Brasil and the Seven Cities sought by John Cabot.

18. Cabot chose an Italian countryman, Juan Vespucci (nephew of Amerigo Vespucci), and Miguel Garcia as joint pilots major during his absence. One year later, in 1527, the post was given to Diego Ribiero and Alonso de Chaves, who became pilots major in 1528 during Cabot's absence.

19. In the Age of Discovery, "Moluccas" referred to a general region of today's Indonesia, not just today's Maluku Islands.

20. Beazley (p. 154 n. 1) quotes Oviedo, who noted derisively that Cabot was skillful in cosmography but ignorant of the "great difference between leading men and handling an astrolabe or quadrant" and possessed no nautical science to navigate the currents despite all his astrology. Seafarers knew Cabot as someone who was emphatically *not* a seafarer, whereas non-seafarers more generally regarded him as expert in all matters pertaining to the sea. Cosmography then was more a mystical and imaginative practice than the science it is today.

21. Ober (*Cabot,* pp. 221–222) writes of Cabot that "his good and his bad traits came out strongly in this expedition. He was determined, yet gentle in de-

meanor; he was in the main humane, but severe in the punishments he inflicted upon his men for disobedience."

22. An alternative spelling is Miguel Rifos. He was apparently a friend of Cabot's.

23. Only eighteen men were on the *Victoria* when it arrived at San Lucar. Thirteen of them had been arrested when it was seized by the Portuguese in the Cape Verde Islands several days earlier. Once the thirty-one men were vouched for by the Castilian court, the thirteen who had been captured were released by the Portuguese and sent to Spain. One of those thirteen was Martin Méndez, who had multiple experiences with mutiny. Cabot must have sensed something about this man, who did indeed eventually participate in a mutiny against him.

24. Unlike Méndez, Rodas was not captured by the Portuguese and did return directly to Seville on the *Victoria* with Elcano. The latter, who participated in the primary mutiny on Magellan's enterprise, did, like Méndez, attend the council at Badajos in April 1524.

25. Tarducci (pp. 158–159) writes that Cabot knew that the mutineers swore an oath at Saint Paul's Church in Seville to replace him with Rojas and then murder him. Cabot's responses to Catherine Vasquez's specific charges are his source; the record appears in Tarducci (appendix 36, interrogatory 3). Three individuals testify specifically that the meeting took place, according to the record, and one individual had general information. No church is mentioned in that primary source, however. Tarducci (appendix 34, interrogatory 6) also offers an account of Méndez's removing his property from the *Capitana* and complaining to the council and includes supporting testimonies by three witnesses.

26. One of these eleven was Hernán Méndez, the younger brother of Martin Méndez.

27. See Harrisse (p. 194).

28. This coastal area is the site of today's Recife.

29. According to firsthand accounts, Cabot's members saw mermen bathing in the surf at Pernambuco. Those mermen were either manatees like the ones Columbus saw more than thirty years earlier or a large breed of seal common to the region. It is probable that the members knew what they were but referred to them as mermen anyway.

30. There were approximately a dozen Portuguese at this warehouse. Because of the tensions between Portugal and Spain at the council held at Badajos in April 1524, it is surprising that local interactions were so peaceful. Because of wind patterns during the time of year when Cabot landed, Portuguese ships

knew not to enter the harbor. Given the location of this harbor with respect to the new dividing line drawn at the council, their presence might have created other difficulties for Cabot's enterprise, however.

31. See Ober (*Cabot*, p. 209).

32. Cabral discovered this bay in 1500 and claimed it for Portugal. It is the largest bay in Brazil and the location of today's Salvador, which the Portuguese established in 1549.

33. Santa Catalina is now the name of a state in southern Brazil. The place described here is the location of today's Florianópolis.

34. This first quotation in the paragraph is from the deposition of a member named Junco answering the fifteenth question at the hearing in Seville on November 30, 1530. The second quotation gives the words of Caro, an ally of Cabot's, who was less critical but no less damning. There are several firsthand accounts of the episode unflattering to Cabot, describing his "la flaqueza de animo" ("weak mind," or cowardice). The primary accounts are accessible in Harrisse (pp. 234–237).

35. A few of these men were survivors of Solís's expedition, but many were from a ship lost in Garcia de Loaysa and Juan Sebastián Elcano's ill-fated attempt to replicate Magellan's enterprise. It departed from Seville on July 24, 1525, shortly after Magellan's *Victoria* returned but nine months before Cabot's fleet departed. The remaining men on Loaysa and Elcano's expedition were presumably working their way through the Strait of Magellan when Cabot met them at Santa Catalina. According to the record of Cabot's hearing in Seville provided in Tarducci (appendix 35, interrogatories 13 and 14), Cabot expressed satisfaction that they had lost their ship, predicted the worst for their enterprise and success for his own, and claimed no intention of helping Loaysa and Elcano.

36. Cabot marooned at least nine men in addition to Rojas, Méndez, and Rodas, including Fernando Méndez (Martin's brother), Christoval de Guevara, Otavian de Brane, Gómez Malaver, Juan de Arzola, and one member listed as "Michael." The other names are lost.

37. See Ober (*Cabot*, p. 219).

38. Biddle (p. 10). Reading the journals and determining the precise movements of Cabot's enterprise is an exercise in intricacy. We have chronicled the events from multiple historical sources to convey the principal themes. Cabot's complexities are also on full display in the record, as he managed to outlast several attempted mutinies.

39. See Arber, p. 288.

40. The island retains this name today.

41. The forts built by Cabot's men were not the type designed to withstand attacks. What the records refer to as forts were more like huts for habitation and a small degree of protection. They were constructed of wood and stones and surrounded by modest moats and walls of dirt or clay.

42. Today this site is the town of Puerto Gaboto, located at the intersection of the Coronda and Carcarana rivers in Argentina. The point is about halfway between Santa Fe and Rosario, which are separated by about 80 miles (129 km). As we shall see, natives attacked and destroyed Sancti Spiritus less than two years after Cabot's enterprise built it, in September 1529.

43. Accounts of these violent events appear in Harrisse (pp. 216, 251); Ober (*Cabot,* p. 234); and Tarducci (p. 231). For a record of the July 28–29, 1530, official inquest of Cabot, Junco, Nuremberguer, and Santa Cruz after their return to Seville on the *Santa Maria del Espinar,* see Harrisse (pp. 415–427, syllabus LII). Their firsthand accounts, in Spanish, relay more details about these violent events.

44. This chief's name is sometimes spelled Jaquaron.

45. Garcia later boasted that he explored in twenty-seven days what it had taken Cabot five months to explore.

46. See Harrisse (p. 218).

47. Garcia's original abstracted narrative of his 1526 voyage to the Río de La Plata appears in Tarducci (appendix 38, p. 373). Different histories of Cabot produce interpretations opposite in tone and sometimes in interpretation. Tarducci's presentation of Cabot's career is intensely positive, whereas Harrisse's is sharply negative. Both works are rigorous and based on the same historical facts. It is not only Cabot's living actions and historic accounts of life that cover the spectrum from positive to negative; so does his legacy and its ramifications.

48. One account lists thirty-four names, whereas another one lists fifty.

49. Hurtado's original letter from Lisbon appears in "Spain: October 1528, 1–20," pp. 805–823.

50. The conclusion that the Río de La Plata was not good for seafaring was already in the annals of Portuguese exploration. Nuno Manuel was likely among the first to discover it along with other seafarers, such as João de Lisboa, as early as 1506. Magellan reached a similar conclusion in 1520.

51. Tarducci (appendix 41, pp. 381–382) publishes the original letter to King John III dated August 2, 1530. Ober (*Cabot,* pp. 244–246) provides a translation.

52. Tarducci (appendixes 34, pp. 353–358; appendix 36, pp. 361–370) pro-

vides the primary accounts of both formal charges. Three of Vasquez's sons sailed with Cabot, and only one returned.

53. This first quotation in this paragraph, by Rojas, is recorded in Tarducci (p. 251), whereas the second one, by Calderon, is recorded in Harrisse (p. 232).

54. Oran is across the strait from Spain. The Spanish occupied it from 1504 until 1708, when the Turks drove them out, and again from 1732 until 1792; a major earthquake destroyed much of the city in 1790. Charles V appears to have softened Cabot's sentence, and the records suggest that Cabot did not suffer at all. A letter in 1533 describes a map he was making for the Council of the Indies, but not much is known about his life from 1551 to 1553.

55. However dreadful Cabot's leadership had been, this expedition supported by Charles V and led by the Spanish explorer Pedro de Mendoza fared far, far worse. Mendoza departed from San Lucar on August 24, 1534, with a huge fleet of twelve ships and about two thousand members. His objective was to enter the Río de La Plata region and find a passage to the Pacific Ocean. Instead, his fleet fumbled around in the region, spending even more time on the journey than Cabot had. Mendoza had advanced syphilis that impaired his mental processes and leadership, and his expedition incurred worse horrors than Cabot's did. Famine compelled his men to cook and eat dead comrades. A devastating epidemic broke out that emboldened the natives to begin systematically exterminating them. Starvation compelled three of Mendoza's men to steal a horse, which they secretly ate with others. The thieves were hanged for the offense. The next day, other starving men ate the dead men's thighs. One member was reputed to have eaten his own brother.

Upon exiting the Río de La Plata, Mendoza developed severe hydrophobia. He died at sea, despairing and sick, in 1539, after eating a dog. Only 150 of his original 2,000 crew members returned to Spain. Their return was so embarrassing that Charles V was not informed of it until a year later. Juan de Ayolas and Domingo Martinez de Irala, who sailed with Mendoza, undertook other disastrous Spanish ventures to the Río de La Plata. The latter was made governor of the region in 1538. Gonzalo de Mendoza, brother of the unfortunate Pedro, succeeded him as governor in 1556.

CHAPTER 4. HUDSON

1. Mutiny also attended this enterprise, which is briefly described in chapter 2, note 39. Had Elcano not departed on this voyage several months earlier

than Cabot's fleet set off, he would probably have been assigned to sail with Cabot. Given how Cabot treated Méndez and Rodas because they had served with Magellan, Elcano would probably not have been welcome.

2. Venturing into this lawless region was risky. Drake himself was arrested and mistreated by the Spanish at Río de la Hacha in 1565–1566. Ships commanded by Hawkins, Drake, and others regularly landed near today's Borburata in Venezuela. The seventeenth-century Spanish Main is the source of today's popular notions of pirates, as well as such dramatizations as the Walt Disney series *Pirates of the Caribbean*. Piracy is not mutiny, although many people mistakenly associate the two. The historic cases of mutiny in this book are largely unrelated to pirates.

3. The Ridolfi plot unfolded in the early 1570s as an elaborate attempt to assassinate Elizabeth I and crown the Catholic Mary Stuart queen of England. Roberto Ridolfi was an Italian banker with many international ties who wanted to bolster Catholicism in Europe. Hawkins learned of Ridolfi's plan by gaining the confidence of Spain's ambassador to England, Don Guerau De Spes. Hawkins's characterization of Drake's actions as described in this paragraph derive from his report quoted in Corbett (appendix c, p. 400). Aside from being an English double agent, Hawkins was an innovator, having improved the construction of ships with removable topmasts, which were useful for weathering storms (as exemplified in chapter 1 by what happened to the mast of Martín Pinzón's *Pinta*, as Columbus's enterprise returned to Spain in early 1493). Hawkins also developed treatment compounds that prevented hull degradation in warm tropical waters.

4. The first quotation in this paragraph is reproduced in Harrisse (p. 322), and the second and third ones are in Nichols (pp. 188–189). It is not clear that Cabot was made an English subject before this point in his life. In this era, one became an English subject by birth or an act of Parliament (letters patent). The historical record strongly suggests that Cabot led the English to believe that he had been born in England. Given the time he spent there as a youth (1496–1512), he would have spoken English fluently but with an accent due to three decades in Spain. He pledged on June 4, 1550, that he had lost the original documentation of March 5, 1496, given to his father, brothers, and himself. He petitioned for new copies. Edward VI easily assented.

5. Biddle (p. 176) cites Hakluyt's documentation of Cabot's summons to the examination of a French pilot visiting England who had some experience navigating along the coast of Brazil. It will be remembered from chapter 3 that

Cabot almost collided with a French ship while navigating the coast of Brazil. This meeting provided Cabot an opportunity to share many minute details and deliver an account, almost certainly embellished but no doubt impressive, of the geography of the Río de La Plata region and his experiences sailing for the Spanish.

6. This second surreptitious exchange between Cabot and the Council occurred twenty-nine years after their first exchange. Cabot's ability to persuade yet again is indicated, for this exchange was facilitated by both the Venetian ambassador to England, Giacomo Soranzo, and the English ambassador to Venice, Peter Vannes. The letters appear in "Venice: September 1551" and "Edward VI: September 1551."

7. See Biddle (appendix c, p. 311).

8. The very old commercial area of Billingsgate, situated between London Bridge and the Tower of London, was where the Merchants of the Steelyard had a warehouse. This area originally contained an important water gate and a dock.

9. Biddle (p. 186) and Burnet (p. 331) show that King Edward VI recorded in his journal that in the year 1551 the Hanseatic League's import trade had grown exponentially, selling 8, then 100, then 1,000, then 44,000 pieces of cloth per year in England, whereas all other importers together (mostly English) accounted for only 1,100 pieces.

10. The easterlings survived plundering by a mob in 1493. In 1598, Elizabeth I moved again to control them as a threat.

11. For example, see Carte (pp. 266–267)

12. In the opening lines of the document, Cabot explains how to avoid mutiny by appealing to the shared values of crew members. Throughout, he emphasizes the importance of trust between leader and members. The document was vital in shaping popular conceptions and misconceptions of mutiny. Its original full text, in English, can be found in Tarducci (pp. 395–405).

13. Novaya Zemlya, approximately 900 miles (1,448 km) long and 90 miles (145 km) wide, is an archipelago north of Russia that extends into the Arctic Ocean. It is about half the size of the American state of Louisiana and home to about two thousand people. In the mid-twentieth century it was the site of secret Russian military activity, including nuclear testing. On October 30, 1961, the most powerful nuclear weapon detonation in history (the hydrogen bomb *Tsar Bomba*) took place on Novaya Zemlya.

14. See J. Sparks (p. 150).

15. A 1555 letter to the Venetian doge and senate from Giovanni Michiel, the Venetian ambassador to England, is translated into English in "Venice: November 1555, 1–15." The original encoded letter, written in Italian cipher, offered an interesting but clearly exaggerated account of Willoughby's ill-fated enterprise. There are still questions about what happened. Gordon theorizes that after Willoughby ordered the hatches sealed to keep out the cold, sea coal was burned for cooking and warmth. Because this kind of coal emits a particularly concentrated carbon monoxide as it burns, the men would have quickly been rendered unconscious and then asphyxiated. The bodies would thus have frozen in situ.

16. Biddle (pp. 197–198) provides the original record of the fearful reactions of the Viking fishermen. Hamel (pp. 29–31, chap. 2) gives a detailed record of the backgrounds of Willoughby and Chancellor. Note that Hamel (pp. 2–3) describes the immense influence of the Hanseatic League in the context of this initial landmark enterprise of the Company of Merchant Adventurers.

17. Ilya Tolstoy was the son of the more famous Russian author Leo Tolstoy. He was no stranger to the intense popular appeal of mutiny or to the unity of extremes in bold human endeavors, since he lived in Moscow during the various mutinies and strikes that led to the Russian Revolution. He immigrated to the United States in 1916, where he continued writing and served as a consultant to several Hollywood film makers.

18. See Tarducci (pp. 301–302).

19. Today this map is in the collections of the Department of Maps in the National Library of France (Bibliothèque nationale de France) in Paris.

20. There are monuments to John Cabot in Bristol, including Cabot Tower, and in Nova Scotia, but almost none dedicated to Sebastian Cabot. We are aware of only the nineteenth-century English sculptor William Theed's (the younger) framed bronze relief in the British Parliament, which shows Sebastian Cabot before Henry VII. Cabot is still a controversial figure. Beazley (p. xii) writes, "Among all the treacherous intriguers and self-advertising nonentities of old time there is no figure more disreputable than that of John Cabot's more famous son." By contrast, Allen (p. 148), in a collection of historic biographies, describes Sebastian Cabot as "one of the most extraordinary men of the age in which he lived" and remarks on Cabot's "gentle, friendly, and social" nature. Today's historians have an opportunity to chronicle Cabot's fascinating life using a wide array of old but forgotten sources.

21. See Thorne's document in Hakluyt (*Divers Voyages*, pp. 33–54).

22. Whereas the "ducks" that Magellan saw in the southern hemisphere

were birds of a pan-alcid species, the ones that Hudson observed were most likely puffins. This particular journal entry is reproduced in Asher (p. 5).

23. See Asher (p. 28). Hudson's account gives this book's third such "fantastical" sighting of what were clearly manatees, dugongs, walruses, seals, dolphins, small whales, or other large marine animals. The Portuguese and Spanish had given up on the idea of mermaids by this point in history. But English seafaring culture was still far behind Portugal's and Spain's at the time of Hudson's second voyage, in 1608, and English sailors were more prone to fantastical notions, just as their neighboring seas were more likely to produce the conditions for effects like Saint Elmo's fire. The idea of mermaids is psychologically and emotionally exciting and can be compared to far-fetched and stirring ideas in entrepreneurial settings where passion is intense and uncertainty is high. Many ideas of today's entrepreneurs and business practices may seem as ridiculous and quaint to future historians as these mermaid sightings seem to us.

24. Today this channel (30 miles, or 45 km, across) is named the Kara Strait. It links the Barents Sea to the west of Novaya Zemlya with the Kara Sea to its east.

25. Willoughby's Island (or Land) had nothing to do with the Hugh Willoughby who froze to death in Lapland. It was a fabled island popular among English mapmakers in the sixteenth and seventeenth centuries. Many maps from this era, amazingly wrong in general compared to earlier Portuguese and Spanish maps, show "Sir Hugo Willougbys Landt" as a small island in the middle of the Barents Sea, east of Vardø (at the northern tip of Norway) and about halfway between the entrance to the White Sea and the Svalbard archipelago to the north.

26. See Asher (p. 43). Hudson refers here to John Davis, one of the many early English seafarers. Davis sought the northwest passage three times in the late sixteenth century. He recorded the discovery of "Lumley's Inlet," Warwick Foreland, and "a furious overfall" at 60 degrees north latitude on the coast of the New World. (See A. Markham, p. xxxvi.) At that time it was uncertain where exactly these discoveries occurred, but Hudson clearly associated them with the fabled northwest passage and, in particular, with what became known as the Hudson Strait, which he discovered on his fourth enterprise.

27. Before the end of the century these two countries would be at war. England would join the war against the Dutch Republic in 1672 with support from the ambitious Louis XIV. However, in 1608, Louis XIV was not yet born, and the peaceful and popular Henry IV was still on the throne in France.

28. Hondius spent significant amounts of time in England and, because of Drake's influence, became a well-known cartographer. He reportedly painted several portraits of Drake. He related well to Hudson and functioned not only as an interpreter for Hudson but also as a witness to his contract with the Dutch.

29. The Davis Strait was named for John Davis (see note 26, above). The 40th parallel was about 2,000 miles (3,218 km) to the southwest of Hudson's position and it crosses through today's New Jersey.

30. See Murphy (p. 49).

31. See Asher (p. 61).

32. Esteban Gómez is the same Portuguese who piloted the *San Antonio* and mutinied against Álvaro de Mesquita (and Magellan) in November 1520. Gómez was killed by natives in 1538 on a Spanish expedition to the Río de La Plata, which we saw Cabot explore ten years earlier (see chapter 3).

33. See Asher's (pp. 45–93) publication of Juet's journal from Hudson's third enterprise.

34. As a result of James I's small capitulation in the name of peace, in 1625 this region was renamed New Amsterdam. The initial settlement was supposed to be a stopover for Dutch ventures headed for Brazil, but it was inconveniently situated. The Dutch began to hold more of the region, and the Dutch East India Company, which had strong commercial and trade interests, governed it for almost forty years. In June 1665, the Dutch surrendered it to the English, and it became New York City. Yet it briefly became "New Orange" under the Dutch in July 1673. Then it finally was given back to England as "New York" in November 1674 with the Treaty of Westminster and the end of the third Anglo-Dutch War. The volatile history of New York involves the English and the Dutch largely because of Hudson's third venture, which he undertook for Holland.

35. Prince Henry was popular in England. He was regarded as a promising heir to the throne and the embodiment of the young Protestant vanguard against Catholicism. In November 1612, at eighteen years of age, he died of an illness that may have been typhoid fever. There were many rumors of foul play. His younger brother Charles became king in 1626, but he was convicted of treason and beheaded in 1649 during the English Civil War.

36. Mount Hekla is a volcano that sits about 25 miles (40 km) due north of the volcano Eyjafjallajökull, which erupted several times in 2010.

37. Frobisher, for instance, led several voyages to the region. He discovered no passage, but his fleet of three ships did discover what seemed to be gold and carried full-capacity loads of it back to England, where the cargo was consid-

ered as immensely valuable as Drake's procurements from Spanish ships carrying gold out of Peru in the early 1570s. A few months later Frobisher received funding for fifteen ships to exploit the resource. After several navigational mistakes and a shipwreck, his armada returned with over 1,000 tons of the mined mineral in late 1578. Amid so much excitement, the immense payload was only then discovered to be pyrite, or fool's gold. It was eventually smelted and used to help pave English roads.

38. On July 3, 1736, for example, the explorer William Coats lost a *second* ship in the ice floes of the Hudson Strait. A veteran navigator, Coats visited the strait several times. His admonition to future seafarers was recorded at the Third Session of the Eighth Parliament of the Dominion of Canada (Sessional Papers, 1898): "Keep well south of Cape Farewell, and carefully avoid being entangled in ice before you enter Hudson's Straits; the ice is hard, and the swell runs miles into it; tides and currents keep the ice in continual motion, make it dangerous to hazard a ship in it until you get 10 or 15 leagues into the straits. In 1727 I lost a ship near Cape Farewell by being nipped, and in 1736 I lost another during a calm, when the ice shut in on me six leagues inside Cape Resolution; the ship sank in 20 minutes." Coats's writings capture the "strange and powerful effects of the ice." He wrote that "we found the ice so large at the entrance, that, being inclosed, we had our ship crushed to pieces; and in the year 1739 we attempted to enter the streights six times between the 1st of July and the 12th, and could not effect it, so compact and close a body of ice lay across the entrance, which obliged us to stand out to sea" (Barrow, pp. 18–19). It is hard to express in words the power of the forces of nature that Hudson faced in the Hudson Strait. They could destroy a ship like Hudson's (or Coats's) very quickly.

39. From Pricket's account. See Asher (p. 100).

40. See Asher (pp. 101–102). The term "hundred" seems to have been used to indicate great magnitude and emphasize a point. Earlier, we saw Hudson describe his intent regarding Lumley's Inlet: to "runne into it a hundred leagues." We just saw much discussion involving one member and Staffe, who argued over the giving of "one hundred pounds" to be back in England. Finally, here we see Hudson's claim that they had "entred above an hundred leagues further than any English ever was."

41. From Hudson's journal. See Asher (p. 97).

42. James Bay, though small compared to the enormous bay that Hudson was exploring, is still very large. It is about 225 miles (363 km) long and 130 miles (210 km) wide. By comparison, Lake Michigan (on whose southwest

coast Chicago lies) is 270 miles (435 km) long and about 80 miles (129 km) wide. Hudson Bay is about 600 miles (966 km) long and 700 miles (1, 127 km) wide.

43. From an original note found in Widows's (alternatively spelled Widhouse or Wydhouse) desk. See Purchas (vol. 13, pp. 411–412).

44. Candlemass, a lesser known Christian holiday celebrated on February 2, falls forty days after Christmas and is part of the cycle culminating with Easter. Historically, it reflects the Mosaic Laws of ancient times, when females would follow a ritual ending in purification and the offering of a sacrifice forty days after giving birth to a son. Juet's sarcastic "Bantam by Candlemasse" reference was thus made with especially clever guile, for it mocked Hudson's pre-departure claim to supporters that they would reach that realm by February 2, 1611. England established a trading center at Bantam, in west Java, in the early 1600s so ships traveling around Africa to the Spice Islands and other points east could have a port of call.

45. See Purchas (vol. 13, p. 387).

46. See Asher (pp. 111–112).

47. See Purchas (vol. 13, pp. 389–390).

48. See Asher (p. 121).

49. See Asher's (p. 119) quotation from Pricket's original account.

50. Hudson's dealings with other natives almost three months earlier was probably known to these natives. If so, that knowledge must have been a factor in the sudden attack on Greene and his companions.

51. Bylot, who replaced Juet as Hudson's mate (and was in turn replaced by Staffe) captained the *Discovery* back to England. He led a new expedition on the *Discovery* in 1615. Back he went to the same bay to seek a northwest passage. The brilliant navigator William Baffin was his pilot, and he concluded rightly that there was no passage out of the bay. The next year these two led the *Discovery* on another attempt to find a northwest passage. They discovered Baffin Bay (between Greenland and Canada) and ventured farther north than any ship would go for more than two centuries. They charted Lancaster Sound in the upper northwestern corner of Baffin Bay, not realizing that it was actually the route to the elusive northwest passage. No known passage to the Pacific from the North Atlantic was made until 1905, when Roald Amundsen, a Swede, with a crew of just six members, took a small ship called the *Gjøa* on an incredible three-year trip through northern Canada, at one point using the ice floes as a means of transport. It was then finally realized that a useful northwest passage did not exist.

CHAPTER 5. THE POWER OF SHARED VALUES

1. This tendency to ascribe a larger and natural purpose to reinforce the conflict in a mutiny was as common in the Age of Discovery as it is today. For instance, as Martyr (vol. 2, p. 154) wrote in his fifth decade concerning the mutiny against Magellan in the Bay of Saint Julian, "According to some, Magellan was within his rights in thus acting, while according to others he was not, and the severity he showed was merely the outcome of the ancient hatred existing between the Spaniards and the Portuguese."

2. As mentioned near the end of chapter 2, there was another mutiny against Elcano, long after Magellan had been killed in the Philippine Islands, as the *Victoria* rounded the Cape of Good Hope on its way back to Seville.

3. Our conceptualization of trust and distrust as orthogonal dimensions is informed by Lewicki, McAllister, and Bies.

4. For the original explication of these points, see Coye, Murphy, and Spencer. One of the contributions of that research was these three actions that managers undertake to prevent mutiny. We know of a large-scale study of mutiny by John Humphreys, Jane Whitney Gibson, and Jennifer Oyler that is based on our 2010 study. Their research provides support for the validity of our findings and extends the conceptual application to an archival examination of mutiny in mining colonies during the Blair Mountain War in 1921. Publication of that research is forthcoming in the *Journal of Management History.*

CHAPTER 6. ARCHITECTURES OF INVERSION

1. For a closer examination of these eighteenth-century maritime cases of mutiny, see Coye, Murphy, and Spencer. On the Indian Mutiny, see chapter 2, note 1.

2. See Biddle (p. 135).

3. For a historic treatment that explains the importance of mutinous activities to the development of the Silicon Valley, see Blasi, Kruse, and Bernstein.

CHAPTER 7. DOUBLE-EDGED BLADES

1. The author of *The Caine Mutiny,* Herman Wouk, served aboard several ships in the South Pacific during World War II, where he learned a great deal about various kinds of leaders and the way people behave in different con-

texts of uncertainty. He was second in command of a vessel almost identical to the one in his book, and he once ran a ship aground to avoid destruction in a typhoon.

2. The Marquesas are part of today's French Polynesia in the South Pacific Ocean. The island in question is Nooaheeva in historic records but Nuku Hiva or Nukahiva today. The *Essex* had become infested with thousands of rats during its voyage. In those days, when a ship had this problem, it was careened and unloaded. Then, fires were burned and the smoke was concentrated and channeled through the hull for days or even weeks to drive out the rats.

3. See Porter (p. 176).

4. See Porter (p. 216).

5. Porter's memoir, cited in the bibliography, provides vivid accounts of this episode and others. The famed Admiral David Farragut was Porter's foster son. He was twelve years old and a midshipman on Porter's *Essex*.

6. We changed the names of the individuals and the firm involved in this actual case of mutiny.

7. Even those in organizations with excellent leadership will still find insights here, but this section is designed for members of organizations with bad leadership, who already understand the problems that personal stress and an unhealthy climate can sometimes create. Deposing a bad leader can help improve those aspects of organizational life.

CHAPTER 8. A FORCE OF HUMAN NATURE

1. See Popper (p. 36).

2. The hierarchy was first proposed by Maslow (1943).

3. A conspicuous example is the case of Morgan Stanley in the early part of this century, particularly the mutiny in 2005. The best chronicle of this case is Beard's *Blue Blood and Mutiny*. As the book's subtitle tells us, the book examines "the fight for the soul of Morgan Stanley." It richly describes a strong organizational culture and shared values of collaboration and adaptivity balanced by tradition and pride. Decisions and actions by the new CEO Philip Purcell violated those values in an uncertain environment of lawsuits with the Securities and Exchange Commission and poorly performing stock. Purcell was seen as a foreigner, and eight people made a highly coordinated effort that finally deposed him. By analogy, one is reminded of Magellan leading his enterprise amid grave uncertainties. As Ober (*Magellan*, p. 154) wrote, "Ordinarily pleas-

ant, and accessible to all, Magellan would have been a favorite with the Spaniards had he been of their own nationality; but they could never forget he was a Portuguese." In this more modern case, the eight people were not subject to Purcell's authority, so the effort against him was not a proper mutiny, but they constituted a significant and coordinated element and represented a different culture and set of values than Purcell did. Like many modern cases, that case reflects many tenets in this book. It illustrates the distinct roles of trust and distrust. It shows a stark gap between leader and members. It highlights affronts to shared values in an uncertain environment, leading to mutiny. And it conveys a sense of the intense subjectivity of participants that frustrates attempts to understand cases of mutiny today.

BIBLIOGRAPHY

Most of the primary and secondary historic sources examined for this book, including original maps, logbooks, accounts, journals, and letters, are accessible via libraries and museums such as the Archives of the Indies in Seville, the National Maritime Museum in Greenwich, and the Bibliothèque nationale de France in Paris. Many sources are also procurable through university libraries. Some of the primary sources have been translated and republished many times. Some of our sources were authoritative notes in large volumes or obscure additions to old trade periodicals or digests. The sources listed here include the works cited in the text and some works that informed our research. They are a representative sample of the many works consulted.

Adams, Charles K. *Christopher Columbus.* New York: Dodd, Mead, 1892.

Allen, William. *An American Biographical and Historical Dictionary, Containing an Account of the Lives, Characters, and Writings of the Most Eminent Persons in North America from Its First Discovery to the Present Time, and a Summary of the History of the Several Colonies and of the United States.* Cambridge, MA: William Hilliard, 1809.

Arber, E. A., ed. *The First Three English Books on America, (?1511)–1555 A.D., Being Chiefly Translations, Compilations, &c., by Richard Eden, from the Writings, Maps, &c., of Pietro Martire, of Anghiera (1455–1526), Apostolical Protonotary, and Councillor to the Emperor Charles V.; Sebastian Münster, the Cosmographer (1489–1552), Professor of Hebrew, &c., at the University of Basle; Sebastian Cabot, of Bristol (1474–1557), Grand Pilot of England: With Extracts &c., from the Works of other Spanish, Italian, and German Writers of the Time.* Birmingham: 1 Montague Road, 1885.

Asher, Georg M. *Henry Hudson the Navigator: The Original Documents in Which His Career Is Recorded, Collected, Partly Translated, and Annotated, with an Introduction*. London: Hakluyt Society, 1860.

Barros, João de. *Décadas da Ásia*. Vol. 6 of *Da Ásia de João de Barros e de Diogo de Couto*. New edition. Lisbon: Na Régia Officina Typografica, 1777.

Barrow, John, ed. *The Geography of Hudson's Bay: Being the Remarks of Captain W. Coats, in His Many Voyages to That Locality, between the Years 1727 and 1751. With an Appendix, Containing Extracts from the Log of Capt. Middleton on His Voyage for the Discovery of the North-West Passage, in H.M.S. Furnace, in 1741–1742*. London: Hakluyt Society, 1852.

Baudier, Seigneur M. *The History of the Court of the King of China*. London: Thomas Osborne, 1745.

Beard, Patricia. *Blue Blood and Mutiny: The Fight for the Soul of Morgan Stanley*. New York: William Morrow, 2007.

Beazley, C. Raymond. *John and Sebastian Cabot: The Discovery of North America*. Vol. 3 of H. F. Wilson, ed., *Builders of Greater Britain*. London: T. Fisher Unwin, Paternoster Square, 1898.

Biddle, Richard. *A Memoir of Sebastian Cabot*. Philadelphia: Carey and Lea, 1831.

Bigges, Walter. *A Summarie and True Discourse of Sir Francis Drakes West-Indian Voyage*. London: Nicholas Bourne, 1652.

Blasi, Joseph, Douglas Kruse, and Aaron Bernstein. *In the Company of Owners: The Truth about Stock Options*. New York: Basic Books, 2003.

Breton, Nicholas. *The Goode and the Badde; or, Descriptions of the Worthies, and the Unworthies of This Age*. London: George Purslowe for Iohn Budge, 1616.

———. *The Works in Verse and Prose of Nicholas Breton*. Edited by Alexander B. Grosart. Edinburgh: Thomas and Archibald Constable, 1879.

Burnet, Gilbert. *The History of the Reformation of the Church of England*. Vol. 2. New York: D. Appleton and Company, 1843.

Burpee, Lawrence J. *The Search for the Western Sea: The Story of the Exploration of North-Western America*. London: Alston Rivers, 1908.

Burton, Richard F., trans. *Camoen's Os Lusiadas*. London: Tinsley Brothers, 1880.

Butterworth, Hezekiah. *The Story of Magellan and the Discovery of the Philippines*. New York: D. Appleton, 1899.

Carte, Thomas. *A General History of England*. Vol. 3. London: Author's House in Dean's Yard, 1752.

Chapman, Charles E. *A History of Spain: Founded on the Historia de España de La Civilización Española of Rafael Altamira*. New York: Macmillan Company, 1918.

Corbett, Julian S. *Drake and the Tudor Navy, with a History of the Rise of England as a Maritime Power*. Vol. 1. London: Longmans, Green, and Company, 1899.

Coye, Ray W., Patrick J. Murphy, and Patricia E. Spencer. "Using Historic Mutinies to Understand Defiance in Modern Organizations." *Journal of Management History* 16, no. 2 (2010): 270–287.

De Córdoba, Don A. *A Voyage of Discovery to the Strait of Magellan: With an Account of the Manners and Customs of the Inhabitants; and of the Natural Productions of Patagonia; Undertaken, by Order of the King of Spain, by A. de Cordova*. Translated by José Vargas Ponce. London: Sir Richard Phillips, 1820.

Eden, Richard. *A Treatyse of the Newe India, with Other New Founde Landes and Ilandes, as Well Eastwarde as Westwarde, as They Are Knowen and Found in These Our Dayes, after the Descripcion of Sebastian Munster in His Boke of Universall Cosmographie: Wherein the Diligent Reader My See the Good Successe and Rewarde of Noble and Honeste Enterpryses, by the Which nhot Only Worldly Ryches Are Obtayned, but Also God Is Glorified, and the Christian Fayth Enlarged*. London, 1553.

"Edward VI: September 1551." In *Calendar of State Papers Foreign, Edward VI: 1547–1553* (1861). British History Online, http://www.british-history.ac.uk/report.aspx?compid=70332/.

Galvao, Antonio. *The Discoveries of the World, from Their First Original unto the Year of Our Lord 1555*. London: Hakluyt Society, 1862.

Gardner, John W., and Helen Rowan. *No Easy Victories*. New York: Harper and Row, 1968.

Gordon, Eleanora C. "The Fate of Sir Hugh Willoughby and His Companions: A New Conjecture." *Geographical Journal* 152, no. 2 (July 1986): 243–247.

Guillemard, Francis H. H. *The Life of Ferdinand Magellan and the First Circumnavigation of the Globe.* London: George Philip and Son, 1890.

Hakluyt, Richard. *Divers Voyages Touching the Discoverie of America and the Ilands Adjacent unto the Same.* London: Thomas Woodcocke, dwelling in Paules church yard, at the signe of the blacke beare, 1582.

———. *Hakluyt's Collection of the Early Voyages, Travels, and Discoveries of the English Nation.* Vols. 1–5. London: R. H. Evans, 1812.

———. *The Principal Navigations Voyages Traffiques and Discoveries of the English Nation.* Vols. 1–12. Glasgow: James MacLehose and Sons, 1904.

———. *Voyages in Search of the North-West Passage, from the Collection of Richard Hakluyt.* London: Cassell, 1886.

Hamel, Iosif Khristianovich. *England and Russia; Comprising the Voyages of John Tradescant the Elder, Sir Hugh Willoughby, Richard Chancellor, Nelson, and Others, to the White Sea, Etc.* [Translated by John Studdy Leigh.] London: Richard Bentley, 1854.

Harrisse, Henry. *John Cabot: The Discoverer of North America and Sebastian His Son.* London: Benjamin Franklin Stevens, 1896.

Herbert, William. *The History of the Twelve Great Livery Companies of London; Principally Compiled from Their Grants and Records.* Vol. 1. London: Published by the author; and to be had of him, at the library, Guildhall, and all of the principal booksellers, 1837.

An Historical Account of the Circumnavigation of the Globe, and of the Progress of Discovery in the Pacific Ocean, from the Voyage of Magellan to the Death of Cook. New York: Harper and Brothers, 1837.

Janvier, Thomas A. *Henry Hudson: A Brief Statement of His Aims and His Achievements.* New York: Harper and Brothers, 1909.

Jones, John W., ed. *Divers Voyages Touching the Discovery of America and the Islands Adjacent.* London: Hakluyt Society, 1801.

Kerr, Robert. *A General History and Collection of Voyages and Travels, Arranged in Systematic Order.* Edinburgh: George Ramsay, 1811.

Kerr, Steven, and John M. Jermier. "Substitutes for Leadership: Their

Meaning and Measurement." *Organizational Behavior and Human Performance* 22 (1978): 375–403.

Lawler, Thomas B. *The Story of Columbus and Magellan.* Boston: Ginn, 1905.

Lewicki, Roy J., Daniel J. McAllister, and Robert J. Bies. "Trust and Distrust: New Relationships and Realities." *Academy of Management Review* 23, no. 3 (July 1998): 438–458.

Markham, A. H. *The Voyages and Works of John Davis, the Navigator.* In *Works Issued by the Hakluyt Society,* vol. 59. London, Hakluyt Society, 1880.

Markham, Clements R. *The Journal of Christopher Columbus and Documents Relating the Voyages of John Cabot and Gaspar Corte Real.* London: Hakluyt Society, 1893.

———. *Life of Christopher Columbus.* London: George Philip and Son, The London Geographical Institute, 1902.

Martyr, Peter [Pietro Martire d'Anghiera]. *De Orbe Novo: The Eight Decades of Peter Martyr D'Anghera.* 2 vols. Translated by Francis A. MacNutt. New York: G. P. Putnam's Sons, 1912.

Maslow, Abraham H. "A Theory of Human Motivation." *Psychological Review* 50 (1943): 370–396.

Maynarde, Thomas. *Sir Francis Drake: His Voyage, 1595.* London: Hakluyt Society, 1849.

Murphy, Henry C. *Henry Hudson in Holland.* The Hague: The Brothers Giunta D'Albani, 1859.

Navarrette, Martín F. *Colección de los viajes y descubrimientos que hicieron por mar los españoles desde fines del siglo XV: Expediciones al Maluco, viage de Magallanes y de Elcano.* Madrid: Imprenta Nacional, 1837.

Nicholls, James F. *The Remarkable Life, Adventures and Discoveries of Sebastian Cabot of Bristol.* London: Sampson, Low, Son, and Marston, 1869.

Nichols, John G., ed. *Literary Remains of King Edward the Sixth.* Vol. 1. London: J. B. Nichols and Sons, 1857.

Ober, Frederick A. *Ferdinand Magellan.* New York: Harper and Brothers, 1907.

———. *John and Sebastian Cabot.* New York: Harper and Brothers, 1908.

Popper, Karl R. *The Poverty of Historicism.* London: Routledge, 1957.

Porter, David D. *Memoir of Commodore David Porter; of the United States Navy.* Albany, N.Y.: J. Munsell, 1875.

Pricket, Abacuck. "A Larger Discourse of the Same Voyage." In Purchas, *Hakluytus Posthumus,* vol. 8, pp. 377–410.

Purchas, Samuel. *Hakluytus Posthumus; or, Purchas His Pilgrimes: Contayning a History of the World in Sea Voyages and Lande Travells by Englishmen and Others.* 20 vols. Glasgow: James MacLehose and Sons, 1905–1907.

Rodrigues, Jorge Nascimento, and Tessaleno Devezas. *Pioneers of Globalization: Why the Portuguese Surprised the World.* 2nd edition. V. N. Famalicão: Centro Atlântico, Lda.

Russell, William O. *A Treatise on Crimes and Misdemeanors.* London: Saunders and Benning, 1843.

Sessional Papers of the Parliament of the Dominion of Canada, Session 1898. Vol. 9: Third Session of the Eighth Parliament. Ottawa: S. F. Dawson, 1899.

Seyer, Samuel. *Memoirs Historical and Topographical of Bristol and Its Neighbourhood.* Bristol: John Mathew Gutch, 1821.

Shippen, Edward. *Naval Battles, Ancient and Modern.* Philadelphia: J. C. McCurdy, 1883.

"Spain: October 1528, 1–20." In *Calendar of State Papers, Spain,* vol. 3, part 2: *1527–1529* (1877). British History Online, http://www.british -history.ac.uk/report.aspx?compid=87579.

Sparks, Edwin E. *Famous Explorers.* Boston: Hall and Locke, 1902.

Sparks, Jared. *The Library of American Biography.* Vol. 9. Boston: Hilliard, Gray, and Company, 1838.

Stanley, Lord of Alderley. *The First Voyage Round the World, by Magellan: Translated from the Accounts of Pigafetta and Other Contemporary Writers.* London: Hakluyt Society, 1874.

Stephens, Henry Morse. *The Story of the Nations: Portugal.* London: G. P. Putnam's Sons, 1891.

Tarducci, Francesco. *John and Sebastian Cabot.* Detroit: H. F. Brownson, 1893.

Tillotson, John. *Adventures in the Ice.* New York: Virtue and Yorston, 1869.

Tolstoy, Ilya. "The Soviet Uses the Allies." In G. H. Payne, ed., *The Forum,* vol. 66, pp. 1–12. New York: Forum Publishing, 1921.

"Venice: April 1523." In *Calendar of State Papers Relating to English Affairs in the Archives of Venice,* vol. 3: *1520–1526* (1869). British History On-line, http://www.british-history.ac.uk/report.aspx?compid=94359.

"Venice: December 1522." In *Calendar of State Papers Relating to English Affairs in the Archives of Venice,* vol. 3: *1520–1526* (1869). British History Online, http://www.british-history.ac.uk/report.aspx?compid =94355.

"Venice: November 1555, 1–15." In *Calendar of State Papers Relating to English Affairs in the Archives of Venice,* vol. 6: *1555–1558* (1877). British History Online, http://www.british-history.ac.uk/report.aspx?compid=100560.

"Venice: September 1551." In *Calendar of State Papers Relating to English Affairs in the Archives of Venice,* vol. 5: *1534–1554* (1873). British History Online, http://www.british-history.ac.uk/report.aspx?compid =94870.

Williamson, James A. *A Short History of British Expansion.* London: Macmillan and Company, 1922.

Winsor, Justin, ed. *Narrative and Critical History of America.* Boston: Houghton, Mifflin, 1884.

INDEX